HOLES IN OUR HEARTS

HOLES IN OUR HEARTS

An Anthology of New Mexican Military Related
Stories and Poetry

SouthWest Writers

ISBN: 9798392360277

Edited by: Jim Tritten, Dan Wetmore and Joseph Badal

Formatted by: RMK Publications, LLC.

Printed in the U.S.A.

CONTENTS

FOREWORD

Holes in Our Hearts is more than a collection of works written by individuals with some connection to the United States military services. Whether active duty, veterans, or relatives of those who served, these short stories, memoirs, poems, essays, etc., are the expressions of deeply ingrained memories and experiences.

It is often difficult for those who have served and their family members to verbally relate memories and experiences to others. Whether too personal, too poignant, or traumatic, these memories and experiences, more often than not, rest in the back rooms of their minds, never to be shared. This lack of sharing is tragic on two levels. First, those who never had the privilege of hearing these stories will never fully understand what it means to serve their country through the military. And the people who had the privilege of serving never have the opportunity to realize the catharsis of sharing their experiences.

This anthology includes offerings from members of all the armed services, as well as family members of men and women who served. It is a beautiful collection of works that are, at times emotional, humorous, frightening, enlightening, or thought-provoking. The reader should be aware that the recollections in *Holes in Our Hearts* are, in many instances, the only way that the authors could share with you their memories and experiences.

And I hope that the contributors to this collection have realized some psychic and cathartic relief through the relating of their memories and experiences.

Joseph Badal

ABOUT THE COVER

The photograph of Steve Borbas' "Holes in Our Hearts" sculpture seemed to be an appropriate cover for our anthology. The outdoor art piece was commissioned by the Albuquerque Public Art program and dedicated on August 23, 2013, at its location at the New Mexico Veterans Memorial. The sculpture is dedicated to the New Mexicans who died in the Vietnam War. The almost 400 large and small holes in the three message walls represent those losses. Steve's piece inspired the following poem.

A HOLE IN MY HEART
Paul David Gonzales

There's a crushing pain in my chest
A piercing pain that denies me rest

I endure not for me
But for those who will never be

Young men and women who died
Paid the ultimate price of war
Now stand at heaven's door

Their future is never more

The evidence of a soldier's presence
Is nothing but a slight residue
Absorbed in the vapor of time

My heart … that vital organ
Pumps anguish over our loss
Each chamber fills with grief
For which … there is no relief

My blood flows like lava from
earth's inner core
Searing my spirit
Knowing your physical presence is
never more.

When the bugle blows its final notes
Toward heaven, your spirit floats

I dare not question the hand of GOD
For in heaven you now trod

Your destiny was written from the start
Your absence will forever leave
A hole in my heart.

PREFACE

According to *U.S. News & World Report*, the U.S. is home to around 16.5 million Veterans, making up about 6.4% of the nation's adult population. These men and women put their civilian lives and dreams on hold to answer the call of their country.

Whether they were actually on the battlefield or not, their day to day lives and the lives of their families were indelibly affected in ways that many of them don't even realize until years afterwards.

With assistance from the state of New Mexico Arts division, SouthWest Writers undertook the task of creating a work of literary art focused not on glorious battles but on the much more complex views of military life. Some personal memoirs are battle related, some are simple stories of what life was like on a military base or living in a military family. Some stories by veterans are fictional, drawn from their hearts.

Here, in this collection of stories and poetry, you will find glimpses of life experiences, feelings and insights of New Mexican veterans, family members and caregivers.

Rose Marie Kern
President, SouthWest Writers

Image by tammyatWTI via Pixabay

INTRODUCTION

Holes in Our Hearts provides snapshots of military life and how the military has affected lives. It is written from the perspective of New Mexico active-duty military members, veterans of the Army, Marines, Navy, Air Force, and Coast Guard, as well as their family members and caregivers. Some of the writing represents the first time many authors have revealed their innermost thoughts to anyone. Some of the stories are written by established authors with numerous publishing credentials. All are worth your time to learn why we continue to honor the military on behalf of a grateful nation.

The contributions are organized alphabetically with memoirs, poetry, essays, humor, fiction, etc. mixed. A total of ninety-five written contributions were accepted from fifty-four New Mexicans. Each represents a tale worth reading, internalizing, and contemplating the experiences we as a nation expect our young men and women, their families, and their caregivers to deal with — sometimes long after their military service has ended and nothing is left but holes in our hearts.

Jim Tritten
Editor

ROSA ARMIJO-PEMBLE

Just Care: A Lesson in Possibilities

Raising a child to be an amazing adult is hard, but to raise one on the spectrum holds many more challenges. He was already his own little man by age three. A thirty-year-old in the body of an extremely articulate and beautiful child's body, just screaming, literally and figuratively, to be let out.

Some days he traveled a long, bumpy road. Other days he was zigzagging back and forth across the median. I followed at a distance where I might keep him from too big a crash. I marked the places we'd been, and the places I didn't want to revisit, all while praying the next road might be an easier one for all of us. When there are a lot of ambiguities in such a child's head, it is very much like packed streets. Cars bumper to bumper. People honking and yelling. Stop and go. No one can break free. Especially stuck is the child at the center of it all.

When the chaos was too much, I'd tell him, "Just care."

He cared about his cars, trains, and planes. He especially cared for his baby sister. But was he listening to how caring for others and other things was also important?

Just care was my mantra for him. And I repeated it often. We showed him we cared by supporting the things that made him happy and calm. My husband and I would take him on train rides even though there was a chance I'd get motion sick. Family road trips lead to museums where planes that once flew in battle were placed just for him to reach. Some he could touch or sit in. A little sister to follow him and

9

a plane in his pocket was the perfect vacation. If we'd lived on a train, had our own plane, and didn't take the car to school, life might have been simpler.

He was free in the air of a general aviation aircraft on one of the small airport's flight tours. The skies offered peace of mind and a judgment-free zone. On the ground, he battled kids, teachers, parents, and family. Though he'd get frustrated with others' misconceptions, he wasn't deterred from meeting the right kids and making great friends or impressing the best teachers. He may have made a few adversaries, but he also learned to earn respect and trust.

As he grew, the gibberish in his brain started to unmingle into sounds and phrases he could comprehend. He dealt with annoyances by finding humor and learning to be a little more considerate as well. He still forgot that correcting a teacher was disrespectful, even if he did know something more. However, the world started to make sense, and he started to find ways to conquer it.

Adulthood gave him the power to drive in the direction that worked best for him. He began to figure out which paths he should drive on and which he should walk towards.

One day he walked into our home and said, "I'm government property."

My joy was the bright light in his green eyes and the pride in his smile. I just had to double-check which branch since he was pursued by all and considered each through his senior year. I cried watching the video of his swearing-in for the first time on the phone that he purchased for himself when he turned eighteen. A step up from the flip phone we'd let him have.

My skinny, beautiful, and still too clever son woke for the first time to a stranger yelling at him to fold his socks, clean his room and pay attention on his nineteenth birthday. He quickly learned that overseeing one's own life and charting new territory, even if it's hard, can be scary as well as rewarding.

Though he sometimes still lacks patience, the highways and skyways are there for him to explore as he serves his country. He stands with more competence than those who didn't believe he was capable of more than tears and tantrums. He is part of a group of men and women who can be proud to say they serve. That takes more than caring. That takes guts.

*****

Author: Rosa Armijo-Pemble

Rosa Armijo-Pemble's son was born and raised in NM, where he lived until he left two years ago for Air Force basic training. She is a photographer and technical writer. She has been a member of Southwest Writers for at least twenty-five years. Raising children put her creative writing on hold.

JOSEPH BADAL

White Dog

Chapter 1

It was a glorious fall day, the kind of day that makes a person glad to be alive. The leaves on the trees along the residential street displayed a Joseph's coat of colors as they desperately hung onto their branches, just a day or two away from becoming Nature's carpet.

"Not bad, hey girl," Bob said, coming up behind Liz and wrapping his arms around his wife.

She murmured with pleasure and pressed back against him. "I never thought I would be so happy here."

Bob laughed. "I told you Greece would be special."

"Don't get me wrong, I do love it here. But after two tours in Afghanistan, anyplace would be *special* to you."

"You've got a point there." He released Liz and stepped back. "I guess I'd better get to work. The colonel is manic about the big inspection next week."

Liz turned and kissed him. "Try not to work too late. I'd like Michael to spend some time with his father before he goes to bed."

"I'll try."

"Famous last words," she muttered.

"Where's the human wrecking ball?" Bob asked.

"*Michael* and White Dog took off down the path." She paused a beat and gave him an imploring look. "He really loves that dog."

"Don't start on me again, Liz. You know we can't afford to ship a dog back to the States. Between shipping costs and putting her in quarantine for two weeks, it'll cost a fortune."

"I can cut back on —"

Three-year-old Michael's screams and White Dog's high-pitched barking interrupted her as they careened around the corner of the fenced path between the front and back of their Kifissia rental home in an Athens suburb.

"My God!" Bob shouted, covering his ears. "How do you stand that all day?" Then he pointed at White Dog. "Look at her. No wonder someone dumped her on our property. Her eyes are different colors, one ear flops down and the other is pointed straight at the sky, her tongue hangs out all the time, and she's got a soprano bark. My God, she looks lopsided. That's not a dog; it's a Picasso painting."

"Oh, Bob. She's a sweetheart. And she's Michael's best friend."

Bob groaned. "I'm telling you, Liz, we can't afford a dog. Please get it out of your head. Find someone who will take her in before Michael gets too attached to her."

Chapter 2

Liz's morning routine did not vary much. After Bob left for the US Army post, she cleaned up the breakfast dishes, made the beds, and walked with Michael to the local market — White Dog trailing behind, sniffing at trash cans. When they returned home, weather permitting, she played with Michael in the back yard, while White Dog moved to the morning sun-warmed back patio.

"Swing, Mommy, swing," Michael yelled in his megaphonic voice, as he ran to the backyard glider swing.

"Okay, big guy," she said. "How high do you want to go?"

"To the sky, Mommy. Up to the sky."

Liz waited for Michael to climb aboard the swing and get settled on the seat, then she pushed it while he shouted for joy.

"Higher, Mommy, higher."

Before she could respond to her little daredevil, White Dog barked, got up and ran to the back door. Then Liz heard the doorbell ring.

How does she do it? Liz thought. *Amazing. She hears people at the front door before they even ring the bell.*

"Michael," she said, "Mommy's got to answer the door. You wait here."

"Okay, Mommy."

Liz looked over at the gate between the yard and the street, making certain it was closed. On a corner lot, the house was completely fenced in five-foot-high wrought iron, with two gates, one on the street by the back yard, and the other facing the cross street fronting the house. Satisfied Michael could not get out of the yard, she climbed the steps to the patio, and crossed it to the back door. White Dog followed her inside. She turned from the kitchen down the hallway to the front door and saw through the sidelight a woman in a long, brightly-colored dress standing on the front porch.

"Not another peddler," she whispered.

She opened the door and saw the woman had spread three *flokati* rugs on the terrazzo porch.

"Missy vant to buy nice rug?" the woman said in a strong Slavic accent.

"No, thank you," Liz said. "We've already got all the rugs we need." She started closing the door when the woman fingered her necklace and shook it.

"How 'bout nice necklace? It have real gold and silver."

Liz scowled. "Not today." Again, she started to close the door.

"Vait, vait," the woman said in a strident voice, "I have other jewelry to show Missy."

The woman was beginning to irritate Liz. The peddlers who periodically came by the house usually knew how to take no for an answer. She said, "I don't want anything today," and closed the door.

"Pushy!" Liz said to White Dog.

Suddenly, the dog growled, something she had never done before. Not like her high-pitched bark, this was an honest-to-God, deep-throated growl. Then White Dog's ruff stood up. The dog launched herself down the hall, in the direction of the back door. When she reached the kitchen and tried to take the turn there, her hind legs slipped out from under her. She skidded and crashed into Michael's little table and chair. White Dog righted herself and disappeared into the kitchen.

Liz ran after White Dog, down the hall, through the kitchen, and out onto the back patio. She looked toward the glider swing. Her heart seemed to stop. No, Michael. She looked toward the street just as White Dog catapulted herself over the gate.

"Michael!" Liz shouted.

Liz thought she heard Michael call, "Mommy," but she could not be certain. She ran down the steps from the patio and across the yard to the path on the side of the house. Halfway to the front gate, she heard voices, and then her heart quickened at the unmistakable voice of her son.

"Mommy! Mommy!" Michael screamed.

Liz peered through a gap in the rose bushes along the fence and saw a car parked there, its motor running. There were at least three people standing, moving around the car.

"Mommy, Mommy!" Michael screamed again.

Liz crashed through the rose bushes, only mildly aware of the pain the thorns inflicted on her face and arms. She leaped up on the top of the fence and rolled over onto the sidewalk, ten feet from the car. She looked into the wide-eyed, frantic stare of her three-year-old son. In the next instant, her vision expanding, she saw a man holding Michael against his chest with one arm while repeatedly hammering his free hand downward against White Dog's back. The man was shrieking. A woman — the peddler who had come to her front door — was trying to cram rugs into the trunk of the sedan. Another woman, screaming something in a foreign language, ran around the nose of the vehicle and ripped open the front driver-side door.

White Dog, viciously growling, fangs clutching the front of the man's trousers between his legs, was jerking her head back and forth, seemingly immune to the man's blows.

Liz jumped at the man and slammed him several times on the side of his head with her fists. When he did not release Michael, she sank her teeth into the bare arm he had around her son. She tasted blood as she bore down with all the strength she had. When the man, cursing and still shrieking, finally released Michael, she snatched him away and ran down the street toward the front steps, calling all the while for White Dog. With White Dog at her heels, she entered the house, closed and locked the door behind her, and called the police.

Chapter 3

Two policemen arrived fifteen minutes after her call. The cops wanted to keep petting White Dog as they called her *Kalo Skylo* (good dog), over and over again. By the time the police left, Liz's heart rate had dropped almost back to normal. She sat on the couch, Michael sleeping on one side of her, his head resting on her thigh, and White Dog panting on her other side, her tongue lolling out of the side of her mouth.

By the time Bob arrived home, shortly after the Greek policemen left, Liz had put Michael to bed and White Dog was finishing off a steak she had planned to serve for their dinner.

Bob rushed in and hugged Liz. "I'm sorry, honey," he said. "I wish I'd been here."

She backed up a half-step and smiled at him. "It's okay; White Dog was here." Her voice croaked as she said, "She saved our son." Tears flooded her eyes and flowed over her cheeks. "If it wasn't for White Dog, we would —"

"I know, honey," Bob told her as he pulled her into him. He kissed the top of her head and said, "I guess we'd better talk about taking her back to the States with us, after all. White Dog's always going to be with us."

Liz's throat tightened and her tears flowed. She tried to speak but words would not come, while White Dog placed her front paws on her lap, licked her face, and barked happily.

*****

 *Author: Joseph Badal*

Joseph Badal is an Amazon #1 Best-Selling Author, with eighteen award-winning suspense novels. He is a two-time Tony Hillerman Award Winner and a four-time Military Writers Society of America (MWSA) Gold Medal Winner. He was named Writer of the Year in 2021 by MWSA.

Rebecca Black

The Sword

We were young. We didn't know. He didn't tell us. Phrases that came whenever I thought about what we had done. The first were excuses, the last putting the blame back on him for never talking about those years. When I try to picture it now, it was exquisite, a work of art much more than a weapon: the sheath strong and elegant, with gentle waves of carving reaching to the hilt, a handle that had been contoured by centuries of battle among men, always men, facing each other, hand to hand, not the killing from high above. The blade itself was shimmering metal of strength, finely tuned for use, yet, on a second look, it was covered with detailed images of imagined combat, laden with fate rather than hate. But I do not really remember; it was a long time ago, and my sister and I were in a hurry, our search through the creaky attic of the old farmhouse not really furtive, as no one else was there, but somehow, we knew we were treading where we did not belong.

Guzzie was his nickname, the guy that had taken my sister's nineteen-year-old heart, or maybe just her body, that summer. The camp where we worked was not far from the farm, my grandfather's hobby, and second home where we had all gathered as kids on holidays. Sometimes my sister and I came down together when our days off coincided, and sometimes each on our own. Maybe it was one of the latter times that she brought Guzzie and whatever happened made her want to give him something to cement their relationship? And it was thus that she and I found ourselves hunting through the dry mustiness for that something among all the mementos of other people's decades.

If he had told us, our father, as he did long after it was gone, that the sword was a gift, a very special one that was given to him at a very important time: the abdication of a country under threat of a third weapon of mass destruction, a weapon he believed had been built never to be used. If he had told us, we might have known better than to give it away to a guy, a nice one admittedly, who I sort of knew and my sister, in that moment of time, felt was her heartbeat. But quickly after, he wasn't so important, and who was he really? I looked some years later when my father wondered out loud about where the sword had gone, but there were so very, very many names like Guzzie in the NYC [New York City] phone book. It was impossible to find him, or it.

If he had told us about his four years on a ship, crossing from this sea to another, hearing and feeling the terror of explosions from the sky, from the sea, seeing people die, maimed, destroyed, some that his orders had made die, we might have thought twice. I don't know what he saw, or what he made happen as an officer in command, that made him so willing to let me wear his officer's jacket over my teenage worn jeans and hiking boots, me not knowing that the stripes on the sleeves were anything until someone happened to tell me how impressive the number of them was. Nightmares haunted his sleep, my stepmother told me, hard enough that each night she built a wall of pillows between her and him to avoid the flying arms. One time in my post-teenage years, I saw a purple heart nestled in with some other medals, ribbons, and metal in a little box. Why didn't he tell us?

It was the late 60's, he was supporting Eugene McCarthy to end another war, and it was the era when I didn't bother, dare, to look deeply at his face; I was too lost in my own growing up. If I had noticed, I might have seen a hint of personal hurt mixed with the rational stoic face he always had on such policy issues. He had left the military after that world war and worked for our government for the rest of his life; he must have believed in what he had fought for. At the end, some photos were left in his belongings, maybe still there because he had no one to give them to, pictures of him in combat uniform, other men around, no one I could recognize. He had not stayed friends, not kept the war alive in his life.

My grandmother told me once much later that he was part of the occupation of Japan and lived for six months on that island, had fallen in love, but came back to marry an American, my mother. Maybe that time helped him heal a little, or maybe only sharpened the edges of memories so that he could never again support war, any war. I don't know. Clouds of regret too often follow my thoughts of him, my father who shaped me, made me much of what I am, but told me so little of what he had lived. Was the sword a reminder that he had helped save his country or that peace was the more important? I will never know. All I do know is that he asked about it once in a while, even just before death, wondering what had happened to the sword he last saw in the attic, and my sister and I could never admit we had so easily given it away.

*****

Author: Rebecca Black

Rebecca Black lives in Corrales, New Mexico. She is the youngest daughter of Robert Bruce Black, a commissioned officer in the US Navy from 1942 to 1946, serving at sea during World War II. Rebecca is a retired Senior Foreign Service Officer.

STEVE BORBAS

A Life Much Liked

The US Army drafted me to Fort Dix back in 1967. I qualified for Officers' Candidate School and waited … and waited to be shipped to Fort Leonard, but the Army told me the wait list was very long. My waiting allowed me to play for the base soccer team, but after a time, I withdrew my name from the list. So, I was sent to South Korea and the DMZ [demilitarized zone] at the end of 1967. We were told it was a dangerous period due to the USS Pueblo (AGER-2), an American ship that was found within North Korea's twelve-mile limit. The North Korean military breached the DMZ and blew up the foxholes. When peace came about, I suggested that the rebuilt foxholes be designed similar to the maze at Hampton Court by Henry VIII in London. I do not know if they accepted such an interesting architectural concept.

My next assignment was at Camp Darby in Italy, working as an architect and continuing to play soccer. Since I needed to complete a few subjects both in architecture and city planning at Pratt Institute, I gave myself strange assignments to practice architectural designs and drawings each month. For example, I designed an island with hotels, shops, entertainment, and such. Another time I designed a lighthouse that I transformed to become a person's home. Pratt was impressed and took me back to finish both an architecture and city planning master's degree. I thank the US Army for allowing me these opportunities to travel the world and create many exciting physical environments. As a fairly poor man, the G.I. Bill was of great help and a confidence builder.

Some eight years ago, I won a design competition in Albuquerque's Veterans Memorial Park to design a Vietnam-era sculpture I called "Holes in Our Hearts," a contemporary sculpture for families and friends of the 400 New Mexicans who died during that war. The visitors

21

can place flowers, notes, letters, or photos in the holes of the three monuments feature 400 holes.

This has been a life of variety, adventure, and learning. I have a book coming out with around one hundred sketches and stories from around the world.

*****

Author: Steve Borbas

Steve Borbas was born in Hungary and escaped with his family during the revolution of 1956. He lived in refugee camps in the former Yugoslavia until the family was allowed into the US. Steve is a US Army veteran, a professor emeritus from the University of New Mexico, and he enjoys traveling and his art.

E. Joe Brown

"Hey Coach"

My Favorite Memory as a Football Coach at Desert High

During my military career, I was assigned to Edwards Air Force Base in Southern California. Desert High School was located on the airbase, and I spent many evenings there as a coach. The following is a true story from that period of my life.

I have many fond memories of coaching youth in football and baseball, but one young man and our shared times are a little more special than most. We met when he played on an Antelope Valley Youth Football League team in Southern California. That league was created for youngsters to play in before they were old enough to be on a high school team. His name was David Flaugher. He was the same age and a teammate of my older son. I saw potential in him, but he lacked discipline. That meant he could not be depended on to execute his part of whatever play the coach wanted the team to run. I couldn't always attend the practices because I was coaching at the high school, but I took David aside on one of the days I was at their practice.

"I'm Coach Brown, and I enjoyed watching you today. You're David, right?"

"Yeah, who are you?"

"As I said, I'm Coach Brown, and I coach football at Desert High. I watched you today during your practice."

"So, why should I care?"

"Well, maybe you shouldn't. But I wanted to know if you planned to play for the high school next year?"

"Yeah, probably. If we're still here, hey, I gotta go." He turned and walked away.

***

That was my first experience with the young man. His attitude told me volumes, but it also created questions. I hoped to see him next year.

I stood on the practice field the following year as the players walked out from the locker room on their first day. "David, welcome to your first practice on the Desert High Scorpion's Junior Varsity team."

"You're that guy I saw at a practice last year. Aren't ya?"

"That'll be, aren't you, Coach Brown? Or aren't you, sir? You can pick; either one works."

That was the start of our time together, covering the next four years of our lives. David became an excellent high school football player. He was big, so he became an offensive lineman. But where he grew most was in his self-control. His respect for himself, his teammates, and the adults in his life became his trademark. I was his coach for those years, and the team successfully won enough games to make the state playoffs every year. But David's senior year was special, and what made it special started in a football game in Bishop, California.

There are four quarters in a football game. You play two and then break for halftime. It was getting close to halftime, and neither team had scored. After we had kicked the football to Bishop's team, David came running off the field, red-faced with his fists clenched ....

"Coach ... Coach ...." He had a crazed look in his eyes.

"What, Flaugher, what's wrong?"

"He's calling me girly and princess and some names I won't tell ya."

"Who is?"

"Their middle linebacker, number fifty-five."

"And that bothers you, David?"

"Yes, sir, he's makin' fun of my hair."

David had beautiful long red hair that flowed out under his helmet.

"What are you goin' to do about it?"

"What do ya mean, Coach?"

"David, I would never tell any player to break the rules, but why don't you KICK HIS BUTT."

"What? How?"

"When we get the football. On the first play, you fire out and knock fifty-five to the ground. I mean to knock fifty-five into 'next week.' Do you understand me?"

"I think so, Coach. What if the play called has me doing something else?"

"David, for this one play, you go get that guy. Got it?"

"With a big grin on his face, he said, "Got it, Coach."

After David walked away, I went directly to our head coach, who called offensive plays, and said, "Leroy, call your first play with Mayfield running off right guard."

Leroy looked puzzled and asked, "Why, coach?"

I smiled and said, "Flaugher is going to settle a score with the middle linebacker."

Leroy smiled back at me, "Sure, we can do that."

Randy Mayfield, our running back, was fast and talented.

We got the ball back about forty yards from Bishop's goal line.

Leroy called the play, and David exploded toward number fifty-five. You heard the sound of the impact of David's block throughout the stadium. The Bishop High coaches had to help fifty-five off the field. Mayfield ran those forty yards for a touchdown. That play gave the Desert High Scorpions a spark, and we won the game. The best part was when David came off the field after the extra-point play. He was beaming.

"Coach, did ya see it? Did ya? Boy o' boy, did ya?"

I was laughing as I said, "I sure did, buddy, and I doubt you'll hear another word out of him tonight."

He didn't. Fifty-five didn't make a good play for his team for the rest of the game. Mayfield had one of his best games running the football behind David.

But the best night of that season for David and me was still to come.

It was a cool and beautiful Friday night in late November 1989. I had been coaching football at Desert High for almost a decade by that time. Something wonderful and unexpected was about to happen.

The team was dressing in the locker room for the final home game of the season. There was electricity in the air mixed with sweat, liniment, and excitement. The team had already qualified for the post-season playoffs, and now we wanted to end the regular season on a positive note.

It was Senior Night, with its ceremony at halftime. Each Senior on the team remained on the field. Their parents come out of the stands. The players give a rose to a parent during the ceremony. That always is touching and adds a great memory to any season. This Senior Class of players had been one of the most successful in decades. Everyone expected a packed stadium.

I was the varsity offensive line coach going over my lineup and plans sitting in a corner of the locker room when I heard a familiar voice say, "Hey Coach, can we talk?"

"Sure, David; what's on your mind?"

"You know tonight's Senior Night, right?"

"Yes, and I look forward to meeting your folks."

David was one of my best linemen, standing well over six feet and weighing 240 pounds. Towering over me, he looked almost embarrassed as he stared down at his feet, saying, "Come on, Coach, how long have you known me?"

"Since you were in junior high."

"That's right, and have you ever seen either my mom or dad?"

"Well, no, I haven't. That's why I said what I did."

"Coach, they're not going to be here. That's why I wanted to talk to you."

"Okay."

"Coach, would you be my dad tonight during the ceremony?"

26

I practically melted. I knew we had become close over the years, but David asking me that far exceeded anything I could have imagined.

I said, "David, it would be my honor. Are you sure?"

With tears beginning to show, "Yes, Coach, and thanks."

At halftime, I counted the people forming the two lines of parents and players so I would arrive at the right time with David. I had not had a chance to let the announcer know what David and I planned, but there was no need. Roger Bean, the announcer, knew David and me very well and had figured it out because when we got to the head of the line, you heard across the stadium. "Next, number 78, David Flaugher, starting right guard, and his friend, Coach Joe Brown."

The stadium erupted in applause, and I experienced a moment I will never forget as this big bear of a guy hugged me and whispered, "Thanks, Coach, this means a lot to me."

*****

 *Author: E. Joe Brown*

E. Joe Brown writes historical fiction and memoirs. He retired from his US Air Force (USAF) military and civil service careers in 2010 as a Senior Analyst advising the Commander USAF Flight Test Center. He is a member of SouthWest Writers, Western Writers of America, Military Writers Society of America, and several other non-profit organizations.

LAUREL BURNETT

Chronological Vista

Baby (born on the kitchen table)
Son
Toddler
Sibling
Dust Bowl eyewitness
Feed Store work hand
Salesboy (punch cards at the rail yards)
High School Graduate
University of Texas Student
Boyfriend
College Graduate
Alumni
Fiancé
Air Force Officer
Groom
Spouse
Penn State Nittany Lion
Meteorologist
Parent
Reservist
Chemist at Los Alamos National Laboratory
Ph.D.
Sunday School Teacher
Bookstore Owner
Grandfather "Daddy-B"
Golden Wedding Anniversary Celebrant
Great Grandfather
Genealogist
Role Model

Volunteer
Writer
Friend
Veteran
Caregiver
Lifelong Learner

My Dad
alone, in isolation
covid death
a vertical list
honoring a panoramic life

Laurel Burnett provided care support for her dad, himself an Air Force veteran, after he was diagnosed with Alzheimer's disease in 2018. He now rests in peace at Santa Fe National Cemetery with his beloved wife of sixty-six years.

*****

Mere Reflections

I was not surprised that I was the youngest person and the only female in the room. At twenty-three years old, I was an Air Force 2nd Lieutenant assigned to the 7th Munitions Maintenance Squadron, a Strategic Air Command flight line with conventional and special weapons (and all that entailed). The field of munitions had been closed to women until 1972, and although it was 1981, maintenance remained a male-dominated environment.

I twisted my body to fit into a cramped school desk chair with a wrap-around writing table. Experiencing a mental food flash to the past, I realized these were the same type of chairs from the Baskin-Robbins 31 Flavors ice cream parlor in Los Alamos, NM. The chairs felt so much roomier when slurping up a rocky road double dip cone after a

Lassie League softball game. Not as comfortable when sitting among thirty-nine senior non-commissioned officers in a stuffy mobile trailer.

The civilian consultant facilitating the "Management and Leadership Techniques" seminar welcomed us and exclaimed, "You are all participants!" My stomach flipped, and I felt nauseous. I preferred workshops where I could listen and learn without having to speak up. My body and mind heaved a weighted sigh. Our consultant divided us up into eight groups of five.

We were given fifteen minutes to discuss and develop a survival plan in the aftermath of a plane crash. It was a straightforward scenario: five survivors, we had filed a flight plan, we took off from Texas en route to California, and we crashed in the desert. We had no working radio and salvaged five items from the rubble: a canteen of water, a six-inch knife, a compass, a broken piece of a mirror, and a handbook entitled *Edible Desert Wildlife*. We were to reach a consensus and prioritize *two* resources. I mentally prepared my list: water, mirror. Simple. Done. I thought, "What is so complex about that? What other solution could there be?"

Our group agreed on the need for water; completion of fifty percent of our activity in less than one minute! We engaged in spirited discussion for the next thirteen minutes and thirty seconds. I was the only group member who found merit in keeping the mirror. The four men were in full agreement that we absolutely did *not* need a mirror. There were mixed inputs about whether a knife or a wildlife handbook would prove handier.

I tried multiple times to inject my rationale for the mirror. I emphasized, "We filed a flight plan. There will be rescue planes. We are in the Arizona desert. There are hours of sunlight, and we can use the mirror as a signal. We don't need a knife to split a saguaro or a book about how to kill a coyote. If we keep the mirror, we will be rescued before lunchtime tomorrow, and you can eat as much as you want!"

To no avail. It was as if I was speaking into a windstorm of a Steinbeck dust bowl. I was a group member yet invisible at the same time. I felt discouraged, realizing that being young and female contributed to my words not being heard. It didn't stop me from trying, but I was talked over and drowned out.

The consultant reminded us we had less than one minute to finish our exercise. There was a last-ditch effort of arguments about whether the "knife or the book" would increase our hope for survival. The manual about how to locate and kill food in the desert won. Reason being that if the knife were used to dig up and consume poisonous plants, we'd still die; thus, the book would provide instructions on how to forage the safest type of food from a desert environment.

By the end of the fifteen minutes, I was not looking forward to even one make-believe night in the desert with my four group members. When the eight groups reconvened, a representative from each group summarized the two survival items that were chosen. The consultant probed, "How did your decision process evolve, and was there a dissenting member?" The consultant stated, "Given the circumstances of the crash scenario, the two wisest and most rational items to select for survival are the water and the mirror."

When we broke for the day, my four fellow survivors approached me, and the most vocal advocate for the wildlife handbook stated, "I guess we should have listened to you." The other three group members nodded in agreement. I was still befuddled. I asked, "*Why* didn't you think we should keep the mirror?" A moment of silence. "We thought you wanted the mirror to see what you looked like."

*****

Author: Laurel Burnett

Laurel Burnett is an Air Force veteran and served twelve years on active duty in the Strategic Air Command and US Air Forces in Europe. She served thirteen years with the Air Force Reserve; and completed her service at the Pentagon Combat Support Center after the 9-11 terrorist attacks. She is a Licensed Mental Health Counselor in New Mexico.

SHERRI BURR

My Brother's Guardian

January 1971: Phoenix, Arizona

"Mom," Ralph yelled at the top of his lungs. In his bedroom, he played with an electronic football game as rain drizzled outside. He had lined up his teams in formation.

"What is it, Sweetheart?" Mom asked as she walked from the kitchen through the living room to Ralph's bedroom. She wiped wet hands on a striped apron.

"Can you please tell Sis to get out of my room." Ralph pressed the play button to start the teams moving.

"But Mom," I replied, "It's not fair. He got the best toys for Christmas."

"Honey, why don't you go play with those new Barbie dolls?" Mom asked.

"I've already cut their hair," I said. "There's nothing more to do with them. I want to play with Ralph's football game."

"Go away," Ralph yelled at me. "I want to play by myself. And take off my cutoffs. You stretch them out."

Mom gave me a full look. At age eleven, I stood a head taller than nine-year-old Ralph and was nearly the same height as Mom. "Honey, please take off Ralph's cutoffs."

"But Mom, I don't have any blue jean cutoffs. And these are good for playing football."

"Honey, girls shouldn't be playing football."

"Yeah," Ralph added. "Go play with your own friends. Leave mine alone."

"But Mom, Linda is the only other girl on our street. All she likes to do is ride bikes and pop wheelies. Besides, it's raining outside."

"Well, Honey," Mom said to me, "maybe you could read one of the three books you picked up from the library."

"I finished those books last night," I said.

"That quickly?" Mom asked. "You just brought those books home yesterday."

"She reads after you tell her to turn off the light to go to sleep," Ralph said. "She gets down by the door and uses the light coming in from the hall."

"Tattletale!"

"Honey, you'll ruin your eyes reading with so little light."

"My eyes are fine, Mom. Can you tell Ralph to let me play with his football game?"

"No!" Ralph yelled. "Go away."

"But Mom, I like playing football. When it's not raining outside, his friends let me play quarterback and running back on their teams. And I'm fast."

"We only let you play when we don't have enough boys," Ralph chimed in. "Besides, you like to tackle us, and we can't hit back 'cause you're a girl. Yesterday, you leaped up and jumped on a boy."

"I was just trying to keep him from scoring a touchdown," I said in my defense.

"It's supposed to be flag football. You're just supposed to pull our flag," Ralph said. As Mom and I left, Ralph demanded, "Take off my cutoffs."

"Fine," I said. "You can have them back, but one of these days, you're going to really need me."

***

33

November 2009

By the time the words of an eleven-year-old proved prophetic, my brother Ralph had finished his military career, and I was in my twenty-first year as a University of New Mexico law professor. On a fall evening, I was back in Arizona for a conference and driving to Ralph's condo in Mesa for a barbeque. About a mile from his home, I dialed his number because I was lost. "Hello," answered an unfamiliar voice.

"Hello. Ralph?" I questioned.

"Is this Sherri, Ralph's sister?" The unfamiliar voice asked.

"Yeah. Who's this? Where's Ralph?"

"I'm an officer with the Mesa Police Department. Ralph had a heart attack. The ambulance just took him to the emergency room. Ralph's friends said you were on your way. I'm waiting for you to lock up his condo and show you how to get there."

"Oh, my God, how's Ralph?" I asked.

After I explained my location, he gave me directions. When I arrived, we locked up. I followed his car to the emergency room.

Ralph lay on a bed looking defenseless. Tears welled up in my eyes and flowed down my cheeks. I kneeled by his bed and started praying. A cardiologist came in and explained they were taking Ralph up to the Intensive Care Unit [ICU] for tests on his heart. While he talked about shooting dye through Ralph's veins to get a picture, my brain felt like he was speaking Serbian.

The ambulance people who brought in Ralph were still there. They mentioned working on him for about twenty-two minutes. "He kept flat-lining," one of them said. "We shocked him. We gave him medicine. We'd get a pulse, and then it would disappear again. Finally, we got him stable enough to bring in."

"Thank you for saving my brother's life," I said. I didn't want to ponder that flatlining meant Ralph had clinically died.

He had first suffered a heart attack after his daughter was born four years earlier. I found out by serendipity. While visiting his home, I discovered a book on how to improve your heart. Just as he had done during our childhood, Ralph kept many things to himself.

As his friends milled in the hallway, I introduced myself. Two of them told me Ralph was barbecuing on the patio when they heard a thump. They found him lying near the grill. They called 9-1-1 and were advised to administer chest compressions. "It took the ambulance four minutes to get to Ralph," one of them said.

Amazingly, Ralph had as many friends now as when we were children.

*****

Minutes turned into hours and hours into days as more tests and procedures were run on Ralph. In the Intensive Care Unit, the doctors cooled his blood to reduce swelling in his brain and then re-warmed him twenty-four hours later. I slept on a cot in the chilled room and was grateful when a nurse brought me warm blankets.

About four days into the ordeal, a doctor and a nurse came into Ralph's room.

"Sherri, we have to talk to you," the doctor said as the nurse stepped to the side.

"Yes," I said, stiffening my back into an erect posture.

"We don't think he's coming back."

"What? What are you talking about?"

"After we re-warmed him, we expected him to awaken within twenty-four hours. Since he hasn't woken up, we think he's gone."

"What do you mean he's gone? He's right over there, breathing."

"We think there's so much brain damage that the part of his brain that gave him his personality is gone."

"What have you based that on?"

"We have studies to prove it," she said.

"I want to see those studies." My analytic brain resurfaced. I wasn't about to accept what she said without an investigation.

"Fine," she said and left.

About thirty minutes later, she reappeared with the paper.

I quickly read the document and observed that it was based on a survey of four hundred people, all of whom had been sent to hospice to die, "This study should have an error rate of plus or minus five percent, but it doesn't state any." I said to the doctor, recalling my statistical studies as a graduate student at Princeton. "I think they all died because no one was given a chance to live. Ralph gets at least a week to try to wake up."

"Fine, you can have a week," she said and abruptly left. I had the feeling that she was unused to encountering a patient advocate like me.

I flashbacked to high school when I was a junior, and Ralph was a freshman. I saw Ralph get on the bus to go home, and he looked like he had been in a fight. He sat by me, and I asked him what had happened. He said that some kid had said something nasty about me, and he fought the kid. It occurred to me that all those decades ago, he had fought for my honor. Now, I had to fight for his right to live.

***

From the ICU, Ralph was sent to a skilled nursing facility, and I became his guardian through a court procedure. My investigation into his finances revealed he had no money. How was he going to support his two kids? I decided to apply for Veterans Benefits.

At the VA [Department of Veterans Affairs], the intake officer mentioned that Ralph had received a General Discharge instead of an Honorable Discharge from the Air Force. She said not to worry, however, because the VA sometimes awarded benefits to individuals with a General Discharge. She gave me a stack of papers to fill out and asked me to wait for another person to review the file.

I wasn't sure what the difference between an Honorable and a General Discharge was, other than General obviously came with less benefits than Honorable.

After a few minutes, a tall guy with a buzz haircut introduced himself. I followed him to a conference room. After reviewing the file, he said there were two obstacles to obtaining benefits for Ralph. I had to prove that Ralph's current condition was connected to his time in the service, and I would need to seek a military review to see if I could get Ralph's discharge upgraded to Honorable.

"My brother is in a coma," I said, "I can't interview him. I didn't even know he had received a General Discharge. All I remember from twenty years ago is that he said there was conflict with his commanding officer."

He looked at me sympathetically. "If you fill out these papers as his guardian, you can request his medical records. Maybe there will be some connection to his current condition. The bigger problem is requesting his service records. They are going to want him to sign."

I stared. *What part of "my brother's in a coma" is this guy not getting?*

He sensed my dismay and continued, "On this form, have the hospital staff mark a thumbprint for his signature and then sign their names."

I immediately filled out the paperwork and mailed off the request. As I drove to the skilled nursing facility, my memory jetted back to April of 1988, when Ralph was stationed at Elmendorf Air Force Base in Alaska, and I was a graduate student at Princeton. He told Mom and me that his job was intelligence related. No details. He also said he was applying, based on his Fisk bachelor's degree, to attend officer training school, but his commanding officer was against him.

At age twenty-six, he was engaged to be married. Mom and I were planning to fly up to Anchorage for the wedding. We were both excited because neither of us had been to Alaska. Then, the trip fell apart.

Ralph called to say he was no longer getting married and leaving the Air Force because they wouldn't let him become an officer.

Now it appeared his leaving the Air Force was involuntary.

Upon arriving at the skilled nursing facility, I informed the case manager that I needed Ralph's thumbprint on documents signed by two nurses. To my surprise, they immediately produced a fingerprinting kit.

Two weeks later, Ralph's medical records arrived. Ralph had been treated for periodontal disease. I had read that there's a proven connection between the condition and heart problems. Ralph had started the periodontal treatment, but there was no indication it had been completed. Had the Air Force booted him out with no access to medical treatment? I didn't understand this. Ralph told me he had purchased a house with a VA loan. Why would the VA permit him to have housing but not medical benefits?

The VA sent back the request for Ralph's service records. The nursing staff had forgotten their license number.

Even with that, the documents came back again. The VA said Ralph's thumbprint was illegible.

I decided to give up. This was an uphill climb, given Ralph's General Discharge. With no evidence to be obtained from him, I was unlikely to get that overturned. I yielded, as I had when I took off his cutoffs all those years ago.

*****

Author: Sherri Burr

After her brother suffered a heart attack, Sherri Burr became his guardian and sought to obtain his veteran's benefits. Her twenty-seventh book, *Complicated Lives: Free Blacks in Virginia, 1619-1865*, was nominated for the Pulitzer Prize in History. She has a Princeton Master's in Public Administration and a Yale Law School Doctor of Jurisprudence.

IVAN CALHOUN

Second to None

Albert's '72 Chevy pickup lurched to a stop outside of his single-wide trailer. Prior to his arrival, the trailer court had been quiet as a church. He fixed that as he began revving the truck's engine, causing his oversized exhaust pipes to boom loudly. Windows in all the nearby trailers rattled from the noise while inside the truck, his 8-track played George Jones' "The Race Is On" — also so loudly folks could hear it. The awakened neighbors were pissed, but Albert's family in the trailer hated it more as they heard the exhausts crackle with every deep depression of the throttle. The digital clock in the truck showed it was 2:20 in the morning — Albert was again home drunk.

In the back bedroom of the trailer, Jim fidgeted in his upper bunk, hoping that he'd get left alone; he had school that morning. The eleven-year-old's bedroom door was open, allowing him to see down the shotgun hallway to the front of the trailer, where a light came on. He lifted his head slightly to look better over the end of the bed and heard the front screen and then the door open clumsily and slam. He pursed his lips as he heard his mom Lilly start trying to settle his father down. Though he could not make out most of the words she was trying, he could tell they weren't helping.

"Come to bed, Albert," Lilly implored from upfront.

Albert mumbled loudly back to his wife and pushed her back. Jim, still looking down the hall, saw the large dark silhouette of his father start down the hallway towards his room. He remained motionless in the bed with the dread that had been building in him all day fully realized since his dad had not come home right after work again. He hoped the night's upcoming events wouldn't involve his little brother Max who also wasn't sleeping any longer in the bunk beneath him.

Lilly shouted down the hall at her husband, "Albert! Stop!"

Albert's black form grew huge as he came down the hall. He turned on the lights in the bedroom to look at his two sons in their beds. Jim stirred, pretending as if he'd been fully asleep; he got up on one elbow. Max didn't move; thankfully, it was harder for his dad to see him on the lower bunk.

"Get yer butt up," Albert barked at Jim. "God-damn-it! Let's go, candy-ass."

Max pretended to stay asleep as he watched Jim clamber down from his bunk and follow their father out the door into the hallway. Jim turned out the lights as they left.

Jim thought, *Man, it's too bright in here,* as he walked into the small kitchen-dining area of the trailer. Being a skinny kid, he looked even skinnier, wearing only his white briefs like he always did to bed. His mom, in her robe, lit a cigarette in the front room. She forced a smile of resignation toward him for what seemed the thousandth time as his father pulled a beer out of the fridge. Jim ducked an unfriendly open-handed swing at his head as Albert came back to the dining table where Jim stood. He had gotten better at not getting clobbered at least half the time.

"I thought I told you to mow the lawn today," Albert growled.

"I did, Dad," Jim replied.

"Did you weed-eat around the trailer?"

"Yes, sir."

Albert motioned Jim to take a seat at the dining table.

"Let the boy go back to bed; he has school," Lilly shot from the front room.

Albert ignored his wife, saying to his son, "Get the game."

Jim opened the bottom cabinet of the particle-board cupboard next to their rickety Formica-top dining table. He pulled out a cardboard box and set it down on the table. It contained a chess set which he started setting up on the table between them. Albert took a drag from his beer while he waited and spotted a book in the cabinet. He reached in and

40

pulled out a worn, tattered copy of *The Last of the Mohicans*, an edition printed back in the '40s. Jim warily stayed out of reach as he finished setting the game. Since Jim had made him white, Albert made the first move. Jim struggled to stay awake as he began playing against his father, who started on a rant — again.

"That stupid son-of-bitch tells me how it was like over there. He doesn't know shit. Officers, all of 'em, over-educated idiots," Albert grumbled fifteen minutes into his tirade to no one. "Are you going to move?"

Jim snapped back to being alert, moving a bishop and taking a pawn.

"Hmmm ...." Albert mused as he castled his King. Looking back up, he saw Jim nodding back to sleep. Angrily he shouted, "God damn it! Are you sleeping or playing?"

Straightening back up again, Jim replied, "I'm playing, Dad." He re-focused on the board.

Albert reached into his trouser pocket and pulled out an oversized bronze challenge coin with the 2nd Infantry Division insignia on one side and a map of Korea on the other. He started absentmindedly twirling it on the tabletop while thumbing through the beat-up copy of James Fennimore Cooper's novel.

After a bit, Lilly came to the table with a T-shirt, a small plate of cookies, and a glass of milk for Jim. She bent down and kissed him on top of the head.

"I've got to get some sleep," Lilly said. "Honey, wake me if you need anything."

"I'm all right, Mom. I'll see you in the morning."

"I know you are, kiddo."

Albert kept looking over the board, seemingly oblivious to his wife, but as she passed him, he grabbed her arm roughly. He pulled her down to him and kissed her. She straightened back up and left for bed without a word. Albert's challenge coin sat in front of Jim.

"Where'd you get this again, Dad?" Jim asked about the coin.

"My company's first sergeant gave it to me when I ran into him a couple of years ago. Means more than my bronze star and purple heart put together."

Thirty minutes later, the chess match continued with Jim wearing his T-shirt, now fully awake; the cookies and milk had done their trick. He sat silently, moving his pieces when it was his turn.

"That dumb bastard. Giving me his take on being an infantryman. That sea-going bellhop doesn't know crap," Albert blurted out, starting another diatribe. He moved a piece and continued talking to the chessboard. "*Chipyong-Ni*, that was a fight. Tell me all about your good conduct medals after you've faced thousands of Chinese charging your position waving flags, blowing whistles and horns for four days and nights."

Jim looked up and studied his father's face.

"Most of 'em Chinese, I bet weren't seventeen years old, and there were girls in with them fightin', and all you could do was keep shooting into their formations and hope the falling bodies in front slowed down the ones behind 'em," Albert went on with a voice that started quivering, "One of those firefights ... one night a half-track backed us up with quad 50s on top. My God, when it opened up. We had at least a battalion of 'em attacking our position, and it was good to have that truck firing ... with the whole platoon dug in and all of us pouring it in, we ground them into hamburger."

Albert paused as his eyes welled up.

"They still got too close. The bastards ... the bastards .... There were too many. The lieutenant called in mortars on top of us. When the shelling stopped, I looked up. There on the plank across the front of my foxhole was a beating Chinese heart," Albert went on as he choked noticeably. Albert looked back at Jim, still studying him. "Do you believe that shit?"

"Yes, sir."

"Well, when that dumbass Lipton at the VFW [Veterans of Foreign Wars] can prove to me he was ever within ten miles of a firefight and not in the rear with the gear, he can start jabbering at me without me jacking his jaw."

Jim glanced at Albert's right hand and only then noticed that the knuckles were bruised. He returned his gaze back to his father's weathered face and saw for the hundredth time the sadness there. It wasn't the first time Jim had heard what happened at *Chipyong-Ni,* and he expected to hear it again another evening.

Albert took one of Jim's pawns. "Check," he confidently pointed out.

"Checkmate," Jim quietly declared after two more of his own moves. The wall clock showed it was almost four.

"Son-of-a-bitch," Albert whispered.

Jim got up from the table, went to his seated father, and kissed him on his whiskered cheek. He then pressed his forehead tightly to his father's forehead, and they stared fiercely into each other's eyes for five seconds. "Goodnight, Dad. I love you."

"Good night, Candy ...." Albert stopped himself. "Good night. We'll all go fishing on Saturday."

Albert picked up *The Last of the Mohicans* and started reading a passage.

"I'm glad I had this in my bag over there. This part I always tried to remind myself of. *Every trail has its end, and every calamity brings its lesson.*"

Jim spun around as he was leaving for his bedroom. "Oh. Here," Jim held out the challenge coin to his father. He had absentmindedly picked it up during the night and been clutching it.

"Thanks, Jim," Albert told his son, taking the coin back.

Headed to bed, Jim almost tripped over Max, who had fallen asleep on the hallway floor listening to his father and brother through the night. Jim bent down to get his brother to his feet.

"Come on, Max, let's go to bed," Jim quietly said.

*****

Author: Ivan Calhoun

Ivan Calhoun's father was a Korean War combat veteran and has a son currently serving in the US Army as well as a Gunnery Sergeant for a son-in-law. Ivan's previous published fiction has been included in the High Plains Writers' annual anthology and *Big Bend Literary Magazine*.

JOHN J. CANDELARIA

A Poetic Study on the Elegance of Military Thinking

I had a twenty-year military life experience with diverse assignments in the United States and three overseas assignments in Thailand, South Korea, and Vietnam. I saw many places, had engaging experiences, and encountered thoughtful leaders as officers and NCOs [non-commissioned officers]. Central to that experience was an unfolding of what I call a military mind. A poetic expression captures that essence.

Sonnet to the Military Mind

A military mind is a deft mind,
Informed by clear, certain truth based on facts.
A wisdom acquired over years that bind
Thought and action into convincing acts.

This mind follows its duty, with honor,
And for country. High standards taken in
An oath to support and defend in candor,
So deeds on the outside come from within.

It's a frame of mind thriving in critical
Thinking that never allows the excuse,
"The end justifies the means." Ethical
Ways evolve to keep the oath from abuse.

This path enables growth in character
And molds each defender and team as victor.

***

My thinking was trained and seasoned always to have clarity of mission, to make plans, and prepare to execute that mission with available resources. Most importantly as a team, when one leader is killed, the next leader is trained and expected to continue the mission.

In the Army Medical Department, "To conserve the fighting strength" is the broad mission; at the 45th Surgical Hospital in Vietnam [the term Mobile Army Surgical Hospital or MASH was used to describe such portable units], it was to have the hospital ever ready to give its patients the best surgical and medical care. A clear poetic view speaks lucidly.

***

A Tribute to the 45th MASH

You endured untold sights and sounds of war,
   But were ever ready to treat and heal, aware
The damage war swept past your door
   Made this MASH a crucial refuge in warfare.
Many soldiers left enemy strikes in despair
   For life or limb, and saw in you gentle
Hands that stitched fighting spirits so their
   Courage was kept intact to fight another battle.

Dustoff's whirling blades were your
   Call to service at the MASH, their midair
Howl an urgent cry for medics to restore
   And mend injured fighters without fanfare.
In surgery, your labor kept warriors in repair,
   As hands cut, clamped and sutured in skillful
Fashion, and salvaged soldiers became aware
   Courage was kept intact to fight another battle.

Your 45th MASH forever tried to be a savior
   To all who came in distress, and whose share
Of worthy efforts now live ever in combat lore.
   Two surgeons died as they toiled with rare
Talents, so warriors could live lives any
   Those who spoke warmly of your hospital,
Reminded others of your superb patient care.
   Courage was kept intact to fight another battle.

Medics, the 45th MASH was a place where
   Soldiers desperate fates were turned hopeful,
So, confident voices would always declare,
   "Courage was kept intact to fight another battle."

***

After those twenty years in service to my country, I repeatedly mused on the idea, "Did my military mind work well in the civilian world, or best kept amid military service." I worked in five civilian work settings. I searched for excellent team milieus to continue as I had in the military. I found most successful efforts were connected to and supported as a team. In some cases, a sense of exceptionalism dominated, and team efforts collided with individual competition.

In 2002 a significant life change occurred as I began writing poetry as a narrative poet. I had poems published in various periodicals, and in 2017 I became the author of the book *War in the Company of Medics: Poems of the 45th Surgical Hospital in Vietnam.*

While writing poetry, I took an opportunity to become an Oasis Tutor, to help elementary school children improve their reading skills. Under the leadership of the Albuquerque Oasis Intergenerational Tutoring Program, I spent eleven and a half years tutoring.

47

In all these times and events, I focused on what my mission was. I know those experiences were driven by a military mind centered on purpose of action. A final poem sketches out those thoughts.

***

On Focus

Tasks unfolded; my mind sprung to inquire,
"What is the mission I am here to do?"
As I sought a clear vision to inspire.

Military ways taught me to aspire
For a sharp focus on what will ensue.
Tasks unfolded; my mind sprung to inquire,

Will our mission succeed in the gunfire
Of combat? Vietnam MASH a prime view
As I sought a clear vision to inspire.

In civilian milieus, feats would require
A refocus on purpose to come through.
Tasks unfolded; my mind sprung to inquire,

And remember times that held a crossfire
For direction, and mission became true
As I sought a clear vision to inspire.

In all those efforts there were surefire
Ways to find success; mission was the glue.
Tasks unfolded; my mind sprung to inquire,
As I sought a clear vision to inspire.

***

I came to admit military thinking works well in any experience as its attention on mission is paramount for success.

*****

Author: John J. Candelaria

John J. Candelaria is a retired Army veteran of twenty years of service. He is a narrative poet, writing since 2002, and his work has appeared in numerous publications. John is the author of a poetry book titled *War in the Company of Medics: Poem of the 45th Surgical Hospital in Vietnam*.

JUDY CASTLEBERRY

My Atomic Vet

If it was not for the atomic bomb and the USO [United Service Organization], I might not have been born. My mother was raised on a ranch near Farmington, NM, but my dad was from a small town in Alabama. They met at a USO picnic when he was stationed at Los Alamos, and she was a student nurse in Albuquerque. They were married for sixty-seven years and had five children.

One of the last photos I took of my father was at the Veterans Dinner at the Farmington Elks Lodge. He had lost so much weight that his seventy-year-old uniform shirt fit. I ironed it, and my nephew gave him a haircut and shave. In the photo, my father is standing up as straight as he can, transported in time to the days when he was a soldier. It had been a hard year; my mother had passed away, and he had broken his shoulder. But for that evening, he was as spit-shined and ready to go as ever. I felt like I was escorting the belle of the ball.

About ten years before this photo, I had interviewed him for a story about Atomic Vets that I was writing for a class. When I was a kid, most of my parents' friends had been in the military, serving in World War II or the Korean War. A few had scars or amputations from combat. My dad was not a combat soldier. Most of his time in the service, other than at Enewetak Atoll, was served stateside. I think he always felt a little guilty for not serving in combat. But atomic vets were a special group, and many bore the marks of their service. This is his story.

When I was a little girl, a life preserver hung on the wall in the den. It was smooth and white, like a mint Lifesaver, with a rope running through loops around the edges. On one side were painted palm trees and the word *Eniwetok* [the US government changed the spelling of the name in 1974]. It was so solid and heavy that I could not imagine it floating in water. I knew it was from when Daddy was stationed on a small island in the South Pacific, like the grass skirts we sometimes wore for Halloween. But I was much older before I understood that this soldier's souvenir had anything to do with the atomic bomb.

Nuclear testing did not end with the bombing of Hiroshima and Nagasaki in August 1945 and the end of World War II. Fresh from celebrating the end of the War, the United States fell immediately under the shadow of the Cold War. New weapons — including atomic weapons — were considered imperative to fight this new menace. Fat Man and Little Boy, the bombs used at Hiroshima and Nagasaki, composed the entire United States atomic arsenal. The scientists at Los Alamos National Lab continued their work developing more efficient and easier to mass produce weapons. Bob Batley, my father, was a young PFC [private first class] from Alabama when he was sent to Los Alamos in May 1946 as a part of the atomic forces.

The wheels of the olive-drab bus scrabble to catch hold of the loose gravel of the corduroy road. The driver shifts into a lower gear, and the motor whines in protest as the bus continues to crawl up the mountainside. The windows along the side are slid open, catching the dust-laden breeze that brings in the aroma of sagebrush clinging to the granite wall almost near enough to touch. Passengers on the far side see only the spear points of blue spruce and Ponderosa pine in the canyon below. "If we ever get where we're going, I'm never coming back if it means coming down this road," a soldier wisecracks. A nervous guffaw runs through the bus.

"They didn't tell us anything," Daddy said, describing that first trip to Los Alamos. "I thought I was going to be stationed in downtown Santa Fe because all I knew was PO [Post Office] Box 1559. It wasn't until we were in the barracks that we were told we were stationed on The Hill. That's all they called it: The Hill."

If they had any doubts, soldiers on The Hill quickly learned how hush-hush their new duty was. One site was so secret that only twelve people were allowed in. My father, as an MP, had to identify each person three times when they entered: the person showed his badge, there was a matching ID [identification] in the guard shack, and a visual ID. Unfortunately, Klaus Fuchs, who later sold secrets to the Russians, was one of the twelve people. Even in Santa Fe, a soldier shooting off his mouth in a bar suddenly found two "suits" on each side of him. He was released only after a long night of questioning.

On the other side of the world from Los Alamos is Enewetak Atoll in the Marshall Islands, the site of many atomic tests. Enewetak is a series of forty islands surrounded by a lagoon-like a pearl necklace slung casually across the aquamarine South Pacific. Complete with sandy beaches, slender palm trees crowned with frowsy clusters of fronds, and the perfume of ocean breezes mixed with tropical flowers; the islands could be the setting for a movie about paradise. The Japanese built an airfield early in the war on the main island and used it for staging attacks on the rest of the Marshall Islands. It was captured by the United States in 1944. My father was assigned to Enewetak during Operation Sandstone and Operation Greenhouse.

"There were one hundred of us from Sandia in charge of security for Sandstone," Daddy recalled. By this time, he was stationed at Sandia Base in New Mexico. "We would be down on the beach at 3:00 AM because all of the shots were before dawn. Every fifteen minutes until the shot, the man in charge of each group would have to visually ID each person. Not a roll call, but by sight, so he would shine a flashlight in each guy's face. This was a safety issue. Everyone had to be accounted for."

Daddy rocked back in his recliner. We were in the comfortable den of the home he and my mother had lived in for over sixty years. I visualized the young man with the curly black hair and crisp uniform in a black and white photo on a shelf across the room. I could see him and his buddies in the pre-dawn hush of a tropical day, kept alert by the flashlights, waiting for the blast. Landing craft pulled up on the beach nearby in case something went wrong and they must evacuate the island.

"What did it look like?" I asked.

"Oh, like the pictures you've seen of Hiroshima." Daddy shrugged like a nuclear bomb is an everyday event.

The radio crackles with the alert. A rumble like thunder grumbles in the distance. A glare as the sky turns from black to blinding white, as if the sun has suddenly burst into the still-black tropical sky. The fountain of radiance shoots up and falls back on itself, forming the iconic mushroom-shaped cloud as the foam of debris churns at its feet.

"What kind of safety equipment did you wear?" I asked, expecting to hear about hazmat suits or the equivalent of the day. Instead, he explained that the higher rank military wore goggles, similar to welding goggles, while the other guys were told to turn their backs.

"What?"

"I had goggles," Daddy assured me, his face crinkled with the grin he used to deliver the punch line to a story. "Rank has its privileges. That's just the way the military was."

Atomic Vets, the 225,000 military personnel who served during the nuclear testing, have a higher rate of cancer than normal. Some veterans' groups have made it their mission to get enhanced medical treatment for these veterans. My father never had cancer and denied that he was exposed to radiation during the testing. They were also warned they might be sterile, but the baby boom following the testing proved that false.

"Of course, when I was stationed at Trinity, there was trinitite laying all over the orderly room and barracks," Daddy told me, referring to the radioactive glassy residue that was left after the first bomb was detonated in the New Mexico desert at White Sands Missile Range. "None of us had any idea about it, just that it was residue from the blast."

These young men on the beach, witnessing the next step in developing atomic weapons, had already seen the devastation of Hiroshima and Nagasaki. What did they feel about the testing?

Daddy did not pause before answering. "I never heard any comments against the tests — not one. You've got to remember that most of us were in our mid to late teens when they bombed Pearl Harbor. They weren't going to do it again."

Eighteen American ships were hit at Pearl Harbor, and over two thousand military personnel were killed. I met one of the survivors of Pearl Harbor when he was an elderly resident in a nursing home. He told me the story of being thrown from his ship docked next to the USS Arizona (BB-39). He said that when he was in the water, he didn't know if he was going to make it out or not. I am sure he and my father would have agreed that they were not ever going to do it again.

My father, like most World War II and Cold War veterans, exhibited the staunch patriotism common in what Tom Brokaw labeled "The Greatest Generation." Daddy was the first to his feet when the flag was raised; he never questioned paying his fair share of taxes and voted in every election. When my father recited the Pledge of Allegiance, I knew he meant every word of it.

The life preserver with the palm trees and *Eniwetok* was just a soldier's souvenir. But for my family, it was also a symbol of the strength and courage of my father.

In the quiet den, he told me, "We were just doing our duty."

*****

Author: Judy Castleberry

Judy Castleberry is the daughter of Sgt. Robert L. Batley, Jr., and Troyetta King Batley. Her story, "The Gosling," is included in *A Diversity of Expression*. She is the author of *The Caregiver Zone, The Yard Sale, Road Trip, Villainy in the Valley*, and numerous business and senior care publication articles.

BRENDA COLE

My Unknown Father

The entire thing was red. From his shoulder down to his fingertips. My dad, two siblings, and I were fishing. Dad always found the most secluded spot under the trees to go fishing. This spot was a deep glistening spillway over the blacktop to the North of the lake. It was a hard scramble down the limestone boulders to reach the spot, guaranteed to house feisty bluegills and bullheads. Sadly, it was also the perfect locale for clouds of gnats. Gnats are normally just an annoyance when you must spit them out when arguing with a sibling. For my father, they were a hospital trip waiting to happen. He was allergic to them, and he knew it. I asked if he'd applied bug spray and got a grunt in affirmation.

An hour later, my sister yelled and pointed at his arm, and I quickly started packing up and trying to get us up the scree field and to the car while he could still drive. This wasn't an isolated case of my father having a seemingly broken self-preservation instinct. Looking back on all the times he became ill or did something we knew he would pay for, I wondered how his own health and safety became so insignificant.

My father was an Army veteran; he had joined in 1952 at the tender age of eighteen. He was assigned to the 555th Engineer Group as a bridge specialist and vehicle driver. His unit specialized in building pontoon bridges, and he spent his tour serving in Germany instead of going to Korea. I heard about his driving the atomic cannon through the narrow medieval streets of Germany and only knocking off a few bricks. He was also on the unit's basketball team as their center. While he said he wasn't injured in the line of duty, he did damage his knee.

According to him, they were building a bridge on a tributary of the Rhine River one winter. There was an ice jam in the river that tore up the bridge. Dad went in the water, and his leg got caught between the ice and the bridge, giving him a permanent "trick" knee. I have a handful of photos of Dad in Germany; he would regale me with driving stories, playing against famous basketball teams, and even taught me a few phrases. Although, as a non-smoker, asking for a light in German wasn't high on my list of useful ways to communicate. According to him, he never fought; he just built, drove, played basketball, and drank a lot.

Dad completed his active-duty tour of service in 1955 and was in the standby reserve until 1961. His first stateside employment was working as a carpenter for Owens Yacht Co in Dundalk on the southeast side of Baltimore. I never could get an explanation from him of how he ended up in Baltimore as he was practically allergic to big cities. He was from Southern Illinois, and he always said he went into the Army to escape from Carbondale. Dad always had a story, so many stories that would lead you in fascinating directions, and always away from whatever in-depth or personal questions his oldest child desperately wanted the answers to. I never did know what was so troubling at home that he would prefer the Army.

The spring I was four, the family packed up and headed west. The carpentry job couldn't support a family of five, even with my grandmother contributing her meager salary as a drugstore clerk. We were heading out to Phoenix. Dad's doctor said the drier climate would help his lungs, and we stopped in Carbondale for a few months along the way. Dad's cousin had talked him into taking a good-paying job with John Deere up in Moline along the Mississippi River. Dad and Ernie took the long drive northward, leaving the rest of the family with my grandparents. I don't think it ever occurred to my dad to wonder if he would like a factory job. He always seemed happiest when he was out in the woods sitting by a glass smooth lake, casting for bass or out hunting with Grampa's Blue Tick Coon hounds. Regardless of what he might have wanted, we crossed the river into Davenport, Iowa, in the brutal heat of a Midwestern July.

When one met my father for the first time, it was obvious he had lived a hard life. When he brought the ever-present cigarette to his lips, the missing and twisted fingers of his right hand begged for an explanation. He lost them when I was six, and my mother had just become pregnant with my only brother. Dad worked as a sheet press operator for John Deere. It had grown dark outside of our second-floor apartment. Since Dad always came home in daylight, I was getting scared. Mom was throwing up every time she got up off the couch to look out the window, and I was tasked with minding my little sister.

The door finally opened after we were in bed. Worry and anger colored Mom's voice as she started shouting at Dad, and then she just screamed. I stumbled out of bed and stopped dead in the hallway. Mom was lying in a chair sobbing while my uncle was getting Dad seated on the couch. I couldn't recognize a morphine haze at this age, but my field of vision lasered in on his right arm. He was holding it against his chest with huge bandages wrapped around what remained of his fingers. It's been almost sixty years, and I still remember that tableau. His machine had malfunctioned, and a three-inch-thick steel plate crushed Dad's fingers. He eventually lost most of his middle fingers but eventually adapted, even coaching my softball team and bowling.

Rickets and emphysema had also etched their signature on my father's frame. At 6' 4," he weighed a scant 151 pounds and had a massive barrel chest. His legs were slightly bowed, and one could see something like a child's beaded necklace on either side of his sternum. These were the tell-tale signs of rickets. The beads were knobs of bone that formed where his ribs met his sternum. Dad was born during the Great Depression and, at some point, didn't receive enough calcium for his bones to grow properly. He was diagnosed with emphysema while my mom was pregnant with me. I never knew him when he didn't have respiratory issues. His cough and the stench of Winston cigarettes color all my memories of him.

For the next thirty-five years, my father worked for John Deere. His body gradually earned more scars, like the bone-deep, puckered white lines from molten steel along his forearms. His knee still locked up, especially when he insisted on squatting down to watch a ball game or cast under a low-hanging branch. To his co-workers and friends, he was jovial and a rambling storyteller, but as always, an hour-long conversation left you with only a glimpse of who he was.

Conversations at home revolved around sports and stories of his exploits or childhood and quickly devolved into arguments. We had three adults in the household: Mom, Dad, and my maternal Gramma. All of them had rough childhoods with alcoholic fathers. As I grew older, the tension in the house was caustic. It became worse as my mother finally took her own path and went to college. She became a nurse, and that only whetted her appetite for academia. She eventually became a chiropractor and received an MS [Master of Science] in Adult Education.

My father completed an associate degree in electrical engineering when I was in eighth grade. Deere was thrilled and immediately offered him a promotion to shop foreman; my father threatened to quit. For the rest of his career, he refused every promotion or advancement. It was as if doing his regular job was the most responsibility he could accept. I remember asking him why he wouldn't want a title and more money. His tirade began and ended with, "Never volunteer, or they'll own you till you die."

By 1974, Dad had survived five or six lung surgeries, multiple pneumothorax events (collapsed lung), and everyone on the pulmonary floor at the hospital knew him. And still, the damn cigarettes called his name. Mom and Gramma stopped smoking when our pediatrician said it contributed to my brother's severe asthma. Dad made half-hearted attempts to quit, but his stash was everywhere; the basement, attic, garage, and hidden boxes, we didn't find until after he had passed.

My entering high school also escalated the idiosyncrasies in Dad's behavior. He constantly berated us if we needed lunch money, and chores were never done fast enough. Yet when I turned sixteen and started looking for work, he threatened to throw me out of the house. I suggested counseling to my mom, and dad wouldn't speak to me for a month. His unstable temper and unwillingness to get help for himself, or us, drove me to the dorms as soon as I could when I entered college. I only returned during the summers because the dorms closed. After receiving my undergraduate degree, I moved to a minuscule apartment and became a starving graduate student; the stress of being around my father was finally unacceptable.

My parents divorced in 1985. They had been going to counseling, but Dad misdirected, evaded, and eventually stepped back. Mom finally realized there was no reconciling and asked for a divorce.

Three years later, I was planning my wedding in Wisconsin. I was back home, and my parents asked me to go somewhere with them. When we ended up at the county courthouse, I was confused. In a long stammering breath, Dad told me that they were getting remarried, I was to be "best man," and I needed to sign the papers. I refused until Mom pleaded with me. I looked at her and softly reminded her about his past actions, and could she live with the results? They made it two years, and Mom literally threw him out of the house. I knew the police had contacted her, but it was another secret as to why.

I saw my father once more before he died. He was barely mobile, using a scooter, and couldn't recognize me even though I am almost an identical twin to my mother. I sat with him and begged for answers about his life, the Army, all the questions that had been rioting in my mind for most of my life. He joked, evaded, or pretended not to hear me for over three hours.

As I left, I realized it was the last time I might see him. On the way out, the staff told me it was time for a full-scale nursing home. He had refused to talk to me again; he was in the final stages of emphysema and only had months left. Thanksgiving night in 2009, my little brother called at 1:30 AM. Dad had been in hospice for a week and wouldn't last out the night; he had to talk to me.

In a ragged whisper, he apologized for not telling me. He said both his father and the Army had trained him not to divulge secrets. After so many years, he had forgotten how just to talk. I gave him my blessing, said my goodbyes, and he passed with my brother and me there.

There is a time and a need for keeping secrets. But when it is so fixated due to alcoholism or hiding what occurred in service, then it can be detrimental to those you hold most dear. I had sixty years with my father, but I never got to meet him.

*****

Author: Brenda Cole

Brenda Cole is the oldest daughter of Corporal Earl Cook, who served with the Army during the Korean War. An award-winning author of non-fiction short stories and essays, her career combined teaching from pre-school through graduate school and professional editing. She is the past President of three nonprofits, including SouthWest Writers.

Shirly Cook (Mom) with 4-year-old Brenda and baby sister circa 1963 in the wilds of Delaware

BRINN COLENDA

Bird Strike!

The cluster of birds appeared out of nowhere, grew huge in the Plexiglas, and smashed through the windscreen at 200 knots like feathered cannonballs. The pain in Lieutenant John Wright Royal's body was incredible and instantaneous. He lost consciousness.

Texas wind swirled around the cockpit of the T-37 jet trainer, battering him with papers and loose objects. He could sense acceleration; G [gravitational] forces squashed him against the side of the cockpit. His left eyelid finally responded. All he could see was the ground spiraling beneath him. Odd.

Where's the sky? Oh, my God! We're in a dive! He groped for the control stick. Pain surged through his shoulder and right arm. *Wings level, pull! Get the nose up!* The ground hurtled towards him, airspeed increasing. "Throttles idle. Speed brake, speed brake!" he shouted into his mask. The pain in his shoulder screamed. He used both hands and pulled harder on the stick. The nose of the jet tracked upwards. *God, this plane is heavy.* He leveled off just before stalling the aircraft.

Royal was woozy, slow, like he had lost fifty IQ [intelligence quotient] points. Air flooded into the cockpit like shrieking banshees.

What happened? Royal counted five, no, six fist-sized holes in the windscreen. His instructor, Captain Swinkels, seated alongside him, slumped against the opposite side of the cockpit, helmet and upper body splattered with feathers and what must be bird guts. His visors were smashed in, blood everywhere. *Dead? Can't tell, but he sure looks bad.*

Royal fought to keep the airplane level. Outside, the horizon stretched as far as he could see. A beautiful summer day, clear and serene. Inside, chaos. A fire hose of high-speed air rocked Swinkels and stabbed Royal in the shoulder like a steel rod.

Now what? My first ride in this damn aircraft! What do I know about flying a jet? His heart raced. Every movement sent shards of pain lancing through his body, and the noise was horrendous. He longed to close his one good eye and slip back into the cocoon of blackness. So easy ….

He jerked upright. *Wake up, Johnny boy!*

He took stock: he was a student pilot flying a wounded airplane that he had never been in before; his right shoulder was on fire, a possible concussion threatened to drag him back into darkness, and something was wrong with one eye. Plus, an unconscious instructor who may or may not be dead.

Great! Just great.

Okay, Johnny, by the numbers: Maintain aircraft control, analyze the situation, take proper action. First thing: slow this baby down. He eased the throttles back a bit.

The roar of the wind dropped with the decrease in speed. Better.

He checked his instruments. He guessed they were all normal and in the green. Fuel still okay. For the time being.

"Oh yeah, transponder." He groped around to find the dial and put in 7700, the code for emergencies. Dialing the proper numbers in the transponder cost him four hundred feet of altitude. "Johnny, you gotta do better than that!"

"Where are we?" He tried to scan the horizon to pick out something familiar. "There's Wichita Falls … there's Lake Wichita. I know where that's supposed to be." His eye traced to the northwest to the flat areas where Sheppard Air Force Base sprawled across the Texas landscape. He dipped a wing. He could make out the runways.

Altimeter check: five thousand feet. More or less level.

He took a deep breath to calm his jumpy nerves before making his first radio call. "Bull Two Four on Guard. I need a frequency."

"Aircraft on Guard, contact Sheppard Approach on channel eight."

He switched the frequency. "Approach, this is Bull Two Four. I'm declaring an emergency."

"Bull Two Four, state your emergency."

"Approach, we took a bird strike. My instructor is unconscious."

"Bull Two Four, Stand by."

Stand by? What do they think this is, a simulator? I need help now!

After what seemed an eternity, the radio crackled into life. "Bull Two Four, this is Colonel Hunt. How are you doing, Lieutenant?"

Colonel Hunt? What's the Wing Commander doing here? "Sir, I've had better days."

"Confirm that your instructor is not responsive."

"He's not moving. I can't tell how badly he's hurt."

Another pause.

"Bull Two Four, Approach will vector you to the bail-out area. Then you will eject. That's an order, Lieutenant. Do you understand?"

Royal's head snapped back in surprise, and he gasped in pain. His heart raced. *Leave the captain? What if he's not dead?*

"Bull Two Four, I've ejected myself. It's not that bad. Trust your equipment, son. It will save you. We don't want to lose you, too."

He thinks I'm scared. Well, he's right! Royal laughed. *What he's trying to do is give me an excuse for abandoning the captain. He's covering my butt for me.* Royal glanced over at Swinkels' inert form.

Maybe he's right. I've never landed anything heavier than a Cessna. Who am I kidding? I'm no Chuck Yeager.

The summer rough, choppy air forced him to focus on flying. It was like driving on a road dimpled with potholes. He knew about uplift from his glider days at the Academy. Somehow the familiarity made him feel better.

The radio spoke again. "Lieutenant Royal, I say again, you will fly to the bail-out area and eject."

I can't leave this guy. He's my instructor, for Christ's sake.

Royal punched the mic button. "Negative, sir, I am now pilot-in-command, and I'm bringing the captain home. I have the runway in sight. Going to RSU [Runway Supervisory Unit] frequency. Bull Two Four Out."

"Maintain aircraft control, maintain aircraft control," he chanted. "Jesus, I sound like a robot." He chuckled, then turned serious. "Okay, Johnny boy, let's get this beauty on the ground." He gauged his rate of descent, cross-checked his altitude, and slowed down.

He called the T-37 Runway Supervisory Unit, which would direct his landing approach. "Cooter, this is Bull Two Four, about five miles northwest, three thousand feet descending. Request emergency straight-in approach."

"Bull Two Four, Cooter. You are cleared for a straight-in approach, runway One Five left. I'll read you the checklist. Do one item at a time. But fly the airplane first and foremost. Got that, Lieutenant? Acknowledge."

"Wilco." *Great! I'll need all the help I can get!*

"Bull Two Four, there will be a small pond on your left at two miles. Put your gear down there. We have you in sight. Just keep flying the airplane."

What pond? Where? Okay, there it is. Gear down. The aircraft wallowed, and he felt the gear extending. Three green lights. Best news of the day. "Trim, Johnny, trim." He added power. "Airspeed, Johnny! Airspeed, attitude. Airspeed, attitude." The leather palms of his flying gloves were all greasy, whether from sweat or bird guts; who knew?

"Cooter, Bull Two Four, three green."

"Copy, Bull Two Four. Go full flaps and start down. Pick up your aim point."

Flaps! Of course! Where's the flap lever? Yeah, got it!

"You're looking good, Bull Two Four. Maintain your aim point, Lieutenant. Keep her coming down. Get that cross-check going. Watch your speed. Looking good. That's it. Keep her coming down."

The concrete runway stretched out in front. All he had to do was to set the plane down, keep it on the runway, and stop. The runway numbers flashed underneath. *Power idle!* He banged down hard, bounced. *Hold the attitude, Johnny!* The plane bounced again. Stayed down.

Brakes! The plane abruptly swerved left. John overcorrected right, then swerved left again. Finally, he stopped the plane and shut down the engines.

Outside, pandemonium exploded as emergency crews rushed at him from all directions. Inside, blessed quiet.

He smiled as he closed his eyes and let himself slip back into unconsciousness.

It had been one hell of a ride.

***

Married

Mary stood on the city sidewalk with a *Sporting News* she had just bought to surprise her husband when she spotted him leaving a restaurant. With a woman! A fancy restaurant with an attractive woman!

They stood close together on the sidewalk. Too close. And happy. Intimate even, like they shared a secret.

No, not my husband.

He waved down a taxi and opened the door for her. As she stepped into the car, she offered her hand, but he brushed it aside for a quick hug. He watched her drive away. As it made the turn into traffic, he did a double fist pump, joy on his face. No, not joy. More like ecstasy.

She ducked behind the newsstand and leaned against a utility pole. It felt like an icepick was plunged into her chest. Her pulse raced, and blood pounded in her ears.

How could he?

***

Six hours later, Mary was in the kitchen preparing supper when she heard her husband's footsteps on the front porch steps.

"Hi, Darlin'," he said as he slouched into the house and entered the kitchen.

He dropped his briefcase on a chair, gave her a peck on the cheek, patted her bottom, then attacked the fridge. He grabbed a frosted mug and poured himself a beer. "Man, oh, man. Do I ever need this. I am exhausted."

"Bad day?" Mary asked.

"Marginal. Very marginal. And long." He popped a cashew into his mouth. "I spent the entire day on that damned Adams account that I told you about. I don't think I've ever had such a mess cross my desk. I finally, *finally*, put it to bed! Holy cow, what a pain. Glad that's over." He stretched, arms up over his head, and groaned.

"Glad to hear it." She laid out the ingredients for dinner. "Anything happen besides that?"

"Nope. Did you get any writing done?"

"A little. I had things on my mind."

"What, no murders, no dismemberments today?"

She smiled. *Not yet.*

"Hey, what's for dinner?"

"Sausage with tomatoes and vegetables." She picked up a slender, hard sausage. "I was downtown this afternoon …."

"Yeah?" He picked up the TV remote and hit the power button. ESPN Sports Center filled the screen.

Watching him, she held the rigid spear of the sausage in both hands and stroked the grainy surface with her fingers.

He plopped down on the couch, placed his feet on the coffee table, and sighed. "What a day."

Mary placed the sausage on the cutting board and extracted a knife from its holder. She studied the back of his head, then slit the casing of the sausage from end to end and flayed it, slowly stripping the skin from the meat. Then she diced the meat deliberately and steadily from one end to the other and placed it in a pot of boiling water.

Her husband changed the channel, and a soccer game appeared on the screen. He settled back into the cushions, now completely engrossed in the game.

She took two peeled tomatoes from a can and held them for a moment, one in each palm. The meaty tomato walls were veined and wet. She squeezed them gently as she rolled each one in her hand, increasing the pressure more and more until both burst. Blood-red juices spattered all over the counter.

"Oh," he shouted, "Oh, my God!"

He jumped to his feet and faced her. "Babe," he said, "how could I forget? Jeez, what a putz." He shook his head in disbelief.

"Remember that trip we won before Christmas, but the charter airline went bankrupt?"

She nodded, still glaring, heartbeats pounding in her chest.

"Well, the tour company sent a broker over to my office today. She took me to lunch, and we worked out the details.

"Surprise! Next month, you and I are headed for *Panamá*!"

*****

Author: Brinn Colenda

Brinn Colenda is a retired US Air Force Lieutenant Colonel. He has published four award-winning books, three political-military thrillers, and one Young Adult thriller. His website is www.brinncolenda.org

JOSHUA COLENDA

Cliffs of Sage

I open my eyes to see the world,
Broken in my mirror.
My heart yearns for a better one.

The path is steep,
And soon I find myself beset by bandits,
Ruining my plans,
They cast me into despair.

This time I open my eyes to darkness.
I am cushioned by a bed of corpses:
The others who have tried.
I started this journey to fix what I could see,
But if I lay here,
With the others who have failed,
Soon, the world will not bother me.

An ancient rumble rouses me from sleep,
It asks if I have finished failing.
It says if I am humble,
It will teach me all it knows,
And feed me what it grows.
But if I become arrogant,
Or burdened by my foolishness,
I will fall into an even deeper pit than this.

"Teach me, train me, beat me, lead me!"
I called out to the sage.
I told him I was not afraid,
But he did not believe me.
Six years passed in that ravine,
Where every day I tried to be,
The good the sage said he saw in me.

Six years passed before I could say goodbye,
Before I was free to live,
And he,
To die.

He crept into a hole,
A grave,
And I,
Alone but for his gifts,
Turned my gaze once more upon the cliffs.

With my new vision I could see,
The cliffs were not as solid as they seemed.
And with the wisdom of the sage,
I began to chip away.

But still it was not easy.
The winds whipped from all around
To knock me from the cliffs,
And onto the ground.

Wildlife came to test me.
Scavengers would bite me if I dropped my guard,
And predators would kill me.

For twenty-eight days I climbed that rock,
Making little progress,
Carving uncomfortable beds out of stone.

Finally,
I stood upon the summit,
And I could see it all!
Below me was the pit,
With all of those the cliffs had broken,
And the teacher who had helped me live.

On my right I saw a river,
Which wound its way to the horizon.

But so much illumination
Sent me to my knees,
I had to close my eyes,
To keep it all from blinding me.

And as I sat there,
In the darkness of my thoughts,
At the peak of my success,
I heard every wind that ever tried to knock me off my path
Together ask,
"But where will you sleep tonight?"

***

Demigod

Worthless!
Alone in my room,
As depression surges.
What's the purpose,
of feeling the promise
Of a better future?
It's a disservice.
The occasional glimpse of heaven
Finds
Its way,
To my conscious mind.
Never content,
It only suggests,
Teasing me,
Taunting me,
Tantalus.
Hope is a fire
They brought to my psyche.
I pay for the price of that lie.
Everyday,
I stand on Olympus.
And look
For the promise,
Delivered.
Eagles with talons,
And malice,
And beaks,
Come down,
To chow down,
On my liver.
One time,

They sent me to prison.
It wasn't my fault,
But they wouldn't listen.
It's just a condition,
They said,
Of cognition.
Of consciousness,
Knowledge,
Of language,
Ambition.
And just when I thought,
I had found my way out,
I took a look at the sun,
And then started to drown.
Never content,
It only suggests,
Teasing me,
Taunting me,
Tantalus.
Sometimes,
I feel like Atlas,
Holding the whole world,
Upon my back.
Sometimes,
I feel like Odin,
Killing myself,
For knowledge potion.
Sometimes,
I feel like Sisyphus,
Breaking my back,
To get to the top,
Then watching my progress,
Roll down the hill,

And back to the start.
Never content,
It only suggests,
Teasing me,
Breaking my heart.
Maybe you feel like Medusa:
Beauty's a curse
That leads to abuse.
Maybe you feel like Cassandra,
Who
Always spoke truth,
But was never listened to.
Maybe you feel like Icarus,
With success so potent,
You're getting sick of it.
Maybe you feel like Atlas,
With the Earth on your back,
Filling you with madness.
Maybe you're a demigod too,
Half-god,
Half-savage.

***

Heartbreaker

Although everything external's fine,
Everything's pessimist,
Here in my mind.

It's like,
Divine decree
Saw all the things,
And said how things should be,
But,
I alone,
Misunderstood,
How hopeless things can seem!

Is it a factor of birth,
Am I on this earth,
To walk around lost,
And then die in the dirt?
So many people I see,
Roam around lost,
Come to a lock,
And then produce keys,
All except me,
Or that's what I thought.

But one day,
When the sun set,
I turned around,
In time to see,
An army
Of opened doors,
Following me,
Like footsteps.

I ran around the planet,
In an attempt to understand it,
I talked to all the people,
Tried to figure who planned it.

And it turns out,
All the people that I talked to,
Everybody has the struggle
That I struggle with.
And even those who made it through,
Know exactly,
What I'm going through.
But there isn't just a single way,
And so even
If I listened,
As they gave me
Their directions,
All our starting points
Are different,
And our destinies,
Are different.

And though
Nobody
Can do it all,
For anybody else,
You can listen,
To how
They made it through,
So you can help,
Yourself.
And then when someone
Comes to you,
You can help
Them too,
Because by then,
You won't
Be selfish.
And one day,
When the sun rises,
You'll turn around,
In time to hear
A crowd of strangers,
Lost,
Asking you for directions.

The Flood

Treading water,
Slowly sinking,
Thinking,
How I came to drink
This foul water,
 I'm now drinking.

Was it fear
That sunk me to such depths?
Was it lack of sense,
Or intellect?
Was I blind?
Was I deaf?
Am I drowning now,
In questions
I was once,
Too proud to ask?

I wonder,
With my death breath,
How I wronged me,
As I slip beneath the waves,
To join my follies,
In our grave.

But alas!
My foot hits earth,
And thus, I am saved!

With my head upthrust to heaven,
And my feet on tiptoes stepping,
I,
Like a spider,
Like an old spider,
Like a hungry old spider,

Moving slowly,
Towards that final fly,
Concoct a pretty plan,
For tonight,
I shall not die!

I explore in each direction,
Seeking elevation in this life-saving endeavor.
Never stopping,
Never stalling,
And though some would send me sprawling,
Sprawling into the abyss!
There was one direction,
Which by chance,
I did not miss.

And as I tiptoed,
On this narrow path,
For hours,
With the little life I salvaged,
I looked above,
And saw my life,
Projected onto the clouds.

A young man,
With thoughts of the world,
Thoughts of himself,
Thoughts of himself in the world,
Committing bad blunders,
And mislabeling them good deeds,
I walk the lands,
A young man,
With much to do,
And much to see.

An older man now,
I see in the clouds,

Above my head,
While I'm drowning.
Neither diving nor rising,
As I attempt to dispel
All the mistakes that surround me.

I move slowly,
But with great purpose,
Testing left and right,
But always forward,
Searching surface.
Hours pass,
The sun is setting,
Mind and body getting heavy,
Getting ready,
For the fate
That I have sent me.

When suddenly,
My eyes,
Which seemed forever doomed,
To search the sky,
Affix upon
A bright beach,
Drawing nigh.

I thrust myself upon the shore,
And shout,
"Surely heaven knows no finer floor!"
These tiny grains of life,
Have saved me from the end,
I will construct a house of them,
And though it will slip into the sea,
The world has returned to me,
And I,
At last,
Have peace.

The Thief

To my children,
I must come clean,
Your humble father,
Was a thief.

When people came into my store,
And asked what I had to show,
I said,
"Sir or madam,
Friend or foe,
I am a simple merchant,
I have only
What your eyes can see."

Every bauble on display,
Was polished bright,
So it would please.
But I kept the best stuff
In the cellar just for me.

If I put my greatest treasures
From the cellar
On display,
I was worried,
They would look at them,
Spit on them,
And say,
"This is garbage,
Old and useless!
Dirty, cracked,
And broken!
I've seen better in a hundred stores!

How dare you call yourself a treasure?"

I'm ashamed to say,
I thought this way,
For many,
Many years.
Terrified,
That if I put my treasures in the light,
They would break my little heart.
So I was only ever proud of them
At night,
Or in the dark.

But something awful happened
To me,
Just the other week.
I went down to my depths,
With my key in my hand,
To open the vault,
To stand there and covet,
To bask in the glow,
Of my lantern of gold.
But imagine my horror,
When I opened the door,
And saw that my art,
Had started to mold!

What could I do?
I rushed,
I flew!
I gathered my treasures,
In armfuls,
And bagfuls,
And started to run.

I knocked all my counterfeits,
Down to the floor.
And hung up my treasures,
So they could be healed,
By the sun,
As it entered my store.

Then people came from all around,
To see the things that I had found.

"This is beautiful,
Magical,
Stunning!"
They said.
You live in our town,
You know what came next.
All of the merchants went running,
To gather their treasure,
And set them to sunning.

Now the little street,
In our humble town,
Is full of nice things,
The nicest around.

And I went to the cellar,
And tore down the door.
And made it a table,
To put in my store.
So go tell the neighbors,
And tell them to bring,
Something dirty,
Or cracked.
I once was a thief,
Now I'm giving it back!

Self-Help Letter From a Friend

My Friend,
I'm so sorry
You are feeling
This way,
But the answer
Still is,
Hard work,
Every day.

With a reason why,
You can live
Through anyhow.
It's awful you're in hell,
And I hope you make it out.

I'm here for you,
But I can't keep feeding you fish.
You need to be yourself,
If you ever want to live.
And I can tell you about
Some things that worked for me.
But I can't lead you,
In fact,
I can barely see.

I want to help,
But I don't know how,
So here are some things
I heard

Wise men talk about:
If you fall off the horse,
Get back on,
Rome wasn't built in a day.
You reap what you sow,
So go plant some seeds.
Water them with sweat,
And then watch them grow.

I'm sorry you're in pain,
But please,
Don't end it all.
Someone out there,
Will buy what you can sell.
And if we lose touch,
I wish you luck,
I'll be here to talk,
When you get better.

*****

Author: Joshua Colenda

Joshua Colenda is a Sergeant in the US Army National Guard. A New Mexican on active duty, he lives in Salt Lake City with his two dogs. He enjoys hiking and playing guitar and has been writing poetry since college. Colenda uses poetry as a vehicle to express himself and talk about mental health issues.

MARK FLEISHER

A Day to Be Remembered

February 18, 1968. I had been in-country for five months, assigned to the Combat News Division of the 7th Air Force Directorate of Information (DXI) at Tan Son Nhut Air Base outside of Saigon.

Six weeks after my mid-September arrival into my one-year tour and after getting acclimated and completing routine assignments, I "made my bones" covering the Air Force role in a major operation at Song Be near the Cambodian border. The mission involved airlifting more than 10,000 troops of the Army's 101st Airborne Division to Vietnam and then deploying them around the country. I endured not only the red dust that seemed everywhere in Song Be but almost nightly mortar attacks from Viet Cong who occupied a nearby hill.

Nearly three months later, in what became known as the Tet Offensive, Viet Cong and North Vietnamese regulars staged countrywide attacks on cities and bases, including Saigon and Tan Son Nhut. I recall bullets ricocheting around our barracks and then mortar rounds overhead, fired from a nearby field that the enemy had infiltrated. As my combat news colleagues and I were considered non-combatants, we were not issued weapons except for .38 caliber revolvers, no match for AK-47s, rocket-propelled grenades, and the like.

Soon after Tet, I was sent on temporary duty to the Air Force Jungle Survival School near Clark Air Base in the Philippines. I felt mentally and physically toughened after a week of training involving living off the land, a simulated parachute drop from a forty-foot tower, and an escape and evasion exercise where I spent the night alone in the jungle before being "rescued" by a friendly helicopter. I graduated on February 12, 1968, and flew back to Tan Son Nhut.

While my experiences to this point were nothing compared to hardships endured by Army grunts, Marines or Air Force pilots, I considered myself ready to handle anything during the remaining seven months of my tour.

But I was not prepared for February 18, 1968.

Shortly after noon that day, a 122-millimeter rocket slammed into a vacant building adjacent to our headquarters. To this day, I swear I could hear the rocket's signature whistle before it exploded. Shrapnel ripped through our walls, with several shards slamming into the wall behind my desk, piercing a cigarette lighter and Tiki figure on the desk. I was a foot or two away and escaped harm.

Rick Ramsey was not as lucky.

Shrapnel tore through his body as he turned toward the sound of the explosion. His insides spilled onto the floor. The concussion knocked me to the floor. Dust filled my eyes, and I could hear nothing. Rick's blood-spattered my uniform shirt. Once I gathered myself, I knew there was nothing I or anyone could do. Rick Ramsey died instantly. Years later, I wrote that Rick did not suffer, nor did he cry out for his mother. He had eighteen days before his tour ended. Instead of returning home, Rick found his final resting place in the Eternal Valley Memorial Park in Newhall, California, fifteen miles from his home in Sun Valley.

I left Vietnam in September 1968 and took a newspaper job in upstate New York. Flashbacks soon followed, but I felt I could handle what came my way. Years later, when I worked as a veteran's counselor in an upstate New York county did I seek help from the Department of Veterans Affairs [VA]. Counseling veterans with symptoms similar to mine made me realize that I probably had Post Traumatic Stress Disorder which the VA confirmed.

The most vivid flashback came shortly after midnight on Christmas Day 2010 when I woke up screaming. February 18, 1968, returned.

Every image, every detail incredibly vivid. I felt like I had been watching a movie about what happened that day forty-two years earlier.

I think of Rick often, especially every February 18th. Of course, I am saddened by the events of that day, but I can't help but laugh at one of our first conversations. For some reason, the topic was religion, and Rick asked what I was. I replied, "I am Jewish." Rick said he'd never met a Jewish person, then let me know he was Mormon. "Well, Rick," I said, "I've never met a Mormon."

I've not had a flashback since that Christmas morning. I began writing poetry soon after, eventually publishing five books containing numerous Vietnam-related poems and works about Rick Ramsey.

Did Rick and nearly 60,000 others die for a just cause, or did they die in vain? That is a subject for debate, and I have no simple answer. What I did finally answer was, "Why Rick, and why not me?" I eventually wrote that "grief and guilt whirl in my mind's maelstrom unable to decipher the impenetrable mystery how bombs and rockets and shells and bullets name their victims."

Writing this piece has been an emotional exercise as I recount an unforgettable chapter in my life's journey. However, I am convinced that writing about that day and other difficult days in Vietnam helped heal the wounds and ease the pain I carry in my memory.

$$*****$$

Author: Mark Fleisher

Mark Fleisher's service in the United States Air Force (April 1965-September 1968) included a year in Vietnam as a combat news reporter. He was awarded a Bronze Star for Meritorious Service, among other decorations. The Albuquerque writer received a journalism degree from Ohio University and held reporting and editing positions in upstate New York and Washington, DC.

PAUL DAVID GONZALES

A Soldier's Friend

A soldier's friend will sit and listen even when the soldier's
eyes no longer glisten.

That soldier's friend will understand and even hold the
soldier's hand.
It doesn't mean the soldier's weak they simply need time to
speak.

While others say they understand; there was no welcome
home or marching band.

To those who are a friend to the soldier ... they hold a special
place in the heavens above and in the hearts of the soldiers
they love.

***

Our Time

Our time is but a vapor absorbed in the
atmosphere and mystery of creation

Leaving only a slight residue as
proof of our existence.

***

Commander of the Relief

[I am the commander of the relief ... my duty runs from 24:00 till
dawn ... I relive the changing of the guard]

I stand in the gap between the Officer of the Day and the Sergeant of
the Guard
Making sure the enemy never enters the yard.

I go from tower to tower as the night slips by ... hour by hour
Even though we're wet, never show a silhouette.

My boots hit every rung of that ladder ... as fast as I can ... ascend
that ladder
I push open the door on the floor and enter the nest once more.

I replace each guard one by one to keep the perimeter clear
Our hearts beat fast with mounting fear.

I drive to each tower in my Willy's Jeep without the lights
So the enemy doesn't know we're there.

Guard by Guard they mount the towers we'll change again in the next
few hours.
We keep it going through the night till dawn breaks with morning
light.

***

Dear Mom

Dear Mom,

JFK [John Fitzgerald Kennedy] and LBJ [Lyndon Baines Johnson] sent me here to Vietnam.
I did what I was told and now I'm wet and kinda cold. It's thick and lush here in the green but not a pretty scene.

You see, Charlie came in the night, we put up a helluva fight. They surprised us as we slept, I prayed to the Lord my soul to keep. I'm safe in his arms, so please don't weep.

Dear Lord, please take my hand, Mom will understand, there is no pain. It's gone away, so here in heaven, I will stay. The preacher said, "What a beautiful place" ... this heavenly place.

You know I won't be home in May, here in Vietnam I lay, but I want to say, "I did my job and did it well." There's nothing more, only time will tell.

Your Son, Dave

When we left Seattle Tacoma airport on a Northwest Orient Airliner headed to Cam-Rahn Bay South Vietnam in November of 1967. I had plenty of time (a seventeen-hour flight) to think about many painful thoughts of going to a War Zone. Barely twenty years old, and the thought of not making it home alive became very real to me. I wanted the message to be very personal to my mother. I wanted to soothe her agony with my own words if I didn't make it home.

Being the firstborn, I possessed a take-charge personality, so I began to think of ways I could talk to her from the grave. I began to pen words on a paper napkin that would eventually become my final words to my mom. When I reached Cam-Rahn, I finished what I had to say, placed the napkin in an envelope the stewardess gave me, and addressed it to my mom in hopes I would never have to send it. I stowed the note away with my gear and told friends in my company what to do … IF. The letter never had to be sent "thank God." The original letter deteriorated over time and the damp weather in Vietnam. However, I did preserve the words for future reminiscing.

***

OSO Negro (Black Bear)

Hello night, you came to chase the day away with all your might and cause this young soldier much fright … so many men of youth with stories yet untold you stride over them at day's end.

You stride with muscle and very bold. You cast your power over those men of youth as you stride throughout the night … cause they dare not cover their sight
The stars are your eyes ... like silver coins that flicker in the moonlight.

Flares dropped from high above, all night long you stride the sky …
as
I watch with opened eye, day comes quick … I sigh.

You stride from horizon to horizon, till the sun comes arising.

The flares floating ever so gently, lighting up the night, POP, paws, and claws pounding and scarring the earth, POP, paws, and claws pounding and scaring the earth, POP, Lord make it stop.

I'm young, quick, and strong with muscle, brawn, and strength, I will fight you, fear, to any length. Hour by hour, twenty-four, forty-eight, my eyes are slowly closin' cause can't do seventy-two tonight. I'm now asleep and at your mercy, I can only pray …
fear stay away.

C'mon, let's win this war and even the score. We'll kill them all and many more.
We'll say there was a need ... "The Vietnamese we freed."

Fear, you have no form, but yet you surround me and do not care, as if to taunt me with a "double dog dare"
I know not my fate, I declare, but into the night I will stare, with one eye open and a clear insight, because I know you ... fear ... will return again tomorrow night ...
OSO Negro (Black Bear).

***

Under the Flag

Under the American Flag lie the bravest of the brave.
They now lie motionless in their Military grave.

Men and Women who stood in the gap ... for
You and me ... their future they will never see.

They died young to keep us free ... never asked for
What was to be?

These soldiers paid the price, never thought of their own sacrifice.

Words of solemn tone ... are forever etched in those
Granite stones.

I stand and view those stones aligned ... while thoughts of "Joe"
Never leave my mind.

Joe was like no other
Rough and tough ... Joe ... was my brother.

The Street is Talkin'

[During the riots of 2020-2023 here in the United States, I
heard the voice of the streets]

Do ya hear the street talkin'? It's sayin,'

Lord, there's trouble walkin' over me.

Many feet a stompin' hard

Lord, there's trouble walkin' over me.

A regiment of boots "Blue and Green" are standing over me.

Lord, there's war marchin' over me.

Heavy wheels of authority,

Lord, there's trouble rollin' over me.

Sticks and stones smoke and bullets;

Lord, there's blood runnin' over me.

Riots, Unrest, Tires Flaming above.

Lord, there's fire burnin' over me.

Angry people screamin' and chanting;

Lord, there's hate runnin' over me.

Statues falling, paint in my face.

Lord, there's anger walkin' over me.

Lord, I'm just a street … a flat spread of stone marred with blood and
tar always looking up and

seein'

your face from afar.

***

There's a Place Where Soldiers Go

[During a visit to Washington DC, I spent some time at
Arlington Cemetery]

There's a place where soldiers go when the battle's o'er.
A place of sunshine, poppy fields and emerald clover.

A place where Generals and a Private First Class
Can hoist their glass after a Requiem High Mass
When the battle is o'er.

There's a place where soldiers go when the battle's o'er
Far beyond the stars, Jupiter and Mars.
A place where there are no scars of war
A place where eagles soar
When the battle's o'er.

There's a place where soldiers go when the battle's o'er
A place where sailors pull up anchor
Planes fly to meet the sky
A place where pilots are cleared for final approach
coming in hot while writing their final note of forget-me-not.

A place where the Marines all scream Semper-Fi
A place where the Caissons go rolling by
A place where the angels stand at attention
when each name is mentioned
A place where all soldiers go when the battle's o'er.

There's a place where soldiers go when the battle's o'er
A place where orders echo throughout the Universe
A place where cadence is sung with rhythm and song
That's the place where soldiers belong
when the battle is o'er.

There's a place where soldiers go when the battle's o'er
At the dawn of each new day the bugle blows reveille and
The angels sing with revelry.

"My Country Tis of Thee ... Sweet Land of Liberty ... of Thee I sing"
The flag is raised to the highest point ... all salute ...
With stiffened arm, polished brass, uniforms pressed
The order is given "Eyes Right" "Dress Right Dress."

When the day ends and the sun surrenders to the moon's brilliance
The bugle blows the final note of "Retreat"
That's the place where soldiers go ... when the battle's o'er.

***

The Taste of War

The Taste of war is foul, nasty, and full of a horrid insult to the palate.
Its odor is that of rotted meat left in the hot sun.
It reeks of decayed flesh and clotted blood.

The recipe for this rotted dish is conjured up by those who embrace
the serpent of power and control. That serpent coils around their
hearts and minds tempting those who are willing to sacrifice others
for their greed.

As every soldier is forced to consume this awful dish, the flavors
seem to marinate together and become more and more palatable. The
servings keep coming from those whose devious ambitions grow
while dancing with the devil.

The soldier is reluctant to accept this unsavory dish served by the evil force, but the soldier is force-fed and begins to nibble at his or her serving of war, morsel by morsel. Soldiers begin to accept the taste of flesh, blood, fear, anger, and revenge.

It is not long before the soldier craves the taste of war and devours more and more. Serving after serving, never getting enough. Much like an addict who craves the needle in a bulging vein. Soon the taste of war sweetens and becomes a staple to the soldiers' souls. Even after the battle, the taste for war lingers on the tongue and forever seasons the meals of tomorrow.

***

Without the Rhythm of the Band
[Coming home from Vietnam was uneventful, and I felt unnoticed in society]

My country sent me to a far-off land
A maturing boy, not quite a man
To fight a war many did not understand
yet we followed your command of
  "United We Stand ... Without the Rhythm of the Band"

I flew in a jet across the ocean
Where it would land I hadn't a notion
"United We Stand ... Without the Rhythm of the Band"

Somewhere in Vietnam, my orders did read
How will I leave?
Alive ... or consolation would my Mom need?
You gave me an order and a gun to shoulder
Orders were few and incomplete

What fate would I meet?
"United We Stand ... Without the Rhythm of the Band"

Three days I traveled on a plane
From Lewis to Qui-Nhon city
No action, no words, no direction
Yet ... you asked me to fight for our protection
"United We Stand ... Without the Rhythm of the Band

The weather was hot, and the rains fell hard
"The Ace of Spades, was that my card"?
"United We Stand ... Without the Rhythm of the Band"

We spent our days doin' what our country commanded
But in the end, we felt abandoned
"United We Stand ... Without the Rhythm of the Band"

John Kerry threw his medals down
Made the rest of us look like a clown
"United We Stand ... Without the Rhythm of the Band"

Soldiers coming home ... to an empty hand ... and
"Without the Rhythm of the Band"

*****

Author: Paul David Gonzales

Paul David Gonzales is a native of Pittsburgh, Pennsylvania. He served in Vietnam in 1967 and 1968 as a medic with the US Army. Writing is comforting and therapeutic. Expressed words are powerful.

LINDA G. HARRIS

My Worst Hard Year

The Air Force had been good to us, especially during the early years when we needed a steady paycheck, medical care, and, most of all, time to grow up. In return, my husband was obligated to go where the Air Force decided to send him. At the time, we were so focused on our own lives that we hardly noticed the building crisis in Vietnam. But by the late 1960s, we couldn't ignore war protesters marching in the streets and on campuses across the nation. We only hoped the war would end soon. Instead, it dragged on, and in early 1969 he got his orders to go. I imagined it would be My Worst Hard Year.

***

Jim and I married during our first year of college. We were both eighteen. While Jim pushed on taking a full load of classes and a part-time job, I was done. I quit at the end of the semester, thinking my passable typing skills would help me land a job of my own. However, at the end of my first interview, the frumpy office manager leaned slightly toward me to ask one final question. "Honey, are you pregnant?" I took a quick breath, then, like the teenager I was — lied. She never called.

By the next semester, we were dead broke, and our medical bills were beginning to pile up. Jim met with an Air Force recruiter, hoping his year of college would qualify for a scholarship. The recruiter replied — Possibly. With that vague promise in mind, Jim signed up, and on June 3, 1963, he boarded a plane in El Paso for basic training at Lackland Air Force Base in San Antonio. It was his first time on a plane.

Over the next four years, our family of four moved half a dozen times. Jim won the scholarship and earned a degree in meteorology and his lieutenant's bars. By then, the Vietnam War was a mess, its tragic costs brought home by the news that Jim's paratrooper cousin was killed his first week in country. When Jim's orders came, he was assigned to an Air Force base in Thailand. From there, American bombers flew missions to nearby North Vietnam, Cambodia, and later Laos.

When Jim got orders, the kids and I moved back to El Paso, where our families lived, except that my parents had up and moved to Arizona for my dad's job. As for Jim's parents, they hardly knew what to do with us. That left me in the company of my pregnant sister and our band of preschoolers. I was on my own.

Back then, there were no text messages or emails, not to mention FaceTime and Zooms transmitted in real-time. Instead, we kept in touch the same way my World War II parents did — by writing letters. Still, it worked for us — or at least for me. Each week when Jim's letters arrived, I'd read them over and over, devouring every word until the mailman's next delivery.

On the other hand, I found "patched through" phone calls too upsetting. Plus, they reminded me of a prison movie where an inmate talks on the phone from the prison hallway. Eventually, I lost touch with the memory of Jim's voice — a bit of a burr mixed with a tell-tale trace of his Arkansas boyhood. I had only myself to blame for this loss. I still have his letters, bound with ribbons, and stashed in an old shoebox somewhere. None of my letters survived, including the one where I wrote that our car was almost totaled in a front-end collision. My face was bloodied from hitting the steering wheel, but I assured him I was fine. The kids too. When he read my breezy account of the accident, he called me in a panic. He was thousands of miles away, and my letter made him feel guilty, helpless, worried, and a little annoyed all at once. I had become all too comfortable making decisions on my own, and I felt awful for causing him so much pain. After that, I promised to <u>call</u> Jim in an emergency. For that year, I was still the decision-maker.

Our frequent moves and their dad's long absence were tough on the kids, especially our son. He was younger than most of his classmates, plus by the time he finished first grade, he had attended four schools, including a trendy "open classroom" school in Florida. Under its open concept, six-year-olds were expected to work at their own pace. Our son, however, spent his time daydreaming. On one visit to his classroom, we were dismayed to find his desk cubbies stuffed with unfinished papers. His teacher assured us he was fine.

That May, we moved to Texas, where at the end of the school year, his old-school teacher sent him home with a report card full of Fs. I was stunned by her indifference, but as I would learn, that attitude toward military kids was all too common. (Once, when I complained to the orthodontist about changing my daughter's braces without my permission, he dismissed me with a comment on our status as "transients.") I vowed then to be a strong advocate for my children, to make sure they received their due attention and respect. Also, I hoped to give them the courage to advocate for themselves, to speak up, but also to know when to walk away from trouble.

Aside from taking care of my kids, the house, and the dog, I knew if I didn't do something for myself, I'd go crazy. I couldn't get a job and felt out of place in the town I'd left nearly a decade before. Since I already had a whole nine hours of college credits, I decided to spend my Worst Hard Year in college. While searching the schedule for courses that sounded interesting and easy, I spotted the name of a former professor who was still teaching history. I signed up for his American history class as well as a geology class I had failed previously, for, among other things, neglecting to memorize the geologic timetable. Over that year, I took courses in sociology and something called New Math. I studied poetry and short story writing. I admired Ernest Hemingway's spare prose and wrote a paper analyzing his work. In the end, college did more than keep me sane; it gave me a taste of life's possibilities, including the chance to write. Because I was happier, I was also more patient and loving with my children. Then, soon enough, My Worst Hard Year was over.

Jim returned to a four-year assignment to the Pentagon, and we bought our first house in a leafy suburb outside of Washington, DC. Our kids' school was ideal in every way. The teachers were professional and caring. Our son's teacher helped him button his coat and saw that he got extra help in reading. He played violin in the orchestra. Our daughter, shy and smart, blossomed. She joined the Brownies, tall and adorable in her uniform. With Jim off at work and the kids settled in school, I drove the Beltway on Mondays, Wednesdays, and Fridays to attend classes at the University of Maryland.

***

I was wrong back then to think 1969 would be My Worst Hard Year. It's not that I haven't seen a few tough years in the half-century since; it's just that 1969 showed me that there is no worst — or best year. That year, for instance, I became more confident in my ability to shoulder responsibilities, to make decisions, and to be a stronger advocate for my children. My return to college opened up my world and revealed my knack for writing, which I still carry with me. Thinking back, I'd call 1969 My Pretty Good Year.

*****

Author: Linda G. Harris

Linda G. Harris is an award-winning author who holds a Bachelor of Arts in journalism from New Mexico State University. She is the spouse of Major James Harris, a retired US Air Force meteorologist. Linda and Jim have been married for sixty years and recently moved to Albuquerque, NM.

M. ELDER HAYS

So Many Wars

"Mom, why is there a box of rocks in the garage?"

"Those are your dad's," she hollered from the kitchen.

"Can I put them out in the yard?"

"No. That's his collection," she warned.

"Collection?"

"Yes. He brought them from California."

"We have rocks here in Washington. Why did he bring a box of rocks? Is there something special about these?"

"Stop yelling! Come in the house if you want to talk with me."

I entered the house through the family room. Dad lay there in his hospital bed, asleep, oxygen on. He looked peaceful — like he did when in his recliner all those many years before. The television was on, even though he hadn't been awake in days. Mom must have turned it on for him.

"Sorry. I said, 'We have rocks here in Washington.' Is there something special about these?"

"No. They're just rocks. He … he really liked them and insisted on bringing them. He's had some of them since he was a little boy in Clovis."

Speechless, I moved on. I had driven down to Federal Way to help Mom complete the paperwork to get Dad's name included in the Korean War Veterans Memorial in Washington, DC. Long ago, Dad had gone to Albuquerque with some of his friends and enlisted in the Navy on 19 January 1951. He got his training on Treasure Island in San Francisco Bay and shipped out on the USS Toledo (CA-133) just in time for Toledo's third combat tour outside Yokosuka. The Chinese forces staged their sixth major offensive of the Korean War that September.

He was eighteen years old.

He spent almost three years aboard the Toledo before he landed in Long Beach, California. He met Mom there. She was a nurse at the Naval Hospital and six years his senior. They married, had five children, and he worked his entire career at the *Los Angeles Times Mirror*. He did the typesetting by hand, then by machine when technology caught up, setting up the classified ads in ten-point type for a hundred pages of print every day. Dad was good at detail.

Mom, however, got a bit confused about paperwork stuff sometimes. She loved writing checks to charity but couldn't keep track of whom she gave the money to. At last count, she had 135 charities to whom she gave $17.00 to each and every month. She was frustrated about getting more requests for new charities in the mail and puzzled as to why she couldn't balance her checkbook. I tried to get her to make out $20.00 checks so the math would be easier, but she didn't want to do that. Her call. Good thing I'm pretty proficient with a calculator.

"So, you wanted some help?"

"Sure. Could you peel these potatoes for me? I'm making scalloped potatoes for dinner, your father's favorite."

"But he's not awake or even eating, is he?"

"No, not for days now, but if he wakes up, I'd like to have some food ready that he likes. You know how monotonous he found the chow in the Navy." She held out a paring knife.

With a shrug, I took the paring knife and began peeling potato after potato. Third one in, I decided to chat with her while I was working.

"Mom, did you also need help with that application?"

"Oh, no. Susan helped me with it."

"Susan's here?"

"She's taking a nap right now. Poor girl was exhausted." Mom then switched to her "whisper" voice which was pretty loud due to her hearing loss. "She had a fight with Alan in the middle of the night and came down here."

I kept peeling and then slicing the potatoes since I was as familiar with the family scalloped potato recipe as I was with our dysfunctional family dynamics. Figured I'd stick around and chat with Susan when she woke up.

***

While the potatoes were in the oven cooking, Susan emerged from the guest room, up from her nap. I was sitting at the kitchen table drinking a cup of church lady coffee (you know, the stuff so weak that church ladies drink it like water.) The kitchen table was just on the other side of the lattice screen that separated the kitchen from the family room. Dad's hospital bed was set up facing the TV and the fireplace, although I doubt he had any awareness of either of them due to his condition.

Susan and I hugged. She got a cup of coffee and sat with me. We thumbed through old books that Mom wanted to donate to charity. Dad had a habit of putting important papers and $20 bills (and occasionally $100 bills) on page 133 of any book. He said it was his time aboard the USS Toledo (CA-133) that inspired this and cautioned us on a number of occasions to never give a book away without checking page 133.

I love my sister, Susan, but we have had a very troubled relationship through the years. Here we were, though, sitting vigil at my father's deathbed. We chatted like old friends.

I told her about my life. She told me about hers.

Susan talked about her husband, Alan. They'd had a big fight the night before. Not as bad as the one where she needed some medical attention because she was eight months pregnant and worried about the stress of the argument. At the time, I worked for her medical provider, and the clinic staff called me in to help her. I worked to calm her down, put a plan together for where to go (to Mom's and Dad's at that point), and helped her get settled there short term for her and the future baby's safety. She stayed there a few weeks, but shortly thereafter, she left, returned to Alan, had the baby, and eventually married him.

Years later now, she complained about what a horrible husband he was. They had a lot of problems in their marriage, including arguments over raising two of her boys from her first husband. So, our conversation was pretty intense. At one point, she said, "I don't know why I married that man."

At this, Dad came out of his coma, sat up, turned his head toward us, and said, "Yeah, why?" Then he laid back down, eyes closed. He had said his piece.

We sat there in a bit of shock. We looked at each other and cracked up.

Mom heard us laughing and came out to the kitchen. "What's so funny?" she asked.

"We were just talking, Mom," Susan responded.

"And apparently, Dad was listening." I chimed in. "He joined our conversation … briefly."

"Really? What did he say?"

"He's still wondering why Susan married Alan."

"Me too," Mom commented.

Susan opted to change the topic. "Are the potatoes done?"

"Oh, I almost forgot them," Mom said. And off she bustled to make sure they didn't get burned.

Right then, the small cow-shaped cooking timer rang, and we busied ourselves with serving the scalloped potatoes along with the turkey Mom had also cooked. There were fresh steamed green beans and a pumpkin pie. Two days before Thanksgiving, this was going to be our family's holiday meal. Dad was a large guy, and Thanksgiving was his favorite holiday.

All that food Dad loved, but he didn't wake again. He missed this last meal with us all.

*****

Author: M. Elder Hays

Mike Hays is an old, out-of-shape, recovering alcoholic gay guy, as well as the son of a Navy Veteran from Clovis, NM. He worked in social work and health policy analysis but now writes short stories, screenplays, and memoirs. He lives next door to his best friend.

A. MICHAEL HIBNER

Navy ET A-School, Treasure Island
San Francisco Bay

After Basic Training — or Boot Camp — at the San Diego Naval Training Center, I headed home for a couple of weeks of rest and recreation (R&R). After that, it was off to Treasure Island (TI) for Electronics Technician (ET) A-school [technical training].

Treasure Island is a man-made island in San Francisco Bay. To get there, you must take an off-ramp from the Bay Bridge that dumps onto Yerba Buena, a natural island. The Navy owned Yerba Buena, and I believe it mostly consisted of housing for retired Admirals. Fleet Admiral Chester Nimitz lived there after he retired and died there.

I flew from Albuquerque to San Francisco shortly after New Year's Day in 1965. I was placed in a holding company until my class formed. I think I spent about three months in that company. Early on, I was ordered to report to the Chief's Club. I was to be their gopher and to tidy up the place. It wasn't tough duty. I had the duty for eight hours a day during working hours.

Every three days or so, I stood a four-hour watch somewhere on the station. Often it was what was called the Surfside Six watch. It consisted of walking along the breakwater from 2000 hours until 2400 hours, or 2400 until 0400. It was cold and foggy most of the time; one night, I was walking the watch, and the fog lifted, and there was San Francisco. I hadn't realized you could see it from Treasure Island. It *is* a pretty city from the water.

I noticed two pool tables when I first walked into the Chief's Club. At about 1400 hours, four or five Chiefs came in and started playing on the tables, but they weren't playing eight ball or nine ball. The Chiefs, I later learned, were playing what was called Carom Four-Ball Pocket Billiards. I'd seen billiards tables without pockets in pool halls before. I don't think I'd ever seen anyone play on one, though. But these were regular pool tables — with pockets.

You can get points by putting balls in the pockets, but that is incidental to the real object of the game and is not always a good thing. Carom is a finesse game. You start by spotting balls on the center spot and on the two end spots. I don't remember where the cue ball was spotted. You try to hit one of the balls with the cue ball, bounce off the cushion and then hit another ball. If you put a ball in a pocket, you take it out and re-spot it. You get maximum points if you hit all three balls, three cushions, and make all three balls. I never saw it happen.

Anyway, I asked the Chiefs if it would be okay if I used the tables when they weren't and I wasn't busy. They said sure. Sometimes I'd practice with one or another of the Chiefs. I figured out the game and found that the best thing to do was gather the balls in an area, worry them around a little, and keep them tight. As long as you scored at least one point, you kept shooting.

Three Chiefs showed up to play one day, but the fourth didn't. After they were sure he wasn't going to make it, one of the Chiefs asked if I wanted to be his partner.

"No, Chief," I told him, "I can't afford it." They played for big bucks; I'd seen as much as twenty dollars change hands on a single game.

"Don't worry about it." The Chief replied. "I'll cover you."

"Okay."

Much to my surprise, we won. And I had been an asset. After that, my stock went way up with the Chiefs, and I was often asked to play with them.

All good things come to an end; my A-School company was formed, and my education began. We met ET-1 [Electronics Technician First

Class] McBride on the first day. We were with him for the first ten weeks. He was very personable and made the class seem like fun. He told many sea stories as he taught us electronics (which was mostly just algebra, geometry, and basic math). We were introduced to Ohms Law and Joules Law and the world of resistors, capacitors, and diodes. I enjoyed it quite a bit and made good scores on the bi-weekly tests. There were no more Surfside Six watches and no more billiards with the Chiefs.

***

One afternoon, ET-1 McBride told us we would have classes with ET-1 French sometime soon. He advised me to attend French's study groups each night after his regular class period. I did that. Only about six others did as well. With French's instruction at night, we had no problems passing the bi-weekly tests. I think we had French for four weeks. He was the only instructor that had study groups.

A few weeks later, my relationship with ET-1 French paid off in a different way. One Saturday morning, I was sleeping in the barracks when another sailor grabbed my T-shirt and dragged me out of my rack. I was in a sound sleep, but I woke up quickly enough to punch him in the nose three times before my feet hit the deck.

I never did find out his motive for doing what he did. We were both Seamen, and he was not in my A-School company. I wasn't supposed to relieve him from a watch and overslept. In any case, he was bleeding all over the deck and had to be taken to sick bay to get it stopped. Since blood and sick bay were involved, a report had to be written, and a hearing had to be convened.

The outcome of the hearing was that we were both required to spend eight hours policing the grounds, which is Navy jargon for picking up cigarette butts and other debris. We were to report to a certain location for Work Detail assignments at 0800 hours the following Saturday.

When I got there, I found that ET-1 French was giving out the assignments to about twenty sailors.

"Hibner, what the hell are you doing here?" French asked me.

I told him what had happened.

"Get the hell out of here!" he said, "and I better never see you here again!"

He didn't.

***

Treasure Island probably wasn't the ideal place to teach eighteen-year-old sailors electronics. There were too many distractions. San Francisco's North Beach was a twenty-minute bus ride from the base gate. One night a couple of my running mates and I decided to visit the Condor Club.

There was a young lady by the name of Carol Doda dancing there on a nightly basis. She was the first topless dancer to grace the stage at any club in North Beach. And she was an immediate hit with the TI sailors. I didn't see her first dance; that happened a few months before I was assigned to A-School. However, I watched her as her bust measurement increased from a respectable thirty-four to an amazing forty-four, due to the wonders of silicone injections, over just a few months.

While my adventures in North Beach, as well as other interesting and educational attractions in and around the Bay Area, were entertaining, they were nearly my downfall.

I flunked a test at the end of the twenty-fifth week of A-School. By half a point. No doubt due to too much alcohol and topless entertainment, and too little studying. The lowest grade you could receive on a test and still pass was sixty-two point five. I received a sixty-two.

108

I was called into the ET A-School Commander's office and told that I would be dropped back by a company and allowed to retake the test and complete the school. But this could only happen once.

"Hibner, if you flunk another test, you will be assigned to a ship and sent to sea. Understood?"

"Yes, sir!"

"Unless you *want* to go to sea. We can assign you to a ship right now. Is that what you want?"

"No, sir!"

"Are you likely to flunk another test?"

"No, sir!"

I didn't. I aced the test the second time; I don't think I had a test score below 90 after that. I gave up my excursions to San Francisco and spent much more time studying electronics.

The rest of A-School came and went. I was now an ETN, as opposed to an ETR. There were two classifications of ETs, some worked on radios, and some worked on radars. Since ETR was assigned to the radar techs, the radio techs were assigned ETN. I don't know why.

Paraphrasing an old axiom, "Thirty-eight weeks ago, I couldn't even spell Lectronix Teknishon, and now I are one."

I thought I was done with Navy schooling and would be assigned to my next duty station, but I was wrong. I was sent to a four-week C-School [in-depth training]. I had been taught electronics, but now I was going to be taught how to fix radio transceivers. Off to C-School, I went on the following Monday morning. I was introduced to the Collins UHF URC-32 transceiver. The UHF stood for ultra-high frequency; I don't know what "URC" or "32" stood for.

The URC-32 was the Navy's first transistorized transceiver. It stood about seven feet tall, and each function had its own cabinet that could be pulled open like a dresser drawer, and the insides could be dealt with. Each drawer contained plug-in modules that could be removed after failure and replaced with a new module. It was an ETNs dream but too fragile for the average Radioman. They were used to radios that could take the beating they gave them. For example, the old UHF transceivers had a frequency dial that could be rapidly spun from the top to bottom of the spectrum, and vis versa, without damage. On the URC-32, if you spun the frequency dial, it could blow through the stops and would require realignment.

After four weeks of learning the gear, we had a test. But this test required the technician to repair the transceiver. We were called in one at a time, given a Simpson 260 multimeter and a set of tools, directed to a transceiver, and told to fix it. The first cabinet I checked had a good input and a bad output. The first module I checked had a good input and a bad output. I pulled that module and plugged in another one, and the transceiver was good to go. I couldn't believe it. Ten minutes into the test and I was done.

About a week after completing C-School, I received orders for my next duty station. It was to be the USS Kearsarge (CVS-33) stationed out of Long Beach. It was now February of 1966; I had been in Boot Camp, ET A-School, and a C-School for a year and a half. But one more interesting event happened that I took part in (in a small way).

On February 20, 1966, Fleet Admiral Chester W. Nimitz died. His funeral service was to take place on Treasure Island. About five hundred other sailors and I put on our dress blues and marched in the funeral procession.

***

Nothing Rhymes With Orange

They say nothing rhymes with orange,
But I find that pretty boring.
I think no one ever took the time to look.
There must be a rhyme for orange.
I will give the search some more range,
And check in every book in every nook.
I know there's a rhyme for orange
In the billion shelves of storage
In the libraries that span across the land
I find nothing rhymes with orange.
I find nothing that is more strange,
But if you will lend a hand, we'll look again.

*****

Author: A. Michael Hibner

As Navy Electronics Technician Radio (ETN-2), Arthur Michael Hibner, spent the first eighteen months of his enlistment in California in Boot Camp, A, and C-Schools, then thirty months on board the USS Kearsarge (CVS-33). Mostly in the South China Sea near Vietnam, thus a charter member of the Tonkin Gulf Yacht Club.

CARL HITCHENS

Time Travel

The fighting spirit of *Unnacokasimon*, a Seventeenth Century *Nanticoke* Indian chief, meets the fighting spirit of Twentieth Century Ho Chi Minh. And in the breaking waves of colliding spacetimes, a trial testing the steel of personified warrior grit is set into motion.

Such warrior spirit comes by way of a journey of consciousness. One often described as the Hero's Journey. All hero journeys begin alike: A baby's crying response of disorientation in exiting its mother's protective biosphere into the greater biosphere of Mother Earth. Facing the unknown, the baby vocalizes its fear and simultaneous defiance. He or she will *"not go gentle into that good night."* (Dylan Thomas)

Every collective group of human beings is a tribe of a sort, whether a nuclear family, extended family, or nation. These tribes have their hero stories planted like seeds for imitation in a child's mind and heart. Such stories become trees anchoring a people to the land and sky of their being. Tales of bravery and unwavering devotion that transport them back and forth in time to preserve their way of life. An identifying selfhood of who they are now and into the future.

It was by such a ripening of child wonder into adult aspiration that I pushed on through childhood rites of passage to the grownup version and entered the crucible of Vietnam warfare and combat. Along the way from childhood innocence to post-combat citizen, I've learned a few things that have sustained me through the light and dark of life's adversities and personal demons.

As such, we all are on a time journey of our own making, a quest to be the highest expression of the ideal person we want to be — that shiny template of human ascendancy. Every tribe has its lineage of paragons who demonstrated those character traits prized by their people in their time on earth. In my Nanticoke heritage, the contributions of Chief *Unnacokasimon* to the tribe's survival and continuance in the *Age of Discovery* are noteworthy history.

It was a fateful day in 1608 when the British captain John Smith — while exploring the Chesapeake Bay — sailed onto the *Kuskarawaok* River, the self-same river known currently as the Nanticoke. Here he made First Contact (the meeting of two distinct cultures unaware of one another) with the ancestors of today's Nanticoke Indian Tribe. This brush with the *Kuskarawaok*, otherwise *Nantaquak* people, would prove to be a harbinger of change and uncertainty.

Nanticoke, translated from the original Algonquian *Nantaquak*, means People of the Tide Water, referring to the Eastern Shore area between the Delaware and Chesapeake bays. Prior to Smith's transmutative expedition, the Nanticoke maintained a lifestyle based on the rhythms of nature and the web of life.

Drawing sustenance from their riparian habitat, they subsisted on fish, crabs, shrimp, eels, clams, oysters, and the farmed harvest of corn, beans, squash, pumpkins, and sunflowers. As hunters and gatherers, they foraged for nuts, berries, birds, eggs, and edible seasonal plants. During the winter, they hunted in the forests and meadows of the Eastern Shore for squirrels, turkeys, deer opossums, rabbits, bear, partridges, ducks, and geese. It was a predictable pattern of seasons coming and going. But like Captain Smith's vessel, that "ship had sailed" and brought to the Eastern Shore decades of upheaval.

Land grabs and displacement by white settlers disrupted the tribe's seasonal way of life. The de facto invaders whittled down the forests and, consequently, the winter game. Their unconfined livestock plundered native farms and crops, precipitating extenuating thievery of their hogs and cattle by area tribes struggling to "bring home the bacon."

Raids and threats of war and open warfare escalated hostilities between area tribes and colonists, boiling over with Maryland governor Thomas Greene ordering militia captain John Pike to attack and destroy the Nanticoke village and gardens in 1642 and 1647 as coercion to leave the area.

All of this took its toll over a seventy-year span, leaving the Nanticoke and their *Choptank* relations the only native tribes still living on the Eastern Shore. This was the world in which Chief Unnacokasimon fought the good fight for his people.

In 1668, the Nanticoke chief signed the first of five treaties to establish peace between the proprietary government of the Province of Maryland and his people. The treaties, however, did not broker harmony, as English emigrants continued their seizing of tribal lands. Being "discovered" exacted tribute in stolen sovereignty.

To remedy this ongoing trespass, the tribe, under the tenure of Chief Unnacokasimon, petitioned the Maryland government in 1684 to grant them specific tracts of land. This resulted in a jointly defined reservation for the tribe's use, situated between Chicacoan Creek and the Nanticoke River in Maryland. Nonetheless, non-native people still encroached upon their lands leading up to the tribe purchasing a 3,000-acre tract of land in 1707 on Broad Creek in Somerset County, Maryland (now Sussex County, Delaware).

Nevertheless, the fortunes of change hoped for in songwriter Sam Cooke's balladeering lyricizing about change coming did not come to fruition. Therefore, in 1742 the Nanticoke crafted hushed plans for a war of independence against the Maryland colony. But a *Choptank* informer's loose lips alerted colonists, who countered with their own threat to take all of what Nanticoke land remained.

The die was cast. Beginning in 1744, a gradual exodus of the Nanticoke took place. Traveling north in dugout canoes to the Susquehanna River, some migrated to the Six Nations of the Iroquois into New York, Pennsylvania, and areas of Canada on the promise of land and protection. Others walked westward. A significant number, including my antecedents, moved eastward into Delaware and settled near the Indian River.

This living history courses through my veins. It is imprinted in my DNA [deoxyribonucleic acid] as a testament to resolve and resilience in the face of grave challenges. It is a living being within me that lived on in Vietnam and my return home.

As a *baby boomer* swaddled in the Allied victory tantara over World War II oppression and genocide, I wanted to reach the apotheosis of will and courage embodied in Marine Corps lore.

The vital force of "Chesty" Puller, the legendary embodiment of Marine *Semper Fidelis*, drove me in an inevitable act of daring to enlist in the United States Marine Corps in November 1967. Five months and two weeks later, I entered the crucible of the Vietnam War. The lifeblood of Chesty and I went up against General Vo Nguyen Giap, Commander of the People's Army of Vietnam.

Battle joined; the adrenaline-rushed instincts of combat mind got me and my brothers-in-arms through each day and month of jousting with enemy forces. Prolonged exposure to serial danger and deathly consequences of repetitive patrols, sweeps, and operations had armed us with a cognitive recall to anticipate danger, react to it, and live another day outsmarting lethal demise. Failing that, we would join the rest of the immortalized fallen listed on the Vietnam Memorial Wall in Washington, DC.

I lived to live another day, all the way to my rotation date (end of deployment). After thirteen months in the jungles, rice paddies, and hills of South Vietnam, I was on my way home: three days at Camp Butler (Okinawa), then on to Treasure Island US Naval Station (San Francisco), and onward to my hometown, Washington, DC.

Returning, I was a different person, and America was a different country from the one I had left. Stateside duty at Camp Lejeune (North Carolina) tasted like a strange brew of familiar and unfamiliar flavors.

The daily regimen of domestic military bases seemed banal compared to their Nam counterparts, where literal ground force attacks, ambushes, incoming rockets, rocket-propelled grenades, booby traps, and mines replaced alert and response drills.

War is always ultimately personal. The finality of premeditated killing strips away any dispassion from war. It is serious business with serious consequences, the ramifications of which the individual warrior bears. I was twenty-two years old, trying to deconflict the arguments between pro-war and anti-war activists to sift out my own truth. Compounding my readjustment challenge was managing combat-conditioned reflexes to external noises and movement stimuli.

Decades have passed since I crossed the Pacific, leap-frogged over the South China Sea, and touched down at Da Nang Air Base, and on to *beating the bush* as a Marine *grunt*. For some, their jousting with immortality ended there far from home.

We had been denied both the "thrill of victory" and the "agony of defeat" per the proviso of the *Paris Peace Accords*, designating the withdrawal of all US forces from Vietnam (January 1973).

President Nixon's ignominious "Peace with Honor" end to the war was laid squarely at our feet as the flashpoint of America's divisive culture war, which tossed us away as collateral damage left to our own devices.

In my private reminiscences, I questioned the good I had done myself and my country, as seen through the transcendental eyes of Chesty Puller. Chesty would be the final adjudicator of heroic worthiness for storytelling around winter fires as guiding posts for future generations.

To *slay the dragon* that stands between every person and their quest, they must jettison their fears, doubts, and feelings of inadequacy. They must claim their power and their future. The hero's journey on the surface may seem singular. But it is the journey of the *one in the many* that becomes the *many in the one.* The hero's tale acts as a force multiplier for reaching our potential.

Still, my fighting an unpopular war that never came to our shores seems inconsequential compared to my ancient forebears. Yet Nam's long shadow on American culture and politics is an order of magnitude equal to that of an event horizon from which we seemingly cannot escape. Like the dinosaurs, our unmistakable traces turn up in any discussion on foreign or domestic policy that has geopolitical significance.

Our ranks grow thinner with the passing of each year, but we are still here as a reminder of the cost of war and the elusiveness of peace. And in that perennial struggle to coexist, perhaps we have earned a place of distinction in the pursuit of the American Dream. Maybe somewhere in the ugliness of the death and carnage we gave and received is the path forward to a peaceful humanity.

Throughout the ages, humankind has been desperately divided by competing identity interests: tribal, racial, ethnic, religious, and national. Conflicts over land, resources, fortune, and influence have damned peaceable cohabitation throughout history. It is because of our disability to recognize our oneness that we are divided between enemy and ally. War can foist itself into the breach when the need to control circumstances mutates into irreconcilable differences. At that point, "Older men declare war. But it is youth that must fight and die. And it is youth who must inherit the tribulation, the sorrow, and the triumphs that are the aftermath of war." [Herbert Hoover, June 1944]

And therein lies the Catch-22 that pervaded the anti-war and pro-war movements. "War hath no fury like a non-combatant." [Charles Edward Montague] What both sides missed was our reality: "It doesn't make a damned bit of difference who wins the war to someone who's dead." [Joseph Heller, author]

Where does that leave us Vietnam vets when all is said and done? I think we can let Chesty Puller, the most decorated US Marine in history, speak for us from another military stalemate (Korean War). When the 1st Marine Division was surrounded and outnumbered eight-to-one by Chinese and North Korean forces. 1st Marine Regiment Commander Lieutenant General Lewis B. Puller declared the following: "All right, they're on our left, they're on our right, they're in front of us, they're behind us ...they can't get away this time. We're surrounded. That simplifies the problem!"

That's nothing new for the Nanticoke Indian Tribe.

AND WE ARE STILL HERE!

*****

Author: Carl Hitchens

Carl Hitchens, US Marine Corps veteran. Through his writing, he strives to act as a voice of cultural/social critique and criticism. His published works include: "Home" (poetry), "The Sun Rises" (poetry), "Our Planet" (essay), "Thinning of the Veils" (poetry), "Shades of Light" (poetry), "Sitting with Warrior" (historical memoir), and "Breath of Fire" (poetry).

KE HOPKINS

Pocket Money

Most kids find some way to earn spending money. You know, mowing lawns, babysitting, washing the car. It was very special that I could work at my father's delicatessen from the age of eight years old. Quite a wonderful little job for four hours a week, and it let me spend time alone with my dad, which I treasured.

But I thought of myself as an ambitious and clever girl. Innovative, too. There were markets out there just waiting for a gutsy nine-year-old entrepreneur named Maggie with a ponytail and a bicycle.

We'd lived in the same subdivision of new houses for several years. Tons of children with whom to play. In the winter, all the kids built snow forts and had snowball wars. We dragged sleds and toboggans to the top of the highest hill at the park by the railroad tracks. In the summer, we played hardball in an empty field across the street. We rode our bikes to the city swimming pool in the afternoons. We were neighbors and friends.

I stumbled on the idea for my business on a summer day when I discovered my brother and a group of the neighborhood boys poring over a dirty magazine they found in a garbage bin. At first, they tried to hide what they were doing, but I soon reminded them I was not a girl who tattled. I checked out the magazine for myself. Lots of boobs and butts and arty cover-ups for the genital area. Not really racy by today's standards, but the guys were very motivated. I listened to them bemoan the fact that this kind of magazine was kept behind the counter at every news agency and drugstore in town. Besides, they were all petrified that their parents would find out if they tried to buy one.

So, a totally amazing marketing opportunity dropped from the sky right into my lap. The deal was that I would purchase any magazine they wanted with a one hundred percent markup. Double or nothing. Money was required upfront. I started my business small — just the boys on the block. As the sole proprietor, I purposely did not confide in any of my girlfriends. Some of them were a little "goody two shoes," if you know what I mean, and I certainly didn't want any moms or dads involved.

The first time I went to the little news agency in our town, I felt a bit nervous. I knew the man who owned it because I bought comic books and fountain drinks there. Looking as cute and smiley as I could, I put my *Little Lulu* comic book and a candy bar on the counter and politely asked for four of the wrapped magazines I could see on a rack behind the cash register. He hesitated, so I smiled even bigger and said, "They're for my big brother. Could you please put them in a bag for me, Glenn?" And he did!

Soon I was shopping at about six locations in our town and the village to the east. My clientele grew by leaps and bounds. There were adolescent boys who lived up to a half mile away who made orders through the guys I knew, my "preferred" customers. Then the boy cousins in the family got wind of my business, and suddenly I was tapping into such a bigger market. The profits were phenomenal, and I didn't have time to spend all the money that came rolling in. Practically on the Fortune 500 annual list.

I had orders for *Playboy*, of course. But to keep the boys interested, I found copies of magazines like *Gent*, *Stud*, and *Bachelor*. *Penthouse* was another standard. Once, when on a trip to downtown Chicago, I found a real prize right in Union Station; I think it was called *Stag* or *Stag Party*. As CEO of this little company, I decided there would be a surcharge for that particular issue. Highly prized and shared among the guys.

I never really worried about my parents. I figured that even if they found out, my mother would ignore it completely if it had anything to do with sex. She wouldn't even say the word. My dad? Well, he might even turn out to be another customer.

Alas, this lucrative enterprise was doomed to hit the rocks sooner or later. I was actually surprised that it lasted as long as it did. Little Maggie kept thinking how dumb the boys were not to figure out they could buy their own magazines. And then, one of them finally did. The business tanked within a week.

Back to babysitting. Damn! It did pay the bills, but I didn't enjoy it at all. I much preferred working for my dad, and he gave me more hours at the store as I got older. With raises along the way.

Once we were all grown up, the secret came out. As I predicted, my mother refused to even speak about it. Dad just laughed his ass off. To this day, when my older cousin, Craig, and my brother get together, someone always mentions my dirty magazine business. I prefer to remember it as an early venture into the world of high finance.

*****

Author: KE Hopkins

Kathleen E. Hopkins is the daughter of an Army veteran. She worked both as a teacher and a research coordinator before retiring in 2017. Since then, her hobbies have included writing and travel. Her volunteering at the Veterans Administration has been a wonderful experience. Kathy facilitates the Therapeutic Creative Writing Group and works with so many great veterans.

JAMES HOUSTON AND MOLLY HOUSTON

Serving On Top of the World

My first experience with the Air Force was when I entered tenth grade in Memphis. In Tennessee, it was mandatory in the nineteen fifties for all male high school students to take three years of ROTC [Reserve Officers' Training Corps]. I decided it would be a good career choice. So, in the summer between my junior and senior years, I went to boot camp at Lackland Air Force Base (AFB) in San Antonio, Texas. During my senior year, I was in the reserves.

After graduation from high school, I only had to take one month of a refresher course, and I was off to special training for a career in logistics at F.E. Warren AFB in Cheyenne, Wyoming. Then, stationed at Fortuna Air Force Station in North Dakota and Offutt AFB in Omaha, Nebraska, for brief stints, I honed my skills in logistics and was promoted to Airman 2nd. Class.

Thule (too-lee) AFB was my next assignment from July 1958 to July 1959. Thule is the northernmost, coldest, and most remote US Air Force Base. It's located on the northwest coast of the island of Greenland between the Arctic Circle and the North Pole and approximately midway between Russia and Washington, DC. Greenland is a self-governing country within the Kingdom of Denmark. Thule is part of the Strategic Air Command, which was integral in response to the Cold War with Russia and is based at Offutt AFB in Omaha. At that time, only three to four thousand people were assigned there.

I arrived by a military transport C-54 Skymaster, the military version of the commercial DC-4. With the exception of dog sled, it was the only transportation available to Thule year-round. My job was in the logistics section of the special projects unit to build radar installations. This was one of the first early warning systems built to detect missiles or planes coming across the North Pole from Russia headed for the United States.

This transport plane came to the base every Sunday, keeping the engines running all the time they were unloading and loading during the colder months of the year so the engines wouldn't freeze. New personnel, fresh food, some other supplies, and mail were brought in. When it left carrying outgoing mail, equipment, and personnel returning to the States, care was taken to ensure no stowaways were attempting to return before their documented departure date.

Ships were able to come in from late June after a Canadian icebreaker opened the harbor, until late September when the ocean began freezing again. They carried larger supplies, equipment, and vehicles for the construction of the radar site as well as for the base. Army stevedores who traveled on ships all over the world did the unloading. Large trucks carried the radar installation supplies over ten miles to the radar site on top of a hill on unpaved roads.

Luckily, I arrived in the summer when the sun never completely sets, so I easily learned my way around the base. Personnel who came in the winter when it was always dark were at a disadvantage in that respect. After being assigned to a barracks, I was issued special clothing: a heavy fur parka, a face mask, mukluks (high-top fur-covered boots), heavy fur mittens, long underwear, and very warm socks.

The barracks where I lived were built for sixteen people, although some were larger. The living quarters were built up off the ground on pilings. The ground below was covered with gravel to allow air to circulate under the floors so the permafrost would not melt; otherwise, the barracks would sink into the mud. The walls, about one and a half feet thick, were constructed of metal on the outside; the inside walls were wallboard, with insulation in between the two. The two outside doors, one at each end of the barracks, were commercial freezer doors, with an airlock area between it and another inside door.

The barracks were divided in half, each with a common room. The common room had couches, chairs, a television, and a radio. Programs were taped in the US and rebroadcast by Armed Forces Network from the main base to the barracks. The shows were weeks old, as was the news.

Each man had their own small room. We had a bunk bed, a desk, two chairs, and a small refrigerator. Each room had one small three-paned window. A heavy curtain was provided to keep out the light during the summer nights. Occasionally we had to double up as personnel came and went.

Each half of the barracks had a common latrine and two shower stalls. Water was a precious commodity. Fresh water was trucked in from an underground source several miles away. It was treated on the base before delivery to the barracks and stored in two tanks, one at each at the end of the barracks. We could shower for two minutes once a week on a strict schedule. The toilets were equipped with a valve and a pump. You would turn on the water and push down on a lever to send the waste to another of two storage tanks at the end of your barracks.

Once per week, servicemen driving the "honey wagon" came to collect and dispose of the sewage tank's contents. Volunteers who drove the honey wagon could leave several months early rather than staying the full twelve months.

For heat, we had steam heat piped to the barracks in large pipes that ran to the buildings on top of the grounds and over the roads. Utilities on the base had redundant sources. The supplemental heat for the barracks was provided by huge electric generators in each building that were very loud. We had to keep all the doors shut to try to drown out some of the noise when they were in use.

We normally had meals of powdered eggs and milk, packaged and canned food. The Sunday plane brought in food supplies, including some fresh food like fresh eggs, milk, and produce. These fresh supplies lasted a day or so, after which we went back to the normal fare. We also bought food and snacks in the canteen to store in our rooms.

The barracks had a storeroom for essentials. Extra water and food were stored there in case we were stuck in our barracks during a blizzard in the winter. The food consisted of canned and packaged food like powdered eggs and milk, pasta, condiments, and C-rations [US Army Field Ration C] left over from World War II, dated 1943-1945. Hot plates were provided to heat the food, but we were not allowed to use them at other times. If you wanted a cold soda, you could just bury it outside in the ice for ten minutes.

There were several occasions while I was there when we had to stay in our barracks or the office for a few days at a time. Army cots and the same type of food were provided there as well.

Laundry was picked up once a week from the barracks. We were allowed to have the bottom sheet and the pillowcase washed. The top sheet became the bottom sheet the second week, and we could send in our underwear and two sets of clothes. However, if you happened to go to sleep exhausted after a long day at work while eating a juicy cheeseburger in bed, then roll over in it in your sleep, making a mess of your bed, they would give you two fresh sheets.

In the winter, when it was cloudy and dark, and snow was probable, ropes were strung along the roads between all the different buildings. We were required to walk at least by twos and hold on to the ropes to guide us. Once, when walking down an icy frozen road with some buddies, I slid so fast that both feet shot out in front of me, and I landed flat on my back. The snow and winds in the dark could totally obscure your visibility, and the temperatures could fall to thirty degrees below zero. Becoming lost could quickly result in death.

In compensation for our remote location, we were offered some extras that weren't always available on other bases. We had a library, a service club, a lounge where you could check out records and the old tapes on reels for listening to music, a movie theater where we got new movies on a regular basis, and the USO [United Service Organization] occasionally gave shows in the theater for us. Once, we were treated to a show starring Bob Hope.

We worked in a large office containing many people with different jobs. Our work was done the old-fashioned way, using paper and pencil. Individual computers were unheard of then, but we had a very large computer. After we finished our work, we gave it to a punch card entry clerk, who transferred the information to punch cards. The cards were then fed into the computer for storage and printing.

Like on other bases, we took our turn at KP [kitchen police]. Once when it was my turn, I was told I would wear my dress uniform. I also had to go to a special training session where I was drilled on serving protocol. Lieutenant General Francis H. Griswold, Vice Commander in Chief of the Strategic Air Command, visited us. Needless to say, I was nervous. When I was done serving dinner that evening, General Griswold looked at me and said, "Sit down, son."

All the military leaders of the base were at the table. The general was pleasant, asking me where I was from, how I came to join the Air Force, and about some of my experiences. I sat there for about a half hour, listening to the conversation and answering an occasional question. That was one of the highlights of my stay at Thule.

We were paid our salaries in cash. Of course, I used some of the money to buy things on the base: clothes and other personal things I might need at the commissary and movie tickets. The rest I sent by mail to my mother in Memphis, either as cash or as a money order. She would put it in my account at the bank.

Quite a few Danish citizens worked on the base doing non-military duties, like working in the commissary. They, as well as the nearby *Inuits*, were allowed to shop at the commissary.

There were said to be a few other animals around the base, but I only remember seeing polar bears. A barracks' mate grabbed his camera one day in spring and ran after a mama polar bear with two cubs. All of us witnessing this folly yelled at him to come back and leave them alone. No one can outrun a polar bear, especially a protective mama. He didn't listen, but fortunately, the bear must have been used to such human antics as she paid him no attention.

I enjoyed my time at Thule because it was different than anywhere I had ever been before. During my career, I served at numerous places around the world with quite different climates and circumstances. But I'll never forget Thule!

*****

Authors: James Houston and Molly Houston

James Houston retired from the Air Force at Kirtland Air Force Base. He then worked for the Albuquerque Police Department and the US Fish and Wildlife Service. He has volunteered with Crime Stoppers, Cops for Kids, and Court Appointed Special Advocates for Children. Molly Houston was a math and science teacher and took up writing after retirement.

"SOUND OFF" The all army show held at Fort Lewis, Washing in early 1944 featured acts and songs by members of the 44th Infantry Division. (even the female parts). It was held to raise money for athletic equipment for the men at the base.

Before "Sound Off" went into rehearsal, long hours of planning were necessa... Pictured above are (standing) Pfc. Donald Blanchard, Pfc. Vitus Kern, Pvt. Al...

The writers and producers of "SOUND OFF" standing left to right...Pfc. Donald Blanchard, Pfc. Vitus Kern, Pvt. Alan Brock, Pfc. Wally Chulock. Seated left to right...Sgt. Jack London, Pfc. John O'dea, and Pvt. Edward Ruman.

Contributor: Rose Marie Kern

When they weren't actively fighting in WWII, some of the soldiers participated in USO shows. Dad was a comedian and had a great singing voice – I grew up with Mom at the piano and Dad singing "Some Enchanted Evening" or "Oh, Danny Boy."

CAROL KREIS

Full Circle

It seemed unreal that I was taking a final trip with Chuck. We had traveled together a lot during our nearly fifty-seven years of marriage. This time I was carrying his ashes in an urn on several connecting flights from the Albuquerque International Sunport to the Reagan Washington National Airport.

Chuck died on May 30, 2021. Our daughter Susan and our son Jeff decided we should have an intimate gathering at my home with our family and a few of Chuck's closest friends to celebrate his life.

I decided the National Cemetery in Arlington would be wonderful for Chuck's burial with honors because it is our country's most memorable national cemetery. I knew my family would appreciate the beauty and the history of the place.

I faxed documents to Arlington to prove that Chuck qualified for a burial there. After personnel at Arlington verified the paperwork, I was asked to choose which options I wanted for Chuck's honors ceremony. I answered yes to everything that was offered.

A caisson might not be available, but if it was, did I want one to take his remains to the grave site? Of course! (There are between twenty-seven and thirty funerals held a day at Arlington, and they only have two caissons from 1918 and 1919.) Did I prefer a niche in a columbarium or an in-ground burial with a tombstone for my husband? An in-ground burial appealed to me.

How about an Air Force band? By all means! I figured that being a retired lieutenant colonel might mean an ensemble of four musicians, but that would be nice. How about marchers? Yes, although I didn't know exactly what they would do. I wanted a protestant church service with music at the Old Army Post Chapel. Chuck and I first met through a singles group at a Methodist Church in Sacramento, California.

I was told it would be six to nine months before Chuck's remains could be buried. I ended up waiting one-and-a-half years. The COVID pandemic forced the delay of many funerals that had been planned ahead of Chuck's.

His was scheduled for January 9, 2023. I worried that the cold, icy weather might be a problem. I was eager for my family to fly in to attend the event.

A friend dropped me off early at the Albuquerque airport on Saturday, January 7, 2023. I wanted to allow extra time going through security with Chuck's seventeen-pound urn that made my suitcase weigh about thirty-five pounds.

While I waited for my plane to Washington, DC, I remembered my first arrival at the Albuquerque airport with our two children in 1977.

Chuck left Germany several months ahead of us to train in the plane he would be flying with the military airlift squadron at Kirtland Air Force Base. We agreed that I would remain in Germany with our kids until the school year ended. I enjoyed teaching kindergarten at Bitburg Elementary, a US Department of Defense School. Sue finished third grade at the school, and Jeff attended the local German kindergarten.

I told our children that we could go on a short holiday to revisit a favorite place. They instantly decided to return to Tivoli Gardens in Copenhagen. We spent most of our time at Tivoli, a gentle amusement park with a merry-go-round, a pantomime theater, a puppet show, and even a tiny flea circus.

For a final memento from Europe, Sue chose a Swiss Army Knife, and Jeff picked out a small teddy bear he named Warmy. We rode the train to the US Ramstein Air Force Base in Germany. The next day we boarded a civilian plane contracted by the US military to fly personnel and families from Germany to Charleston, South Carolina.

Our plane had a flat tire when it landed in Charleston. We had to wait on board until the buses arrived to take everyone to the airport terminal. Finally, the luggage was removed from the plane. By then, we had missed our connecting flights on other airlines and ended up stuck in the El Paso Airport very early the next morning. I still remember Chuck answering one of my calls from a pay phone and saying, "Where are you now?" Finally, we were on a short hop from El Paso to Albuquerque. I spotted Chuck on the roof of the Albuquerque Sunport, watching our plane as it touched down on that glaringly bright, sunshiny day.

By the fall of 1977, we had bought a house in Albuquerque and enrolled our kids in school. I met couples at the airlift squadron's social events. When anyone asked me about joining the Wives' Club, I remember saying that I would when I had time to go to one of the meetings. That never happened. I took college courses and held a variety of challenging positions through the years in education and as a writer.

How different my life was when Chuck and I married in 1964 in California. I learned to play bridge to socialize with other wives, and I wrote for the Officers' Wives Club newsletter. I was impressed with the traditional, formal dining-out events. A bell rang to signal that it was time to sit down. Toasts were made to the US Commander in Chief and other important dignitaries. I still remember wearing a pale-blue satin gown and long, white gloves on one of those occasions.

When Chuck had to be away for four months, I studied Spanish in Mexico. One of my most memorable years was when Chuck was sent to Vietnam. I spent the time traveling in the Orient with our two young children.

Now Sue and Jeff have families and live in different parts of the country. On Sunday, the day before Chuck's funeral, we saw a few sights in Washington, DC. Jeff wanted to know if Dad lost friends whose names were on the Vietnam Wall.

We found Charlie Davis's name. He had been the senior member of Chuck's class at the Air Force Institute of Technology in Dayton, Ohio. After graduation, Charlie, and most of the class, including Chuck, had been sent to Vietnam. Charlie never made it home; his plane was shot down.

Several years later, Chuck made a business trip to Dayton and saw Charlie's widow. She told him that she dreamed I was going to have a baby. When Chuck returned to our home in California, he asked me if that could be true. I was surprised, but yes, it turned out I was pregnant. And the baby was our Jeff!

On Monday, January 9, my family and I checked in at the Fort Meyer Army Post at 10:00 AM in order to get through security at the gate. After we were cleared to continue, we slowly followed narrow streets on the post that led to the Old Fort Chapel just outside the Arlington Cemetery. Such a picture-perfect, small church with a tall spire, stained glass windows, and white walls!

Just as we parked, riders arrived at the side of the chapel, pulling a caisson with beautiful, white horses. I hoped they were there for Chuck's funeral.

We were ushered into a small room with a big leather couch and chairs before the service started. I recalled how early one morning in June 2009, I dreamed that Chuck's nephew Craig had died. I asked Chuck to call his nephew to make sure he was still alive. Craig's wife, Adele, was crying when she answered the phone. Craig had just died. I thought about prophetic dreams and felt comforted by the thought that there might be more to life than I would ever understand.

The chaplain, a US Air Force Lieutenant Colonel, greeted us. He wore shiny medals instead of ribbons on his dress uniform. Our organist arrived. I passed out programs for the service with a portrait photo of Chuck on the cover. The organist had a template and offered to create the program with my input. She included *Bible* verses I requested for the chaplain to read.

We walked into the chapel. Two young soldiers quietly marched in and placed Chuck's urn and the US flag on a stand in front of the altar. The chaplain gave a fine, brief sermon. Toward the end, he was upbeat and told us to be glad that Chuck and our grandson, who died six months after Chuck, were no longer in pain. He shouted out three hallelujahs. He had us rise and shout hallelujah. At the conclusion of the service, the same soldiers who placed the urn and flag in the chapel marched in and silently removed them.

We were led outside in a single file. At the chapel's entrance, solemn military guards lined both sides of the carpeted entry. We walked past them and stopped. The caisson now had a large coffin on top of its wagon. Soldiers in dress uniforms were on three of the horses. They held the reins of the horses on their left side. Traditionally, the goods were loaded on the left side, and the riders were on the right. Other soldiers were standing aside the caisson. One soldier opened a small door at the back of the large metal coffin and placed the urn in a tray inside it.

Near the caisson stood sixteen members of a US Air Force band. They started playing military marching tunes. Next to them were men with flags on a pole. A group of military marchers was by their side.

We were directed to pull up our cars to follow the procession. We went by a variety of old tombstones and noted a few dating back to the 1800s. Every grave in the entire cemetery had a big, green wreath with a large, red bow at the base of the headstone. Our procession slowly wound down a windy road. Jeff opened his car window so we could hear the drummer's repeated "rat a tat tat" as all the US Air Force soldiers marched in unison.

We finally stopped by an awning with covered seats for our group. The band played again. In the grass field in front of us, a distance from the musicians and other marchers, seven riflemen fired a volley of three rounds of blanks (twenty-one shots). Afterward, I was given eleven of the blank cartridges that the soldiers retrieved from the grass.

The two young soldiers who placed the flag and urn in the chapel now stood erect and made no eye contact with anyone. Chuck's urn was on a table in front of our chairs with the ceremonial US flag over it. They folded it up in the traditional, triangular shape. Our chaplain suddenly appeared and knelt to present me with the flag. He said the words that are always said at military funerals. "On behalf of the president of the United States, the United States Air Force, and a grateful nation, please accept this flag as a symbol of our appreciation for your loved one's honorable and faithful service."

He sprinkled a little sand on the ground and recited the *Bible* verse about from ashes we come, and to ashes, we return. He shouted out a hallelujah! We spoke the Lord's Prayer just as Chuck and I had said it when we married on another Monday, August 3, 1964. The bugler played taps.

Jeff said I chose the right place to bury Dad. All of us were completely impressed with the military honors service for Chuck. That night Sue sent me a text message saying that she missed Dad.

After we left Chuck's remains in such a beautiful place, I was suddenly flooded with memories from when we were first married. I had found comfort in the military traditions included in the peaceful ceremony in Arlington for my late husband, just as I had appreciated military traditions when I was a young bride.

*****

Author: Carol Kreis

Carol Kreis is the widow of Lieutenant Colonel Charles Worner Kreis, US Air Force, retired. They married when Chuck was a Captain in the 904th Air Refueling Squadron at Mather Air Force Base. He flew KC-135 tankers at that time. Chuck always supported Carol's desire to travel whenever he had a remote assignment.

CAROLINE A. LeBLANC

The Hands of War

Some men say an army of horse and some men say an army on foot
And some men say an army of ships is the most beautiful thing
On the black earth. But I say it is what you love.

Sappho as translated by Anne Carson
If Not Winter: Fragments of Sappho

1

In this Christmas snow, if planes get off the runway
their PA systems will crackle, "Some of our military
personnel are with us. Let's give them a big hand ….
We thank you for your service in our nation's stand

against terror." When I fly, I wonder if others share
my doubts, my angst about the horrors of warfare.
Does the evening news make them think a round
of cheer will dispel our soldiers' troubles? I don't

know soldiers who expect a hand from civilians.
True, special programs give "Families of the Fallen"
"survivor support" after a beloved's sacrifice of life or limb,
& some count on food stamps to help feed their children.

Strapped in my too narrow seat, I sit stock-still & stare.
What would a Quaker at Meeting do if enemies were there?

2

Is an enemy near or am I a Quaker at Meeting not yet
moved to stand & speak about the last meals I ate
with my deployed husband & son? About how I savor
each crumb of memories? While they were safe at home

I read poems about Vietnam when my husband fought
as a Green Beret. The year before in DC, *Tsou Tai Tai*
taught Chinese to his group, & we treated demonstrators
at the War Moratorium on the Mall. After, I nursed "lifers"

& draftees in Okinawa while my husband & team traveled
on missions. Years later, "back in the world," the Army's nickel
sent him to med school, while I left our toddlers in the family's care
& went off to Army Nurse Basic. They inoculated me against rare

diseases, but not the grief, not the terror. Vietnam loomed too large —
our hours apart, the days & nights I had nursed troops in my charge.

3
Whatever the hour, Army Nurses are charged with the health of US
troops.
We fired & cleaned Colt 45s, practiced Mass Cals & debrided
wounds.
Future test items, DIs signaled by pounding the podium. "Nuclear
& chemical attacks. You can survive, if you follow proper
procedure."

We watched hours of slides — Japanese maimed by the first nukes,
Americans burned & gassed. We put on & removed charcoal suits.
Troop trucks took us into deep woods for our own taste of the gas
swelled in a windowless shed. We needed no order to don our masks.

"Proper procedure will save your life," admonished our Sergeant
once again, before he led us into the fog. Too soon he barked,
"Remove your mask." Each of us gagged on gas, tears, & snot.
"Replace your mask," his hoarse bellow came like a welcome shot.

The possibility of saving troops gassed in combat felt unreal,
even if we did not die from our own battle theater ordeals.

4

Of course, I survived Basic Training — my heart's ordeal
— traveled from Texas to Massachusetts where I filled
my arms with my sons' soft bodies. In Fort Dix's temporary
housing, roaches kept us awake. At work, I treated basic trainees —

even peace wounds psyches. My hands stroked my sons,
& I nurtured them with all the left-over vigor I had. Some
things were almost too much. Like the night our babysitter's
boyfriend stole my dead grandmother's rhinestone pins

while my sons slept in the next room. High on pot, the thieves
left a trail of Klondike Bar wrappers. It snaked from my freezer
to their stolen stash of guns. Then, the Corp's threat when I refused
a "joint" assignment four hours from my husband. It's true.

Tender enthusiasms matter little to the Army, after all.
No surprise — common wisdom has it women's wars are small.

5

Though common wisdom has it women's wars are small,
I resigned my commission while my husband answered the call
to serve in new wars where he treated kids maimed in battle.
At home, I managed the family & gave others like me counsel.

One son had blond, the other brown hair. Both grew up
with war & chose sides — one preferred weapons,
one the medical profession — healing & wounding, front
& back on the coin of the warrior's struggle with violent forces.

At the Fort Drum gym, I've watched healthy looking men
sit to play volleyball & slide when others would run.
Their net was low, as it would be for children, as it must be
for troops who have suffered traumatic brain injuries

when bombs bounced their brains inside the caverns
of skulls, shaped so much like crucibles of cupped hands.

6
Soldiers' skulls, so like chalices of cupped hands
bake inside Kevlar helmets worn in contested lands.
At three this morning, before their charter plane
touches down, soldiers trade Kevlar for soft caps.

It is minus nine degrees on the tarmac as the last
of the Third return from their tour in the desert —
their fourth. Bareheaded, they march into the gym
below high flying American flags & military emblems.

"You are my hero." "Welcome home," signs blare.
Adults & children wave tiny flags made of paper
in hands that do not care to stay warm under covers while
husbands & wives, father & mothers, brothers & sisters arrive.

An Army band fills our wait-time with patriotic ditties.
Wavy white screens cycle slides of soldiers "in country."

7
In waves cycling behind white screens, my soldier is lost
& a distance farther than the mission's stands between us.
Still, we dare not cross the divide until the Command
Sergeant Major shouts his order: "DIIISsss-MISSED!"

Phalanxes spill, wave into wave, onto the converted court.
At jump lines, I join others who have their children in tow.
Each of us searches the crowd for that beloved face
not touched — in how long? Almost before we can trace

hair or lips, photographers snap shots for papers & TV,
thrust hand-held mikes before our faces. They ask us clichéd

139

questions while hand in hand, we embrace each happy moment
we're given. Soon enough, our lives could be a different hell

if the sand in their boots & gloves won't go away. We know.
Christmas delays on runways? Clap your hands! It's only snow.

*****

Author: Caroline A. LeBlanc

Caroline A LeBlanc is an Army Nurse Veteran, daughter of a World
War II veteran, wife of a retired Army Officer, and mother of a Special
Forces Officer. She is past Writer in Residence of the Museum of the
American Military Family and co-leads Regaining Balance Retreats at
Mountain Gate Zen Center.

JACQUELINE MURRAY LORING

Before and Now

My father believed the mush he concocted in his garden shed
convinced roses to bloom twice each season,
hydrangeas and rhododendron to reject their nature,
bugs to die, he taught me to strip thorns from raspberry bushes,
to prevent puncturing my small fingers. I learned to split stems,
place each severed spike in discarded cans, dye stalks
with black or blue food coloring. He promised me protection,
a sky-blue-pink world, control over what I could not yet imagine.

The deep pleated furrows of the aged elms and oaks refused
my father's chemical creation's attempt to alter their seasons,
his expectation, prevented this child from climbing. Once fall
was late and a December night blustered, our yard was blanketed
with their bounty. I gathered the leaves by hand, piled them
on the earth as high as my eyes, then as my father screamed
his disapproval, I jumped from the porch railing. I tell you
this with pride but there is more.

The smell in the mound bound me
with the clarity of living things,
became a mesh that caught me,
a net into which I could disappear
momentarily. This memory
keeps me from falling through,
taught me to withstand, accept
what was to come.

*An ekphrastic poem based on the painting
"Happiness" by Fran Krukar.*

Braving the Storm

Northampton VA Hospital

Until the blizzard hit on the Mass Pike
the four-hour drive north to visit you goes well.
Packed in the VW, the kids and I play games,
vote to continue to brave the storm.
> *Remove your watch. Place your house keys, wallet,*
> *and comb on the desk. Sit. Unwind.*

I'll say the coaches asked for you at the awards
banquet, won't mention that the boys' punching
upset the trophy table before dinner was served.
You'll see them play next winter.
> *Place your clothes in the sack. Put on paper*
> *slippers. Hand over your car keys. Keep the coins.*

Don't have money to buy our daughter a prom corsage,
to dry clean your sister's borrowed gown
and lacy shawl. Sandals won't show
in the photos your mother will send you.
> *Lock your belt and laces with your meds and shoes.*
> *Pee now.*

West of Worcester the storm worsens,
the frightened kids and I guess
the meaning of good tours, war-
games, outward bound, locked wards.
Remove your dog tag flashbacks. Tuck them with your nightmares
under your pillow. About face.

Today is Always Yesterday

Emperor Jade Pagoda and Ba Thien Hau Temple,
Vietnam welcomes my cousin who posts photographs
of her weeklong vacation. My husband's shoulders
stiffen as he clicks through pictures,
Hanoi, Da Nang, Hoi An and Ho Chi Minh City.

More pictures as my cousin and her grandson
sail a junk in the Gulf of Tonkin in Ha Long Bay,
enjoy dinner in a fresh air market, hold live tarantulas,
tour the Reunification palace and under holiday lights
attend Christmas Mass outdoors.

Near the end of their visit the teenage boy, his grand smile
beaming, captures the attention of foreigners as he wedges
his slim body into a square in the earth, threads his way
through the Cu Chi Tunnels. Once outside,
those who surround him applaud.

I try to refocus my husband, keep his hands from the keys
but he types, "In '69 VC rats poured out of those holes.
Killed my friend ..." stops, reads, "We visited a monk
who gave us a sacred water blessing," looks up at me,
says, they're home. Safe. Right?

To Have and to Hold

Just now, my boy,
you lie
and stare at me.
    Once, a friend
    you held
    screamed armless,
    leaned into your eyes.
    His badge of courage
    clots your mind.

Soldier boy,
you said they said,
"Next time,
do not hold dying
so close
you remain behind."
    More boys
    in your embrace
    lay lifeless,
    stare.
    "Hold on!" you begged
    but were denied your chance
    at heaven.
    Your screams announced
    their souls.

Boy, you said they said,
"do not hold death
so close." Next time,
remember tonight,
still in their embrace,
you offered
your wrists to heaven.

No Other Choice

Welfare said we have no choice,
sell my Rabbit, my guitar and pride,
your guns and toys must go.
List for them my assets and your debts,
add my ability to work,
have my parents certify
they can't afford to help
and yours won't
let us move in.
Don't list tricycles.
A Barbie car and Fisher Price Farm
won't count toward our poverty.

You say there is no choice —
if I want surplus food,
fuel to keep us warm,
insurance to pay
for wounds and braces,
for the baby's delivery.
I must hide the boys' bonds,
given by our best man
before he crashed his bike.
One wall will bear his name.

You say I have no choice
but to rave to my friends
about your newest job,
pretend I don't mind borrowing
formula, shopping with stamps,
insisting to your parents
that we are well
and things are fine.

My only choice is to follow orders,
sell the house I bought
before I thought about fighting
battles and the waste of war.

*****

Author: Jacqueline Murray Loring

Jacqueline Murray Loring is an award-winning poet and writer. In 2019, McFarland published her book *Vietnam Veterans Unbroken: Conversations on Trauma & Resiliency.* *https://mcfarlandbooks.com/.* She has been married for fifty-three years to W. Gary Loring, who served in the US Army in Vietnam from Christmas 1967 to Christmas 1968.

BUTCH MAKI

Bob's Last Flight

In November 1967, four regiments and one artillery brigade of the North Vietnam Army's 1st Division crossed the Laotian border into the Central Highlands of Vietnam. That started a battle that became catastrophic, disastrous, and controversial,

To counter, we mobilized the 173rd Airborne Brigade, two brigades from the 4th Infantry, and a battalion of the 6th Army of the Republic of Vietnam. In all, some 16,000 of our troops were in the field. History would call it Operation MacArthur, or those there would forever refer to it as the Battle of Dak To.

I was a Huey crew chief in the 170th Assault Helicopter Company, based at Camp Holloway in Pleiku. Our entire unit was ordered to Dak To for air support.

My pilots were Chief Warrant Officers Snow, call sign Bikini two-two, and JD Morgan. My gunner was a jolly hillbilly from the panhandle of Florida, Russel Taylor, and I am Donald Makinen or Mack from Phoenix, Arizona.

Immediately after arriving in Dak To, we started flying "ass and trash." Ass being men and the trash being supplies. In the second week of flying all day and repairing battle-damaged helicopters most of the night, I was catching cat naps during return flights to the resupply depot. After dropping off a full load of water and mortar rounds near the Laotian border, I had just leaned back in my seat to enjoy the sun's warmth and closed my eyes when I was rudely interrupted by a radio transmission from a 4th Infantry Unit. "Any aircraft near Hill 764? This is Bravo Alpha Six. We have an emergency."

Half-awake, I keyed my intercom button and scoffed, "What ain't a stinking emergency in this screwed-up war?"

Snow responded, "Bravo Alpha Six, this is Bikini Two-Two. We're ten minutes away."

"Bikini Two-Two, we are in contact with an NVA [North Vietnamese Army] force and need an emergency medical evacuation."

Snow got the coordinates, and I felt the chopper bank hard left as we headed for the infantry company's location.

Snow brought us in low and fast over the trees. He waited to flare the bird until we dropped into the LZ [landing zone]. That flaring maneuver, similar to rearing a horse, used to reduce airspeed quickly, didn't make the landing one of his best. We hit the landing zone hard enough that we rocked forward and back.

I keyed my mic and quipped, "I'd say that landing was D-minus."

Snow defended himself, saying, "We didn't take any hits, chief, and we're all in one piece, so I'd say it was damn good."

Once I made eye contact with the men kneeling in the grass, I motioned with my hand in a fist and arms bent, pumping it up and down, the universal sign to hurry up. Four men stood up and carried a blood-soaked wounded trooper in a poncho towards us. The injured man used his arm to motion for a sergeant to come to him. When he got there, he bent over the bloodied soldier and then ran back to the tall grass.

A few rounds zipped past us, which quickly got my attention. Russ came from the other side of our bird to grab one edge of the poncho with the wounded man to help lift him into his last hope: our flight of mercy.

The sergeant ran up to me with the wounded soldier's helmet and said as he handed it to me, "He insisted I get this to him before you left."

I thought, *why does a man on his way home need this?* My breath caught in my throat when I looked down and saw it was Bob. I was his best man at his wedding to Leah in Bangkok.

I glanced down and saw Russ go to work on Bob's bloody lower abdomen.

I spun around the seat's attaching pole and pulled my face up to Bob's. "Bob! Bob! It's Mack!" I screamed above the roar of the rotor blades. He spoke, but it was so soft I couldn't hear, so I put my helmet's microphone close to his lips and opened a continuous com on the hot mic position of our intercom system.

I heard, "Thank God, it's you."

"Don't worry, Bob. We'll be at the aid station in a few minutes. In the meantime, Doc Elliott is taking good care of you," I said, having just given a grunt gunner a degree in medicine.

"Mack, give me my helmet," he requested weakly.

I went back to my seat and retrieved it for him. He took it and grabbed two envelopes out from under the interior webbing.

Struggling, he said, "Please, Mack, make sure you mail these."

149

I patted his shoulder, the only part of him that wasn't bloody, and assured him, "Don't worry, Bob. In a few days, you'll mail them yourself."

"Remember what you told me in Bangkok one night …" he coughed up some blood, "… don't bullshit a bullshitter, so stop the happy talk." He swallowed a mouth full of blood, choked a little, and said, "I've seen enough here to know it's not good."

I looked at Russ. He slowly shook his head, indicating that he couldn't do much.

Bob's eyes rolled back in pain as he struggled to say, "When you're home in Phoenix, please go see my parents and let them know how much I loved Leah and take care of her."

"I promise you anything you need. I'll be there to have your back. Your home in Arizona ain't that far from Phoenix. I'll tell them about the best love story I have ever witnessed."

Bob looked straight into my eyes and said, "You know I loved Leah like nothing I've ever known before her." He spasmed, his back arched, and then he was gone.

We landed at the aid station. The medics, out of routine, checked Bob's pulse and, of course, found none. They started to take him off the bird when Russ stopped them. Then something odd happened. I heard the Huey's engine shut down. It was unusual because we would only shut the engines down to conserve fuel, and I knew we had plenty of flight time left before refueling. Once at rest, it suddenly hit me. I jumped out, ran back by the tail boom, and, holding on with one hand, threw up my guts.

Russ came back, put his hand on my shoulder, and consoled me. "I heard everything on the hot mic, Mack, and couldn't let them stack him with the others at the temporary grave registry."

I wiped my mouth on my sleeve and turned to him. I had never seen him soft. He was genuinely affected by this one death more than the others we were clocking daily.

"Thanks, Russ," I said, patting his hand on my shoulder.

I went back to the front of the ship and found Snow and Major Burke, our CO [commanding officer], talking.

When he saw me, Snow said, "I heard everything over the intercom, so I called our CO to meet us here."

The CO interrupted, "I understand this was a friend of yours?"

"Er … Yes, ah, yes, sir. I was best man at his wedding."

He came close, put a hand on each of my shoulders, and looked me straight in the eyes. "I think you ought to accompany the body back to Pleiku," the CO said in an uncharacteristic compassionate, soft voice. I looked down at Bob's body. He was having an interesting effect on everyone.

"Yes, sir. Thank you." I sniffled and blinked my moist eyes.

I took out the two letters from my side pocket and saw they were bloodstained. When I showed them to the CO, I remarked, "Sir, I can't send these like this."

"Son, if I were you, I'd write another one to each and put them both in a clean envelope. Your crew is to place Bob on aircraft Zero-Two-Zero. It is going back to Pleiku for maintenance. Get on it. Grieve tonight but remember: the other Bobs who are still out there need you back here at 100% tomorrow."

I started to salute, but he grabbed my hand on its way up, and we shook hands, man to man. "Thank you, sir."

As I boarded the Huey to Pleiku, I couldn't help but notice that my on-and-off antagonist, Lieutenant Rose, was at the controls. *How odd, I thought, that the one officer I had little to no respect for was serving as Bob's and my chauffeur on such a horrible, sad day.*

I was in deep thought about Leah, Bob, and what I would say in the letters I had to write when I heard Rose's radio squawk, "Pleiku Tower. Drydock Five requests landing instructions to 71st Evac."

"Drydock Five cleared straight into 71st pad."

"Pleiku, please advise the 71st. We have a VIP [very important person], KIA [killed in action], onboard and request full honors."

"Drydock wilco, understand a killed-in-action VIP on board."

I looked at Rose in amazement over his thoughtful actions and said, "Thank you, sir."

He just looked at me and nodded.

Then I looked down at Bob, "See, they know how special you are, my brother."

We landed on the hospital pad. As I opened the cargo door and stepped out, I heard another unusual flight procedure for the second time today when the aircraft's engine went to idle. I wondered what Rose was up to, putting the bird in neutral. Two corpsmen wheeled a gurney out, accompanied by an Air Force lieutenant in his full-dress uniform.

Rose had idled the bird so he could climb down to stand by my side. As the corpsmen took Bob out of the helicopter to be placed on the gurney, Rose barked, "Atten-Chun! Preee-sent arms!"

Rose, the Air Force lieutenant, and I came to attention and saluted as the corpsmen gently placed Bob on the gurney.

To end our salute, Rose then hollered, "Orrrr-dah-arms!"

The corpsmen wheeled Bob's body away with the Air Force lieutenant, informal parade-style, marching behind.

That night, I sat alone in my hooch, writing to Leah and Bob's parents. I wrote Leah first. After several attempts, here is what I came up with:

Leah:

It is with the most profound grief that I tell you that I was with your love and my dear friend Bob when he passed away today. It saddens me enormously, and I can only imagine how this terrible news affects your young heart. I am sure it is beyond what you think you can stand, so I want to share something with you in this time of your bitterest agony and grief. I hope this brings some comfort to your anguish. Leah, Bob's last words were, "I love Leah like nothing I've ever known before her."

Leah, you must now trust that your faith will get you through this. You need only to believe that Buddha loves you, and so do I.

Your loving friend,

Mack

I struggled more with the letter to Bob's parents, but after several tries, I got one I was satisfied with:

Mr. and Mrs. Bandelier:

I feel I must write to ask you to accept my sincere sympathy for the sad news of the death of your son, Bob. I was with him when we were in Bangkok together, and I was with him today when he passed away.

Hemingway wrote that every man's life ends the same way. Only the details of how he lived and how he died distinguish one man from another. When I was with Bob, he lit up the room with his big smile and loving personality. When he passed today, it was with dignity. I hope I can live up to his example.

Sincerely,

Specialist Donald Makinen

Placing the last letter in an envelope, I mumbled, "Back in Bangkok, I said it would be an honor to fly you someday, Bob. I never thought it would be like today. God damn war."

*****

Author: Butch Maki

Walter "Butch" Maki served in the US Army as an aircraft crewmember in Vietnam. After discharge, he joined the National Guard again on Huey aircrews. After thirty years of owning businesses, Butch is retired and lives with his wife, Patty, in Los Lunas, New Mexico.

ELAINE CARSON MONTAGUE

Marionettes

Marionettes march in precision
Ne'er a one out of step
Marionettes march with decision
At what they do, they're adept

Who pulls their strings for whose cause?
What change does steady cadence bring?
How does marching precede new laws
From which life and death are sure to spring?

Marionettes set a steady pace
Regardless of tenet or religion
Marionettes' steps defy one's race
A testament to social provision

March in community together as one

Pulling strings in tandem

Right-left into the sun

Leaving nothing random

Let me not be a mindless marionette

Under compelling control

Let me pay my own debt

Watchful ever on patrol

***

1954, (clockwise) Elaine, Charles (top) , Bob, Ellen

The Colonel's Daughter

I liked being the colonel's daughter, but I didn't want to be considered uppity. I liked the respect others showed my mother and me because of who he was. He's been gone longer than two decades, but I'm still the colonel's daughter.

During World War II, Mama made me a cute outfit with a skirt, a full-length coat with shiny buttons, and a military-style cap; the kind creased at the front and back and looking like an upturned rowboat. I lifted my left hand to salute because I had injured my right arm. I remember when Daddy came home from the war in a jeep driven by his commanding officer, the man I called "My Colonel." He was the first colonel I knew, long before my father earned the rank. His family operated a company that made leather oxfords.

I was Daddy's girl and clingy. Mama said they pulled me out of kindergarten when I cried every morning for the first month. I had a restless sleep and listened to the radio late into the night, which I still do. Nightmares and loneliness troubled me.

I liked moving and seeing new environs but worried about making friends. I had to give up my dog because she got carsick and couldn't travel. Houses were hard to find. The new one had brand-new carpet, and I resented that my parents didn't want another dog.

B-36s flew overhead and fascinated me. Windows rattled, and one broke. Our first New Mexico home was a few doors from that of Ernie Pyle, a war correspondent, and I was the first to check out a book when his opened as a library.

My angry heart ached whenever Daddy left for temporary duty. He was my hero, and I didn't know when he would return. I was sad and grieved being left behind. I felt abandoned, although I couldn't label it then. At a young age, I missed the bedtime stories he concocted and games he created, chocolate sodas and funny papers on Sundays, and his laughter when he played tricks on me. I missed hearing Dr. Seuss and being delighted by green eggs and ham for breakfast.

The aloneness continued after he returned and became lifelong. At the same time, I learned to live with myself.

My favorite travels were in the mountains, where Daddy led us in rousing choruses of "I Like Mountain Music" and "She'll Be Comin' 'Round the Mountain." We tried to catch clouds by sticking our tongues out the windows and counted the states as we drove.

Customs, accents, and rules of behavior were different in the Midwest, the East, the South, and the Southwest. Societal attitudes differed. Some distinctions were tricky. Virginia and Alabama had segregated schools, but Ohio and New Mexico did not. I needed to figure out the culture quickly to be successful. I tried unfamiliar foods and learned new vocabulary, saw cardinals in Ohio and roadrunners in New Mexico, smelled the sweetness of magnolias, played among buttercups, and avoided the needle-like prickles of cacti. The climate ranged from lots of snow to arid desert. Living off base was different from living on a base that offered its world of safe isolation and a close-knit community. I lived in Montgomery from 1955-1956, but the base separated me from boycotts, lynchings, and bus violence, so I remained relatively uninformed about what happened outside my door.

Our family was to adapt. We did not acknowledge the stress of readjustment. My parents expected me to respect the role of authority, continue onward, be independent, and never think that I should do a thing because everyone else was doing it. I was to mirror their values, ideals, and attitudes in my good behavior and to be responsible and assume leadership. I was encouraged to serve and value duty, honor, and country. Military ideals of sacrifice for a greater good and service without expectation of reward fit very well into Girl Scout training and my chosen Christian faith.

I was an Air Force "fledgling." Army kids were called "brats." A fledgling is young, new, and inexperienced. That was a good description of me. I was ignorant about what was going on, except for the teenaged terror and confusion I felt when I met my first in-person and up-close rabble-rouser. He protested the enrollment of a young woman at an Alabama university. I recall how shocked I was when I later learned about the civil rights movement. It was not discussed in my segregated high school or home.

Military life guided me to accept most differences and challenges as gracefully as I could and not look back with regret. As a teen, I didn't want to lose my room with lavender walls and turquoise accents and that special boy next door who wove a tiara of clover for my head. Replanting myself in high schools in three states was fun, however, because I met so many people, but I wasn't a class officer due to the moves. Nevertheless, sixty-five years later, I have several friendships formed during attachments and not broken despite separation. These friends helped me heal from losses, especially that of my husband during the COVID-19 lockdown.

Rituals and regalia on base, epaulets and eagles, sharply creased uniforms, flags and parades, salutes, and little calling cards on silver trays enchanted me. One evening, I was impressed when a Navy officer arrived at our home in uniform with a sword at his side. My ID [identification] card made me feel important. I admired the scrambled eggs on the visor of Daddy's dress hat — that's what we called the golden leaf-shaped embellishments that signified his rank.

We had routines and a strong sense of right and wrong. Breakfast was every weekday at 6:30 AM. The base bugle blew retreat at 5:00 PM, and I turned in the direction of the flag with my hand over my heart because I knew the flag was being lowered, whether I could see it or not. I learned about government, United States history, laws, and international relations. I learned the humility of not taking freedom for granted, to be grateful for those who serve, the importance of respect, and to have pride in family, country, and self. I knew I was protected.

At times, there were too many rules. Mama had to follow strict protocol when planning a party. She couldn't spend time with a woman she liked because the woman's husband worked for Daddy and was lower in rank. I didn't understand that and thought it hurtful, but Mama and her friend accepted the situation. It was years before I realized the importance of her role to put Daddy's career first. She was to be strong physically and emotionally, to be brave and generous. Like a military child, she was to choose what could be difficult and be resilient and resourceful.

Daddy's language was disciplined. As Officer of the Day, he took a phone call at home when I was about ten. He exclaimed, "Gosh!" I was shocked because that was the only expletive that I'd heard him use. He tried to keep work separate from home life and valued family time of Sunday dinner, long drives, and classical music, and made them mandatory for the rest of us.

Usually compliant, Daddy went to school to talk with my sixth-grade teacher because she didn't want me to use turquoise ink. She wanted only black. He thought I should be allowed to use the upscale fountain pen with turquoise ink he gave me for Christmas. He convinced the teacher.

We soon moved near Washington, DC, and crawled under our desks in Cold War duck and cover drills to prepare us for an atomic attack on the United States. The same year I stepped down into a bomb shelter beneath a private Georgia home near my grandparents. Those experiences highlighted the importance of the military.

School content was not uniform. On my first day at the new school, I scored zero on a timed test in multiplying fractions, a skill I'd not been taught. I was mortified. Three days later, I scored 100 after Daddy showed me how.

Conversely, I learned enough Spanish in elementary school in New Mexico that it carried me all the way through Spanish 1 in Virginia's high school. As song leader, I taught the class "*La Cucaracha*," a song I'd learned in New Mexico. To the chagrin of my teacher, it was the "*marijuana-que-fumar*" version. To my chagrin, I learned it had to do with smoking marijuana.

I was egocentric but recall proud glimpses into Daddy's work: World War II, Africa, Tunis, Italy, and Sicily. An audience with the Pope. Theoretical physicist. Ft. Bragg. The Salton Sea. Banana River. Los Alamos. Mercury capsule and the space program. Pentagon. Wright-Pat twice. Atomic Energy Commission. Sandia Base's Field Command. Astronauts. Coordination with civilians at Sandia Labs. Administrator. Back to the Pentagon. Belgium. Holloman's Guidance Track. German scientists. With greater clarity, I remember that he spent hours explaining chemical interactions, physics, how I must keep my numbers aligned in calculations and write without erasures, and that a point drawn in geometry is to be no larger than a speck.

Some warriors returning from World War II brought back guns. My hero came with cameos for Mama, an Italian doll almost as tall as I was with open lips and rolling eyes, and a painting of arches in Tunis for himself. His photo albums show many places and scenes: Palermo, Mt. Etna, and a bombed school and house in Catania, Sicily; Egypt, Libya, Tunis, Algiers; cathedrals and artwork, a public toilet, and a market; Naples and Rome in Italy, the Wailing Wall in Israel, and a catapult. There is a pillbox, which is a concrete blockhouse with loopholes that defenders use when firing weapons in trench warfare. Pillboxes are being used in Ukraine in their war with Russia.

Daddy was a thinker but also helpful around the house and surprised me. He purchased fabric and sewed chartreuse and neon pink curtains for my overwhelmed mother after moving into a new Virginia apartment.

He taught me to embroider French knots as we sat on Granddaddy's porch in the mountains of north Georgia.

In New Mexico, he replaced a windowpane my brother had broken and told him to watch because he would never see him do it again.

As far apart as these locations were, so were the events because I saw him do each only once.

The brilliant, dedicated colonel was a strict but kind and devoted father and husband.

I liked being the colonel's daughter.

*****

Author: Elaine Carson Montague

Elaine Carson Montague of Albuquerque, award-winning author of prose and poetry, and her late husband Gary won six domestic and two international awards for *Victory from the Shadows, Growing Up in a New Mexico School for the Blind and Beyond.* Her father was Charles Edgar Carson, Colonel, US Air Force.

SAM MOORMAN

Surprise Way

Gingerly on a bum ankle he walks   in flip-flops without water into
low creosote   toward Nipple Peak named for its shape   with a glance
back to sight a line   through camp to Snowtop Mountain   to orient
safe return

His straight path strays though   onto a faint cross-trail through weeds
a burro track spotted with clods as regular as cairns   in simple
wonder where it goes   For don't all paths lead somewhere   and all
end much the same?

No! a remnant of his soul complains   Life must go somewhere   and
mean something   not just fade into a clump of sage   Or what's the
use, the sense of it? Yet the weary man plods the path   he's dubbed
Surprise Way   bound to see its end

Skidding down scree to a gurgling stream   runoff from his camp's hot
spring   he rests panting   hands on knees   while his lone drip of life's
mirage is sucked   like dew into the sand's burnt craw

Oh! he cries when a jackrabbit flashes   from her hiding bush and
bounds away   Oh, beautiful! and suddenly remembers his place in
our wilderness   this vast world we love and cling to   if only for warm
water muttering   of sun medallions fluttering dark ripples   like
fireflies swarming the river of night   So there he stays   until his dry
body's glow   lets him know it's time   it's always time   to follow the
warm stream home

Sylvia Plath

Confused Muse

cooked her book

in an oven

nook   poor lass

but what a gas!

      Last boast

      I'm white toast!

      from the bake

      rack   such luck

      in that ode to not explode

Resurrected

maybe   as Jew

anew or Peggy

Sue with screw

you hairdo

      Hope she recalls

      each birthday candle

      bluff Careful!

      Blow it

            and you're snuffed

*****

Author: Sam Moorman

Sam Moorman joined the Army after graduating high school in Seattle in 1963. He trained at Fort Ord, California, and Fort Belvoir, Virginia, before posting to Dachau, Germany. He graduated from San Francisco State University with Journalism and Creative Writing degrees, then worked in construction until returning to writing in his senior years.

EVELYN NEIL

Hitch Hiker

His mind a jumble of conflicting memories, Ken whistled along to John Denver's "Country Roads Take Me Home" on the radio and negotiated the curves through Tijeras Canyon. In high spirits, he was headed home to Kansas for the Holidays for the first time in fifteen years. After this long, he still felt guilty for abandoning his parents and the family farm after coming home from Vietnam. But he'd needed to escape the persistent questions that spawned the nightmares of mud, blood, cries of wounded comrades, and the stench of death. "What was it like over there? What happened to erase the twinkle from his eye and render him so quiet? Was he there when his cousin Davy died?" So many questions about things he wanted to forget.

So west was the direction he'd taken as far as Albuquerque, where no one knew him. There he found employment driving a truck towing a manure spreader. He spent long days shoveling manure from the stock pens at Valley Gold Dairy and Karler Packing Company in the South Valley and spreading it on the North Valley alfalfa fields irrigated by water from the Rio Grande. This manual labor in the out-of-doors quieted his mind.

With very little traffic on this winter morning, the ride was pleasant and uneventful. Ken stopped in Santa Rosa to top off the gas tank of his new 1993 F-150 and to stretch his legs. The brisk wind from the eastern plains cut through his red and black plaid shirt and tugged at his black Stetson. The gray New Mexico sky promised rain, maybe even snow.

A few miles east of Tucumcari, Ken whipped the pickup onto the shoulder at the sight of a hitchhiker in an olive-drab dress uniform. The soldier, who resembled Davy, lowered his right thumb, picked up a canvas tote, and sprinted to the truck. Ken leaned his stout body across the seat and shouted out the passenger window.

"Where're you headed, Son?"

"Kansas City," the shivering young man responded.

"That's close to where I'm headed. Hop in." Ken observed how loose the uniform hung on the young serviceman.

"Thanks, it's really cold out there." The stranger climbed in and clutched the tan bag on his lap. He wiped his nose with the back of his hand, tossed his hat onto the dash, and ran grimy fingers through his cropped ginger hair. His teeth chattered as he fidgeted with the bag.

Ken turned up the heater. "We'll get you warmed up in no time." He reached into his new denim bibs and extracted a pack of Marlboros. "Cigarette?"

"Uh, no thanks."

"Mind if I have one?"

"No ... no, not at all."

Ken took a long drag and exhaled slowly. With steely blue eyes, he surveyed his red-eyed, pimply-faced passenger. The patch of the 226th Signal Company on the left sleeve of the jacket caught his eye. Realizing this kid was wearing an old uniform with an outdated Korea-era unit patch, he asked, "Where've you served?"

"Oh, uh, here and there." The kid reached into the bag and pulled out a Smith and Wesson .38, and pressed the cold steel barrel of the revolver into Ken's temple. "Pull over. I need this truck."

"Over my dead body." Ken spat the cigarette to the floor, clenched his teeth, and stomped on the accelerator. The speedometer needle climbed — seventy, eighty, ninety-five.

"Hey man, slow down. You're gonna kill us." The stench of sweat and fear filled the over-heated cab.

"Go ahead! Pull the trigger." Ken yelled. "We can go together."

"Please, mister," sniffled the kid. "I don't wanna die."

The needle held steady at ninety-five.

"Okay, tell you what. Roll down your window. Toss out the weapon."

The cold December air rushed into the cab as the gun sailed into the barrow pit, racing away from them. They continued to fly over the uneven pavement, around curves, and over bridges. As he swerved around slower-moving vehicles and struggled to maintain his calm, Ken longed for the flashing red lights of a black and white cruiser.

"Now, you damned imposter, take off the uniform. Toss it out."

The shaking youngster wriggled out of the wool jacket. Out the window it flew down the highway behind the speeding Ford like a run-a-way kite. Next out was the tie and shirt.

"Now, the shoes and socks. And pants, too," demanded Ken.

"Oh, man. Slow down."

Ken slowed the truck and pulled it onto the side of the road. The kid gasped with relief and leaned his head against the passenger window.

"Get your sorry ass outta my truck," commanded Ken. "Oh, and take that hat and filthy tote with you."

"But, I'll freeze out there," the nearly naked kid whined.

"That's the general idea, you little son-of-a-bitch."

Ken put the truck into gear. Spinning out and kicking up gravel, he pulled onto I-40 and turned up the radio. "Teach him to disrespect the uniform," he muttered as he looked in the rearview mirror to see the hitchhiker in his wind-swept boxers wildly searching the barren landscape.

***

The Price of Freedom

There's a beach in Normandy called Omaha. Legend has it that when the European Invasion was in the early planning stages, the commanding generals were looking for code names for the beach landing areas. General Eisenhower asked a young PFC [private first class], "Where are you from, Son?"

"Omaha, Sir."

Thus, this beautiful stretch of sandy beach on the northern coast of France along the English Channel will forever be known as Omaha Beach.

Recently I walked this beach under dark rain-laden clouds and gazed west across the choppy waters of the cold gray English Channel. On the cliffs above the beach were the remnants of the Nazi concrete bunkers, some of which still held the big guns that once guarded this coast. On the beach were graceful stainless-steel sculptures reminiscent of the razor-sharp jagged steel obstacles placed there by the enemy. The wind-driven rain splattered against my glasses and ran in rivulets down my hooded raincoat. The tide was out. The moon would be full just as it was on that long-ago night when I was a child.

What was lost that day — June 6, 1944 — when over 150,000 young men were expelled from landing crafts onto the beaches into water over their heads? They were the infantry — draftees and volunteers. Most were away from home for the first time. Many could not swim. Pulled under by their heavy packs, they drowned. Most that made it to shore in the first waves were mowed down by machine gun fire amid a steady barrage from the big guns on the cliffs. Some survived only by using the bodies of dead comrades as shields. These eighteen, nineteen, and twenty-something-year-old soldiers were precious sons, brothers, husbands, fathers, uncles, lovers, fiancées, and best friends.

The invasion was set for early June because there would be a full moon to light the way and a low tide to help the landing craft avoid the mines and steel obstacle courses. The German forces were stretched thin at this time. In addition to struggling to maintain their position in Western Europe, they suffered heavy casualties on the Eastern Front. Their reinforcements along the Normandy coast were still a work in progress. The next opportune time for this landing would not be until September. The allies feared by that time that the location of the landing beaches, Gold, Juno, Sword, Omaha, and Utah, would no longer be secret. Rommel would have his fortifications and armament in place. He would be waiting.

The Higgins boats, or LCVP landing craft, were loaded on schedule. Everyone awaited the signal to set sail. A fierce storm blew in across the Channel. The mission was put on hold for twenty-four hours. Thousands of troops — American, Commonwealth, and Canadian — waited. Crowded onto the flat-bottomed vessels that would transport them across the treacherous miles of stormy waters, they were unable to lie down or sleep. Their time was passed smoking, talking, worrying, writing letters, telling jokes, horsing around, suffering from sea sickness, and being terrified of what the next day would bring.

The new day slithered in under a cloak of darkness, bringing more wind and more rain. Still, they waited. They had come too far to turn back. Finally, the order was given to proceed. All through the stormy night, the men were heaved and pitched across the turbulent Channel to be dumped at daybreak onto the beaches to meet their destinies, the Canadians on Juno, the UK on Gold and Sword, and the Americans on Omaha and Utah.

How many messengers did it take to knock on all the doors to bring the news that derailed families? Did the planners of these missions take into account death's aftermath, fallout, and repercussion? Did they plan ahead to find dozens upon dozens of chaplains to help the bereaved absorb the violence of the news, or did they drop their mind-numbing bombs and disappear into the safety of the world? What proof was given the disbelieving young wife holding a crying infant or the devastated parent that the unfathomable was true? What about the letter written home just before the mission that would arrive weeks later?

Later that same day, during my visit to the D-Day beaches, I went to the American Cemetery overlooking Omaha Beach. While standing in the soft rain, I read many of the thousands of names of the missing inscribed on the stone walls surrounding the Memorial.

When the rain stopped, the sun came out, and a rainbow formed over the sea of white marble markers standing sentinel over America's lost heroes. With patriotic pride, I faced the American flag, right hand over my heart, and listened to the clarion bells play the Star-Spangled Banner and Taps.

I walked among the acres of military-straight rows of stately markers, searching for the right one — *Here Rests in Honored Glory a Comrade in Arms Known But to God.* At its base, I placed a long-stemmed red rose.

What was the price? Who among the lost could have been a future world leader, doctor, priest, rabbi, or teacher? Who could have won an Olympic Medal or a Nobel Prize? Who might have found a cure for cancer or a solution for World Peace? We will never know. But we do know they were never afforded the opportunity to enjoy the simple things in life, like watching their children grow or experiencing the joys of having grandchildren.

The ones who persevered and survived that day gained a foothold on the European Continent and began the march to Paris and, ultimately, to Berlin. They were instrumental in the signing of a Peace Treaty to end yet another War that was to end all Wars.

*****

Author:Evelyn Neil

Evelyn Neil, an award-winning author of numerous short stories, was married to Don Neil, a Korea-era army veteran, for fifty-eight years. Her memoir, *Dancing to the End of Our Rainbow*, an indelible tale of love and despair, explores end-of-life choices and is available on Amazon.com. Learn more on www.rmkpublications.com/evelyn-neil

Thomas Neiman

Libations, Elixirs, and Gulps, Oh My!
Recipes from a mildly inebriated storyteller

Tom's Smoothie

Ingredients:

      2 orange carrots

      2 red apples

      2 pears

      2 stalks of celery

      6 ounces of 100% apple juice

      10 ice cubes

What's next?

      Chop up fruits and vegetables

      Add apple juice

      Blend until desired consistency is reached

      Add ice cubes

      Blend for additional thirty seconds

      Refrigerate (my choice) or drink immediately

Commentary

I use a Vitamix® blender, and the result is very tasty, with the consistency of pulpy orange juice. Nothing is wasted, and everything is processed minus the stems and cores. Adjusting the number of ingredients will change the taste. Consider the truth in the quotation, "Variety's the very spice of life, That gives it all its flavour." Toss in leftover or ripened pieces of fruit, and substitute orange juice for apple juice. My friends love it. You can't screw this up.

Kale Smoothie

Ingredients
> 1 yellow carrot
> 1 stalk of celery
> 2 red apples
> 2 pears
> 2 or 3 kale leaves
> 6 ounces of 100% apple juice

What's next?
> Chop up fruits and vegetables
> Add apple juice
> Blend until desired consistency is reached
> Add ice cubes
> Blend for additional thirty seconds
> Refrigerate or drink immediately (your choice)

Commentary

The Vitamix® creates a delicious smoothie. My wife, Gretchen, likes it except for the green appearance. "Don't look at it — just drink it," I told her. Seriously, if the thought of having raw kale stored in your refrigerator bothers you, why not purchase a premixed substitute like Naked Juice® Green Machine at your local grocery store? You don't know what you're missing until you try it.

Postscript
Take caution when adding orange carrots, strawberries, or other red, purple, or dark fruit. The finished product, although yummy, will resemble baby shit.

Orange Margarita

Ingredients
    2 ounces of orange juice
    1 ounce of tequila
    1 ounce of orange curacao
    ½ ounce of lime juice
    5 drops of liquid stevia Valencia orange flavor

What's next?
Mix ingredients and rim glass with margarita salt (optional)
    Add orange, lemon, and lime slices to taste.

Commentary
Use pulpy orange juice and keep an eye on your neighbors; these margaritas taste so good they'll drink them rapidly. Cut back on the alcohol, and everyone makes it home in one piece. Makes one potent cocktail.

***

Kale Margarita

Ingredients
    1½ ounces of silver tequila
    1½ ounces of triple sec liqueur
    ½ ounce of lime juice
    10 drops of liquid stevia
    2 ounces of Naked Juice® Green Machine

What's next?
    Mix ingredients
    Garnish with Cilantro leaves
    Rim glass with Himalayan pink salt (optional)

Commentary

Similar to the orange version; substitute one or two leaves of kale; if you add too much Naked Juice®, it will taste like a tossed salad mixed with alcohol; my advice — stick with the orange margarita; makes one cocktail.

***

New Mexico Painkiller

Ingredients

9 ounces of rum
6 ounces of pineapple juice
1 cup of pineapples
1 cup of mangos
1 cup of peaches
Fruit may be fresh or frozen
1 or 2 large kale leaves
3 limes, peeled and quartered
1 medium avocado, peeled and pitted
20 drops of liquid stevia

What's next?

Chop up fruits and vegetables, and add rum and stevia
Blend until desired consistency is reached
Add 20 ice cubes
Blend for additional sixty seconds
Refrigerate or drink immediately (my choice)

Commentary

It's creamy because of the avocado and has the right level of sweetness. Substitute five ounces of Naked Juice® Green Machine or equivalent for kale. For those who cannot stomach the color, cover the drink with a cocktail parasol and suck it up with a biodegradable paper straw. Then dispose of the straw in a biohazard container. As a last resort, serve only after dark. Makes approximately six painkillers.

Postscript

The truth be told, you really can't make a respectable Mojito with kale. And if a lack of time, patience, or ingredients gets in your way, prepare a kale smoothie, and toss in a jigger of rum. It works for me.

Postscript

The sound you hear after the first sip: "YOOOOOOOOOOOOOOOOO."

***

Blue Crystal Meth Margarita

Ingredients

12 ounces of silver tequila

12 ounces of blue curacao liqueur

6 ounces of Nellie & Joe's Famous Key West Lime Juice®

48 ounces of MiO® Berry Blast Water Enhancer

What's next?

Prepare berry blast colored ice cubes (optional)

Add blue food color to salt. Salt rim to taste (optional)

Commentary

Invite your friends to enjoy these exquisite cocktails. Avoid contact with members of law enforcement or organized crime. Should you need assistance preparing the recipe, please consult Walter White or Jesse Pinkman. Transport at your own risk. If arrested, you better call Saul. Makes twelve margaritas.

Cheers

What Would Il Duce Do?

The men's group finished on time. At previous meetings, the amateur money managers discussed how to get the most from their stocks and other investments without, as someone mentioned, squeezing a nickel so tight the buffalo roared. My next appointment was going to be much more exciting. I was getting together with my writing partners to review stories and update future activities.

As I exited the restaurant, one of the old gents asked, "You're a master gardener, aren't you?"

I'm proud of my life since retirement, marrying Gretchen, becoming a published author, and joining the master gardeners. But before I could respond, another man chimed in.

"Why the hell would you join a women's club?"

What the

My blood was up. A comment like that would never be tolerated if the writers were here. After working together for over five years, we behaved like family and had a serious power bond. I remembered when we excused a journalist from one of our meetings for tampering with an author's whiteboard outline.

You never mess with another writer's yellow stickies.

The members had also chosen me to be their business manager, not for a month or a year, but for life, and bestowed a title on me, *Il Duce*, the leader.

A thought crossed my mind.

What would Il Duce do?

Out of the blue, a voice spoke quietly and with purpose, directly at me.

It is better to live one day as a lion than one hundred years as a sheep.

I was startled, at first, and then responded.

Il Duce?

Sí.

I took a deep breath and felt a peculiar energy coursing through my veins. Closing my eyes, I experienced the sensation of being lighter and elevated. I was transformed and immediately knew what needed to be done. I turned toward the man who asked the question. Although the query was intended as a jab at my masculinity, my answer got the remaining audience's attention. "Yes, I'm a Sandoval County Master Gardener, and one out of every four of us is male. But that's not important. I like the idea of being able to plant a seed in the ground and watch what grows from it, whether it's something as beautiful as a flowering Cosmos or food like corn or apples."

The voice inside my head spoke again.

Seize the moment.

I felt invigorated. I strode over to the glass doors and pointed outside toward the Rio Grande. "How about something that your family can enjoy today and leave as a legacy to the community for generations to come? Look down at the green ribbon along the river, our Bosque, and all those beautiful Cottonwood trees."

Others gathered around to listen. The voice called out to me again.

Be the lion.

Someone inquired, "Is your wife a master gardener?"

I answered, "Yes, Gretchen and I attended class one year apart, although she had plenty of experience transplanting her ideas as well as herself from the East coast to New Mexico. I'm relatively new to gardening, and it's something we can share every day."

Once again, the smart aleck attempted to get a rise out of me, asking, "What do you really like to grow? No, wait. Let me guess. Is it roses or tomatoes?" Then came the smirk. "Or maybe cannabis?"

Remain steadfast.

I shall.

I turned my head and stared down at him. I didn't utter a word until I was sure we had locked in eye contact. Only then did I speak with pride. "I prefer sunflowers, corn, and green beans. Whoever would have thought legumes would be fun to grow? There's no better feeling than eating the fruits or, should I say, the vegetables of your labor. My wife and I also grow trees. Gretchen prefers fruit trees, and I plant Desert Willows and other low-water species." The heckler turned away.

Another person asked, "I heard you say you have a training class?"

"Yes, and twenty-five percent of last year's interns were men. Our next class begins in January and runs through April."

"What do you learn?"

"How to grow and maintain plants for their beauty, crops for their food value, and to improve the overall health of the planet. The County Extension office works closely with the State Land Grant University. The school provides us with up-to-date information, and we, as master gardeners, pass the knowledge out to the community through public events and demonstration gardens."

They're eating out of the palm of your hand.

I know.

The smart aleck asked one last question. "What if I end up with too many ... potatoes?"

Swine.

Calm down. I've got this.

"Yes, I know the feeling. A year ago, Gretchen and I had more eggplants than we could possibly eat in one season. No problem. She preserved some for winter meals and donated the rest to the food pantry."

Another fellow asked, "What if I don't want to plant in my own yard?"

"The Sandoval County Master Gardeners collaborate with non-profits like the Seed2Need Project, where acres of ground are planted and maintained by volunteers. Tens of thousands of pounds of food were donated to the local food pantries last year."

Full of pride — my own pride, the lion within roared again.

"We can always use a little more testosterone in the garden, if you know what I mean." The cluster of observers laughed. As we walked to our cars, I waved my hand over my head with a flourish to the crowd and shouted, "Goodbye, my people."

The lion spoke once more.

Il Duce has left the building.

The truth be known, I was feeling pretty ballsy. As I approached my car, I noticed a folded piece of paper behind my windshield wiper blade. I opened the note and read it. The hairs on the back of my neck snapped to attention. The note said: "Keep the trains running on time — or else!"

***

Rendezvous

Close your eyes
Picture a slice of land
In the valley
Near the Rio Grande
An acre or two
Apache plume, Blue grama, and Purple sage
Assortment of trees
Perhaps an apple orchard, possibly a vineyard?
And community gardens
Can you smell lavender, roses, and mint?

A crossroad for insects at a Butterfly bush
Listen to the Honeybees winging from one blossom to another
Roadrunners hunting swiftly, a coyote on patrol
Cooper's hawk circling
Gamble's quail and her chicks dashing for cover
A gathering spot
To relax, breathe, reflect
With benches and picnic tables
And shade cover — thank God!
Children playing and laughing
The smoky scent of chiles roasting
A Mariachi band entertaining
With guitars and silver trumpets
Open space
Walk your pet
Pathways for people
Trails for cyclists, and horseback riders
Works of art on exhibition
Near the library
Educating kids
Our future
Preserving the land
Adding beauty to the neighborhood
A defining feature
Open your eyes
It's on the horizon

*****

Author: Thomas Neiman

Thomas Neiman was born and educated in the Garden State of New Jersey. He is a master gardener, tree steward, certified arborist, zoo docent, and a published author. Tom is a United States Army veteran living in Corrales with his wife, Gretchen, and their cat, Charger.

C.L. NEMETH

Memories

I estimate that I have driven somewhere between five and six million miles in my lifetime. But no more. So, it was with nostalgia that I stepped out into the garage the other day and beheld our family Kia sitting in its black glossy glory. I ran my hand along the shiny metal, around the rear, and forward up the left side. I opened the driver's door and sat. Sitting there looking out from over the steering wheel, I began to reminisce about the days when an auto seemed like an extension of my body.

I then remembered how, as a little guy, I would open the Model A Ford sedan door and crawl up into the seat behind the steering wheel — sitting there moving the steering wheel back and forth and pushing the gear shift lever mimicking my dad's driving. The fantasies of my trips were heroic, and I would sit there making engine noises. The world was my oyster.

Sitting in the Kia, I didn't move the steering wheel or the shift selector — memories of trips in good weather and bad. I have driven coast to coast twice and driven autos in all but a handful of states. I changed tires, repaired flats right there beside the road, fan belts, thermostats, dragging mufflers, overheating, and out of fuel. These things came flooding back. Memories forgotten came forth clearly. I must have sat there for some time before reality pushed the past back into its niche in my mind. I sighed, got out, and closed the door. My reverie was over. Maybe again sometime.

Memories are to be enjoyed. Even sometimes, the bad ones. It is a catalog of your life. Enjoy them. They are priceless. Each a one-of-a-kind history of a life. Your life.

Coping

I, and as I'm sure others, wondered from time to time just how I would react to a situation that threatened the very way I lived my life. Well, lucky me, I found out. Or rather, I'm finding out since it's an ongoing process.

It was in 2008, and I was just about to turn eighty, when my ophthalmologist, while looking into my eye, said, "I see some onset of macular degeneration. We need to check this out."

He sent me to a specialist, who, as I soon learned, affirmed the diagnosis. I had Age-related Macular Degeneration (AMD). I had read about AMD and knew it was the deterioration of the "rods" in the center of my eye. They control the focus, so you can zero in on an object and see it in detail. My doctor asked if I had noticed anything about my vision. I replied that when I closed my eyes and opened them, a sort of black spot was present for a brief second but soon dissolved. I didn't tell him I was having problems, such as putting a screwdriver on a screw so I could turn it. In fact, this one little thing was the main problem I began to face and what made me finally realize that "Chuck, old man, you've got a problem."

When I thought about a life-changing episode, I usually thought I would throw myself on the floor, kicking and screaming about my fate. That's an exaggeration, but you know what I mean. The fact is, I found myself quietly considering just what the onset of AMD would mean to my daily living. I was running a business, driving all over the state, personally manufacturing the equipment I sold, and then servicing them.

I was already well past the average retirement age, and I think the fact that I must retire soon kept me calmer than a younger person could expect to react. Looking back, I'm astonished that I actually kept on for five more years, retiring at eighty-five. I see now that someone with a brain would have done so a few years before I did. But, as they say in France, "*c'est la vie.*"

So, I closed it all down and found myself retiring in October 2013.

A customer who turned into a good friend had been urging me to enroll in the VA [Department of Veterans Affairs] Medical program. I had never utilized this service and agreed to do so. It was one of the best decisions I have ever made. The low vision programs provided by the VA far exceed anything available in the standard medical services available to the non-military population.

I could easily write another paper on the VA Blind Rehabilitation programs but let me stick to the subject of this writing.

I really thought that I would react poorly to my affliction. After all, although I was assured I would never reach complete blindness, the thought of using a cane, feeling my way along, and having others help me with everyday daily living, didn't do much to increase my enthusiasm for the future.

Again, with the onset of my retirement almost simultaneous with vision problems, I found myself musing over what this would mean as I lived out my term. To my surprise, I found I was looking toward serious changes in my day-to-day living. I had always been an impatient man. I couldn't suffer fools very well. I was an avid antique clock collector and repaired clocks as a second career. That was now gone — no more clock fixing for me. Home repairs and the like also had to be put to rest. Hell, I was having trouble seeing the weeds in the yard. Just what would I be able to do from now on? I used to stream fish and planned to return to it, but that's out too. I loved to drive, and driving was now a huge no-no. No doubt changes they were a-coming.

I enrolled in the VA Medical service early in 2014. This one act has been the core of my activities and continues to be so today. The very act of going to the Blind Rehab Center in Tucson removed all misgivings of how I would cope and showed me that, with the help of experts and the use of specialized equipment, I could, in fact, do a lot more than I had realized.

If there is one single thing that I can point to that has changed the way I go about daily, it is this: I learned, no, I'm learning, patience.

Friends with the same vision problems laugh that what used to take five minutes to accomplish now takes thirty to forty minutes to do. If you lack patience, you're in for it for sure.

The first year of retirement found me doing small jobs I never had time for. I started a daily walking program. I could use a computer, but seeing the screen was getting harder and harder.

I first went to Tucson in June 2014. The VA operates thirteen Blind Rehabilitation Centers. The Tucson unit serves our area. I spent thirty days in what I call their basic training program. Returning that September, I learned Zoom-Text, a computer magnification program that also reads the screen to you. This opened up the use of a computer.

In May 2016, I was looking for something to do. I was bored, and sitting around was not my style. So, I asked Trudi at the VA if I could help her or someone else. She recruited me, and I was elected secretary/treasurer of the New Mexico Group of the Blinded Veterans Association (BVA).

I am now in my seventh year. To quote an old saying, "It has kept me off the streets."

In 2018 I began Tai Chi at the VA. We had to wait until the writer's group meeting ended on Thursdays before we had the floor to ourselves. Upon inquiry, I was invited to join, which became another decision that profoundly affected my life. And the friendships sustain me daily.

So, I began to write. And to my surprise, I found I could do so and was encouraged by my writing group associates to persevere. Kathy Hopkins, the volunteer leader of the writer's group, took me under her wing. She read my efforts to the group since I could not see the printing.

And she did a lot of editing of my work. I have since learned to edit by listening instead of reading. And, to my surprise, in 2019, I won national honors at the VA Creative Arts Festival. I attended the national symposium in Kalamazoo, Michigan. There I met many other veterans with creative skills. And I'm trying like the dickens to win again. Writing and working on BVA matters are what keeps me looking forward.

I'm a poor candidate for distributing advice. I am still in the midst of learning how to live with my affliction. The deterioration of my vision is an ongoing, day-to-day situation. What I could see last month may or may not be seen next month. So, adjustment is the order of each and every day.

As improbable as it may sound, I actually think I am more accepting of my lot in life than I had ever been before AMD entered my world.

I find I am more tolerant of my fellow man. I can accept minor inconveniences more easily than I could in the past. I consider every day I live as a gift. Would I rather I didn't have this affliction? Yes, but it has expanded my life in ways I could only imagine. Even with conflicts daily in my path, I am calmer than ever. I cherish my friends. I can only hope they find it in their hearts to reciprocate.

*****

Author: C.L. Nemeth

Chuck Nemeth served in the Army in Germany during the Korean War. He is legally blind. He is a VA Creative Arts Festival national winner for a short story. He has also appeared in *Veterans Voices*. Chuck is active in the Blinded Veterans Association.

PAULA NIXON

Peacetime

What in the hell did you ask for?

That question boomed out over a loudspeaker the day my dad, Paul, got his orders at Fort Belvoir in February 1957. Ninety-nine curious guys turned to look at him.

Paul was headed to Elmendorf Airforce Base.

Most personal news was communicated by letters in the fifties. If it was really important, there was always a Western Union telegram. Telephone calls were expensive and rare. But this news warranted a call to his wife, Joyce, back in Kansas. The two had been married for less than a year. Paul had asked for Fort Riley, sixty-five miles from Joyce's hometown. He had to break the news to her that they were headed for the territory of Alaska, 3000 miles from Kansas.

***

Paul started college in 1951 after graduating from Cimarron High School on the windswept plains of southwestern Kansas. His parents had moved to Dodge City and then Cimarron during World War II, looking for new opportunities. They had left behind the family farm and their extended family in Oklahoma.

Paul's dad drove him 250 miles to Manhattan, home of Kansas State College, the state's land grant school. Paul had loaded his Cushman scooter into the family's 1949 Ford trunk so he'd have wheels when he got there. He enrolled in math and science classes with the idea of majoring in engineering. As required, he also signed up for Advanced

Reserve Officers' Training Corps (ROTC). The Air Force classes he hoped for were full, so he opted for the Army instead.

He was young, not yet eighteen. Within the first week, he had found a job as a houseboy that would provide him with room and board at Van Zile Hall, a dormitory for girls. He lived in the basement and worked in the kitchen. He would return to the job every fall until he graduated.

***

While Paul was a sophomore taking calculus, surveying during the day, and washing piles of dishes in the evenings, Joyce was finishing her senior year at Topeka High School. She lived in a close-knit family with one grandmother next door and another less than twenty miles away. She played oboe in the high school orchestra, sewed most of her own clothes, and rode the bus downtown to work at Pelletier's, a local department store. She arrived at K-state with a bevy of high school friends and pledged to the Alpha Xi Delta sorority. Her major was foods and nutrition.

Joyce also needed a job and found one at Van Zile, serving in the cafeteria. It's not clear when she and Paul met, but it would be some time before they went on their first date. By all accounts, that first date was to a movie, but the two could never agree on which movie it was. Not in question was their second date at Cohen's Chicken House in Junction City, twenty miles from Manhattan and home to Fort Riley.

***

In the summer of 1953, before Paul and Joyce met, Paul got a three-month contract to work for the Alaska Road Commission. His engineering coursework and prior surveying experience with the Kansas Highway Department qualified him for the unusual summer job. He and three buddies drove a car to Washington State, where they parked it with a family member for the summer and then flew from Seattle to Fairbanks.

From Fairbanks, it was a trip of 250 miles east. Towns were almost nonexistent out on that stretch of the Alcan Highway approaching the Canadian border. Their work on the highway was mostly surveying and calculating road cuts. There Paul learned firsthand the challenges and best practices of working on permafrost.

The closest fresh water was fifty miles away and had to be trucked to the road camp where the crew lived. The pay was decent, and most of Paul's expenses were covered by a daily allowance of $6. It was valuable work experience, and Paul could throw a fishing line in the Tanana River in his spare time.

Paul returned for a second summer in 1954. He and a buddy lived in a cabin to try and save some of their per diem by doing their own cooking and laundry. Bear steaks and salmon were on the menu, but fresh vegetables were nowhere to be found.

***

In 1955 Paul was a senior, and Joyce was a junior, both still planning to graduate on schedule in their original fields of study.

Joyce returned, as usual, to Topeka for the summer to work at Pelletier's. Paul had a six-week ROTC active training camp to attend at Fort Carson in Colorado, so he would not be returning to Alaska. During that spring, he published an article in the March issue of *Kansas State Engineer* about working on the Alcan. He described the challenges of road building in the far north, along with details about living in rustic conditions. He highly recommended the job to his fellow students.

Paul and Joyce stayed in touch and agreed to meet at his parents' home over the Fourth of July weekend. Joyce and a friend rode a bus from Topeka while Paul and a buddy drove in from Colorado.

In December, before the holiday break, they "passed chocolates" to announce their engagement at the Alpha Xi Delta house.

***

On a sunny afternoon in late May of 1956, Paul graduated with a degree in civil engineering. Earlier that day, he had received his commission in the Army as a 2nd Lieutenant. His parents and Joyce were there to celebrate with him. Within days he reported to work with Phillips Petroleum in Borger, Texas, a job he would hold until the Army called him up.

Joyce returned to Topeka to finish planning their mid-summer wedding. It was a formal event on a Saturday evening in July at the Westminster Presbyterian Church not far from the neighborhood where she had grown up. Joyce was one week away from turning twenty-one. Paul was twenty-three. At a luncheon on the afternoon of the wedding, the Lester and Nixon families met each other for the first time.

No time for a honeymoon, Joyce and Paul drove to Borger, where Paul was back at work on Monday morning. By November, the couple had moved to Alexandria, Virginia, where Paul reported for Basic Military Officer Training at Fort Belvoir.

Paul left his job at Phillips, knowing he would have a position with the company when his active duty ended. Joyce was still pursuing her degree via correspondence courses. It was a slog, and she dreaded returning alone to K-State for the spring semester.

During her time in Virginia, while Paul was in school, she got to know another officer's wife in the apartment complex where they lived. She and Dawn became friends, not knowing if they would see each other again after Joyce returned to Kansas.

***

What in the hell did you ask for?

Three of the one hundred that day, including Paul, got the same assignment. The Army Corps of Engineers in Anchorage, Alaska. Each, maybe for a slightly different combination of reasons, high marks in officer training, and/or experience in cold weather construction. Of the three, Paul was the only one who had actual experience in Alaska.

The assignment was considered overseas duty, but since it was peacetime, Joyce would be able to go with Paul. She must have been cheered by the news that her friend Dawn would also be moving to Alaska.

***

Joyce's parents may have feared they wouldn't see their daughter again. After all, the title of Paul's article about his experiences was "Alaska: Wild West of the 20th Century." Paul returned briefly to Kansas before driving, once again, to Washington, this time to Seattle, where their 1956 Ford would be ferried to Alaska. Joyce still had a few weeks of classes and then finals before she could join him.

In a letter to Joyce's parents from Anchorage, Paul expressed his regret for not being present when *she walked across that stage.* He told them about his trip north and the broken taillight the car had suffered on the journey. Much more serious to him was the fact that both of his fishing poles were stolen out of the car. He ended the letter by saying; Please *send my wife as soon as you can — I really need her here.*

Joyce's trip was not without mishaps and miscommunications, but she did arrive in Anchorage within weeks of Paul's letter. A short time later, when their belongings arrived, Paul found a new rod and reel from Joyce's father, a fellow fisherman.

Life in Anchorage was nothing like life in the road camp and provided most of the same comforts of life as in the Lower 48. Although some things, like fresh fruit and vegetables, were hard to find and expensive. The young couple lived in officer's quarters on Fort Richardson and formed long-term friendships with the other officers and their spouses.

Paul's projects included the design of airport runways and nose wing hangars. The work gave him the experience he would need for his professional license. It was one of the few times in his life that Paul would work at an 8:00 AM to 5:00 PM job.

Finally, the couple could enjoy their young married life. They loved the long days of summer, and it marked the beginning of their many years together, fishing and picnicking, spending as much time as possible outdoors next to mountain streams.

By the end of the summer, they were expecting their first child. Joyce bought a used Singer sewing machine and started making maternity and baby clothes.

In the dark of winter, Joyce picked out a female puppy at the local pound on the Fort. Punk was named for the striking pumpkin-colored eyebrows and markings on her legs and chest that stood out against her black fur.

***

In April, Joyce and Paul sent a telegram to her parents: PAULA KAY ARRIVED AT 0429 HRS ON 18 APRIL 7 LBS 8 OZ 21 INCHES.

Joyce and Paul and all of the grandparents were thrilled. Punk was not. She took to ripping diapers off the clothesline.

Paul was promoted to 1st Lieutenant shortly before his active-duty service concluded. In November 1958, he built a wooden-framed crib that he could set securely in the backseat of the Ford for the trip back to Kansas. The four flew to Seattle (Punk in baggage) and picked up the car for the long road trip back to Kansas, Paula and Punk in the back seat.

Paul and Joyce, college sweethearts, married at a young age and returned to Kansas as a family. Their first stop was Cimarron to introduce their newest family members to the Nixons. Then on to Topeka to meet the Lesters.

Paul served his remaining four years in the Army reserves while working for Phillips, later starting his own consulting business in western Kansas, where he and Joyce raised their three kids, the two youngest Kansas born.

***

A few weeks ago, I visited Paul in Colorado. For months we have been going through photo albums, scrapbooks filled with newspaper clippings, and the occasional handwritten letter. Joyce died in 2020, and we have missed her as we have tried to piece the family stories together. On this day, Paul opened a battered Army-issued footlocker. Inside we found his pinks and greens, his dress uniform with its two castle pins on the lapels signifying his service in the Corps of Engineers. And a file folder filled with Army correspondence, including Punk's first rabies certificate. She lived sixteen years, a much-loved member of the family.

Also in the folder was a letter to Joyce from Major Baumgardner with her travel orders. I picture Joyce standing at the mailbox on a breezy Kansas day with the letter in her hand, contemplating how her life is about to take a turn she hadn't anticipated, apprehensive but also excited about what's to come.

*****

Author: Paula Nixon

Paula Nixon lives in New Mexico. Her dad is Army veteran Paul Nixon. Writing this gave Paula a greater appreciation for the sacrifices her folks made — no gap years or summers in Europe! Instead, they relished the adventure and opportunities the Army gave them.

Harper O'Connor

Roadside Temples

My dad was stationed at Osan Air Force Base, South Korea, in 1977, and it was a cultural eye-opener for my seven-year-old self. It wasn't until decades later that I found out we lived off-base, not because it was an unaccompanied tour, it was unaccompanied because the family housing was still a year away from being built. Living, playing, and shopping away from the insular community of American military families meant experiencing an entirely new world.

Dad, Mom, and I took the occasional road trip in South Korea if we had a long weekend in good weather. Each excursion was only for the day, but we'd go see other parts of the country besides Osan. We only went to Seoul once because going by car was a very unpleasant way to discover the congestion and lack of good parking in the capital city. We didn't go to Busan, where the US Naval base was, since it was literally across the country, but other trips revealed many treasures. He would make sure Mom held the best road atlas he could buy to help navigate, and off we'd go in random directions. While I can no longer recall our specific direction or name various destinations, I loved seeing the countryside and found fascinating things along the way that made an impact.

We discovered a Korean graveyard once away from the cities that looked quite different from an American one. I remember curiously staring at a field of little hills with slender stone markers up against the foot of each mound. Why it looked so different was both to save space and to bury the dead in the ground, preferably in the mountains, standing upright in a coffin and mounding the earth over it. The gravestones were also tall slices of stone a few inches wide, again to save room. It was much more natural and organic-looking than rows of crosses or granite slabs. It had only been a few months since we lost Grandpa to a heart attack and sent his body back to Colorado, so our drive became rather somber and quiet after moving on from the cemetery.

Later that day, we found a small roadside Buddhist shrine. While Dad wasn't really religious, and we didn't go to church, he was generally respectful of other beliefs while we were overseas. Maybe something in the peace of Buddhism called to him. I can only imagine what the two bald Buddhist monks in their gray layered robes thought of the white family driving from out of nowhere and stopping at the temple. Between gestures and very minimal English, they managed to convey to us that no pictures were allowed, but we were welcome to enter. Dad bought sticks of incense for each of us for the equivalent of about fifty cents.

The building was unassuming from a distance, with its weathered paint on carved wood walls, latticed sliding doors, and grayish-brown tiled pagoda-like roof. But as I walked closer from the car, my eyes were delighted with the layers of shaped wooden buttresses under the eaves like stacks of nesting birds and the sun-faded red paint on the doors and walls to just above head height. The middle two doors were open and slid aside to let in bright sunlight and air into the dark interior. A low table sat on the ground in front at the bottom of the steps. It held engraved metal bowls resting on little embroidered sapphire silk pillows, piles of freshly cut orange flowers, and a wooden bowl of fresh fruit. All this sat behind a low ceramic dish full of sand with even more sticks of half-burnt incense stuck upright with their smoke curling lazily upward.

The older monk with deep crow's feet and smile wrinkles around his mouth brought a long fireplace-style match over to light our sticks and the one he held as well. He quietly carried the incense with the wooden bottom section between his palms and demonstrated how to close our eyes, bow, then stand the incense in the sand. Dad went first with a quick but polite bow. The monk then beckoned him up the few steps to the open doors and showed him where to take off his shoes. Dad stood back up and followed the monk inside as Mom bowed smoothly over her own incense. She stood at my side for a moment as I carefully bowed, slowly inhaling the rich and beautiful aroma of sandalwood and something else earthy. The scent calmed me, even at seven years old, and I breathed a little slower. When I straightened back up, an impulse came over me to cup the smoke in my little hands to draw it over my head and face. Mom whispered for me to come on. When I opened my eyes, I saw her moving around the table and toward where Dad had entered the temple. The younger monk standing off to the side caught my eye and gave a small approving smile that I shyly returned.

I went up the steps and toed off my sneakers, going to Mom's side. My breath stopped in my throat at the beauty inside this weather-beaten building. More incense burned, and full offering tables sat in front of more gold than I've ever seen in my life. Brass bowls and polished candlesticks reflected the light. Small gilded carved panels were set everywhere into the back wall, and banners hung on the sides with large

Korean letters painted in scarlet and yellow. Other panels on the walls and wooden tables were painted in bright, beautiful colors. Kelly green, white, scarlet, a blue more vivid than cobalt, sunny lemon yellow … color and gold were everywhere.

But the large figure in the center of the back wall on a raised deep shelf was the reason for all of it. My eyes widened at the statue of Buddha. Dominating the room, he sat in lotus position with one hand's fingertips almost touching the dais and the other raised beside his painted black curly hair and thin black arching eyebrows. His skin, his robe, the single jewel in front of his hair's bun, everything glowed warmly gold as if the sun itself sat in his place. His eyes were not quite closed, and he had really long earlobes. His lips and a small dot in the center of his forehead were a bright scarlet, and I was utterly entranced.

Dad and Mom whispered to each other about the carvings, trying not to point at everything they saw. (Pointing with a finger was considered rude in South Korea.) My eyes were glued on the Buddha alone. I stood slightly behind Mom and off to her right, my hands clasped behind my back. The whole place radiated calm. I was normally only this still while I was reading, but it felt strangely comfortable just to be there and breathe. I tried half-closing my eyes like the statue, and I relaxed even more. I stayed there as Dad and Mom looked closer at the carvings in the side walls. Minutes felt like hours and like seconds, all at the same time.

When they were finally ready to go, Mom touched my shoulder. I took a deep breath, then followed her to put my shoes back on. As we stepped down near the offering table again, something impelled me to ask, "Mom, can I do one more stick of incense? Please?"

Dad frowned next to us, and I crossed my fingers behind my back with one hand.

"We need to go," he said.

There was something about this, something important that made me ask again, and I thought as hard as I could that I *needed* to do this. "Please, just one? It'll only take a minute."

He sighed as if an extra minute and a half would be an extreme inconvenience but relented. I was actually shocked when he agreed, "Fine, just one." He dug the coins out of his pocket and dropped them one by one into my outstretched hand. "I'll be in the car. Don't take long." Dad turned and headed for our vehicle. Mom just nodded and urged me with a gentle push toward the monks who were watching us.

They glanced at each other, then the younger one (It was a little hard to tell them apart with their identical shaved heads and gray robes, but he definitely had fewer wrinkles) went over to get another stick and a shorter match as the older one took the coins and smiled at me. The younger one put the incense between my palms, and I felt a strange little hard lump next to the stick. He caught my eye and shared a calm look with me as he lit the incense, then held a finger to his mouth in a hushing gesture before gesturing to the ceramic dish. I smiled at him and closed my eyes for a moment, then bowed before putting the incense in the sand. I used my empty hand to draw the smoke over my face again. After a breath, I turned to him and smiled a final time. "Thank you." He understood the sentiment, if not the words, and bowed to me.

Mom called out. "Come on, Maggie." I ran over to her, and we got in the car. I knelt in the seat and stared out the back window at the temple building and the monks as Dad did a three-point turn and pulled away. They were saying something to each other. I imagined them talking about how the Americans were so nice, not rude at all. Once Dad had his eyes on the road, I carefully opened the hand with the little lump. Surprise jolted through me as I saw a tiny, hand-carved, unpainted rough Buddha figure. I carefully put it in my jeans pocket, turning around and sliding down to sit so nothing would happen to it.

I don't know what eventually became of that small wooden Buddha. What a beautiful gift, though. No translations were needed to see that a child could feel a peaceful spirituality and instinctively understand kindness and respect. I was very surprised to realize that I had none of my usual shyness or uncertainty whatsoever with those two adult strangers. Even when the younger monk touched my hands, they felt … safe. Kind. Caring. It was definitely an energy I appreciated and wanted more of.

*****

Author: Harper O'Connor

Harper O'Connor is a watercolor/sketch artist as well as a writer, living with chosen family and two stubborn cats in Albuquerque, New Mexico. They were a military dependent until age eleven and lived in multiple states as well as South Korea, the Philippines, and Japan.

JEFFREY OTIS

Bottles

It was 1962. I was a sixth-grade pop bottle-finder at Cannon Air Force Base in New Mexico. My base of operations was our house on Queens Loop in the Non-Commissioned Officers housing area, an address that doesn't exist today. I'd haul a box of pop bottles to the Base Exchange, get a few bucks for them, and buy some comics. *Sad Sack* and *Superman* were to my taste. There was usually enough change left to buy some Double Bubble gum and a cold refreshing bottle of Seven-Up.

I picked up stray pop bottles near the baseball diamond or the bowling alley and got a return deposit at the exchange. Soon, I realized the trash cans at these places were a richer source of bottles. All I had to do was reach in, pull out the few bottles I could see, and get my reward. On one particular day, I went further. I checked out a trash can, picked up a bottle on top, and then dug down, where I found several more. I was no longer a casual opportunist. I was now a miner. At first, I made sure no one was around to observe, but later, it no longer mattered. I think the excitement of the search was like the thrill guys get when they scour a beach with metal detectors.

Every day became an adventure. I was a bloodhound, hot on the trail of escaped bottles as I wandered all over the base for hours. The work was hard, and soon so were my muscles. I'd come home hot and sweaty, climb to the top bunk of my room, and enjoy a good comic. What a life.

Eventually, trash cans weren't enough to satisfy me. I realized that dumpsters were just big trash cans. They were filled with bottles. I became accustomed to the stench of wet ashes and pieces of old fried chicken. I would actually climb into the dumpster and dig like a coyote after a prairie dog. When I got paid for the bottles, the thrill was immense. I was making my own money. Hard, honest work. Around this time, my mother bought me the first can of deodorant.

Dumpster diving wasn't exactly cool. That's why I didn't have any competition. It was work most other kids didn't want to do. Not exactly high-status. After a big day, sometimes I felt guilty, like I was doing something I shouldn't. But I kept at it, even after an airman closed the door of my dumpster. I hollered and begged to be let out. I could hear him laughing. I thought I was going to be stuck until a garbage truck swallowed me up, never to be seen again. After a few seconds, he opened the door, and I toppled out. The funny thing is it didn't stop me. I was back at it the next weekend.

Sometimes I found more than bottles, such as model airplanes, records, books, and once a silver ring. I remember finding a *Doc Savage* paperback with a cover so well-painted you could see every wrinkle in his ripped-up shirt. Once, I brought home an album by a famous lady singer; I think it was Sarah Vaughan. My mom loved it and played it on our stereo. As I listened, it occurred to me that I was now able to provide things my parents appreciated. It warmed me. These things were the whipped cream on top of a root beer float.

My dad attended an out-of-state training course for a month or two, leaving my mom alone to deal with all five of her children. I messed up when I should have been on my best behavior for my mom's sake. I'd seen pop machines in the G.I. barracks with a rack of empty bottles attached to one side. *Why am I dumpster diving? This was a gold mine!* I convinced a friend to help me and share in the spoils. We did a trial run, took several bottles from the rack, and put them in a box on the lawn. Nothing happened. No one yelled at us. Within a minute, we were gleefully tossing the bottles out of the snack room door onto the grass. We were efficient and fluid in our movements, careful not to send a bottle crashing into another on the ground. We'd hit the jackpot.

I should have asked myself why a vending company would go to the trouble of providing a special place for empty bottles. I wasn't sure if it was wrong, but the possibility was enough to make me nervous. On the other hand, the potential rewards were staggering. I guess I was testing the waters. When the Air Police (AP) showed up, I knew I'd blown it. *Could the G.I. on the barracks phone during our secret operation have been the whistle-blower?* I thought I was going to jail. Now I was either a criminal or a juvenile delinquent. The opportunity of a lifetime to expand my business had failed miserably. I was embarrassed. Disgraced. I remember looking at my friend as the Air Police truck pulled up to the scene of the crime. He stood frozen, looking for me to save us. It was my fault, after all.

My stomach curled in knots while I waited to be taken to the place where criminals were interrogated. Instead, the Air Policeman called my mom and took me home. The same for my friend. No forceful push against the vehicle, no knee in the back as I lay on the ground, no handcuffs, no threats. Those guys were professional, even kind.

My mom had never received a call from the APs, let alone answered our door to find one standing there with her child. That night, my mom and dad had a long talk on the phone.

I served my time; I think I was grounded for a few days. But I went straight and never tried for the quick buck again. A new line of work was what I needed. So, I began delivering the newspaper. It paid well, but it demanded complete dedication. It meant waking up at six in the morning on weekends. No sleeping until nine and then watching cartoons. That was how I really paid for my mistake.

I'd walk the barracks floors yelling, "get yer paper." In one barrack, I passed by the exact snack room where I'd been apprehended. A deep temptation mixed with regrets left me uneasy. Machines filled with cigarettes and candy lined the walls, and near the door stood the pop machine, its rack filled with empty bottles. I wondered how many comics I could buy from that stash. I put my papers down and bought some candy instead.

***

The Mission

A million years ago, the land where Miro and I stood would have killed us. The Valles Caldera was born of explosive volcanic eruptions that collapsed everything into a massive crater. Still geologically active, forces quietly stirred below the surface. For us, it served as the beautiful backdrop to a day of fishing. The air was cool and crisp, with a damp, earthy smell.

"We teachers need to fish," Miro said, putting more bait on his hook.

I snickered. "Yeah, students can wear me out." I hadn't caught a single fish, but I knew they were there. I could see them watching me.

"My military training helps me with the students."

"Maybe that's what I'm missing. It didn't help my dad. He had military training, but I was still a difficult kid." I paused. "I once wanted to be a pilot, but my eyesight betrayed me."

"Good eyesight is a must. Especially in fighters."

"You once said you flew Phantoms," I said, tossing my line downstream. The early morning mist was fading, giving the caldera's rim more clarity.

"F-4Es. Good plane," he said, pronouncing each word clearly with a lingering accent.

I decided the fish were smarter than me, so I laid my pole down and sat in an aluminum folding chair. "I think I'd have a better chance using my hands."

We were quiet for a while. "My brother had a model Phantom," I said.

Miro continued to fish.

"So, what was flying like?"

"Here is what I'll tell you. A pilot never passes a restroom without using it."

"Funny," I said.

"I got to see Europe from the air. It was fantastic."

"Nice." After a while, I asked, "Was this during the Cold War?"

"Yes."

"My dad was stationed at Rhein-Main Air Force Base and later Ramstein, Germany," I said. "I guess I was oblivious to the threat of war. Teenagers have other things on their minds."

"Your dad a pilot?"

"Air traffic controller."

"That can be a tough job," he said.

"Yeah, I think it was stressful. I imagine your job was difficult, too."

"It could be. The most difficult mission I trained for, in the event of war, was to bomb Czechoslovakia. The target was a city where my dad once worked."

"Was … was your family still in Czechoslovakia?"

Miro reeled in his line, set his pole aside, and sat in a folding chair next to me with a sigh. "My family made it to the West when I was a boy. We were refugees."

Now he had my complete attention. "Was it difficult to target your homeland?"

"I hated the government. The bastards took everything, leaving my parents to struggle."

I knew that tone. I could hear the anger. "Sounds like life was hard for people in Czechoslovakia."

He nodded slowly.

Inside me, the ground shifted. "I've seen pictures of Phantoms loaded with all sorts of bombs."

"They trained us to carry a nuke."

My stomach tightened. I remembered hiding under my desk during school drills. "Can they explode on you? I mean, while you were flying?"

"We never took off with a live nuke."

I hesitated to ask more questions. We were here to relax. But the mood had changed. "Can you tell me about that?"

"We trained all the time. If a war broke out, then we'd have a nuke. As we neared our target, the weapons systems officer and I had to arm the bomb using codes. We both had to flip a switch in the air to consent to completing the mission."

"This is pretty heavy-duty stuff, Miro."

"Yeah. I tried not to think about the people in the cities I might bomb. I was paid to fight. You have to do your job."

None of my jobs ever came close to the burden he shouldered, I thought, or had the possible consequences. I watched as a bird slowly circled in the distance, wanting to believe it was an eagle.

"My mission was to fly fast and low. We were to climb 45 degrees with our afterburners on when we reached a certain point and release the bomb." He mimicked the plane with his hand. "Then we got the hell out of there. We wore an eyepatch over one eye to avoid being totally blinded in both eyes by the blast."

"Jeez."

"By then, our own base would have been destroyed. No place to land. We would bail out and try to make it to friendly forces." He fixed his gaze on the horizon.

I tried to process what he said. He had been prepared to die. Prepared to accept responsibility for a task that might have haunted him for the rest of his life, possibly a short one. It was humbling and terrifying. Neither of us felt like talking anymore. I gazed at the distant rim of the caldera, trying to grasp the monstrous forces that made it. Would we ever unleash such things? Would Mother Nature care? No.

In a million years, she would cover our ashes with grassy meadows surrounding fish-filled streams.

*****

Author: Jeffrey Otis

Jeffrey Otis is a family member. His father served in the Air Force and retired in Albuquerque, New Mexico, in 1970 when he was sixteen. Jeff was born at Wright Patterson Air Force Base in Ohio and spent my youth in Okinawa, California, England, Germany, France, and New Mexico.

DONNA PEDACE

Nancy Wake: "The White Mouse"

Everyone agreed that Nancy Wake was a force to be reckoned with during World War II, including the Gestapo. She was one of the most decorated women of the war.

She volunteered for resistance work with an eclectic personal history. Nancy was born in Wellington, New Zealand, on August 30, 1912. She carried Māori blood from her grandmother, who was believed to have been the first Māori woman to marry a European. When Nancy was two years old, her family moved to Sydney, Australia. Her father soon returned to New Zealand, and she and her five brothers and sisters remained in Sydney and were raised by her mother.

Nancy was always what was called a "tough cookie" who loved adventure. She was rough in her manner and her language. She had a raucous laugh that she retained throughout her life. Nancy ran away from home when she was sixteen and found work as a nurse's aide. She received a small inheritance from an aunt and used the funds to travel to New York City and then to London.

Nancy trained to become a journalist and worked in that capacity for a local Paris newspaper in the early 1930s and later for Hearst newspapers as a European correspondent. In 1933, her paper sent her to Vienna to interview the new German Chancellor, Adolf Hitler. After that interview and witnessing the awful violence inflicted on the local Jewish population, she vowed to fight against his persecution of Jews.

In 1937, she met a wealthy French industrialist, Henri Edmond Fiocca. After a long courtship, they married on November 30, 1939, and she became a local socialite. They were living in Marseille, France when Germany invaded. To be of help, she volunteered as an ambulance driver until 1940. Nancy and her husband began working to support the Resistance and help endangered locals and Allied troops escape from German-occupied areas. Her escape network was called the Pat O'Leary Line.

Nancy in her war uniform.
Photo courtesy of the
Australian War Memorial

She was said to be one of the war's most fearsome French Resistance fighters. In 1942, the Gestapo put her at the top of their most wanted list, offering a five-million-franc bounty for her capture, dead or alive. The Germans began calling her "The White Mouse" for her ability to remain hidden from capture. She later said that she often flirted her way out of difficult situations with German troops. She said, "A little powder and a little drink on the way, and I'd pass their (German) posts and wink and say, do you want to search me? God, what a flirtatious little bastard I was."

Her Resistance group was betrayed to the Germans in November 1942, and she fled the country by crossing the Pyrenees Mountains to Spain. Her husband thought his position would protect him, so he stayed behind. The Gestapo later arrested, tortured, and killed him in August 1943, but Nancy did not learn of his death until the end of the war.

Nancy reached England, where she joined the Special Operations Executive branch (SOE) and was assigned to special spy training. Vera Atkins, the senior female recruiter in SOE, described Nancy as "An Australian Bombshell." Her training included hand-to-hand combat and espionage. Her ratings were very high throughout her training, with excellent shooting skills and fieldcraft. A note on her record said, "She put the men to shame by her cheerful spirit and strength of character." She was also said to be able to outdrink any man in the training group.

After finishing her training, Nancy parachuted back into France on April 30, 1944, as part of a three-person team. The team's purpose was to be a liaison between London and the Maquis (local French) Resistance group. Her specific duties were to select the locations where material and money would be dropped by parachute from Allied planes. After she retrieved the items from the drop, she would allocate them among the Maquis, including pay to individual fighters. She also kept a list of physical targets the Resistance was to destroy before the Allies invaded. Included were communication lines, transportation sites, and gun factories.

In May 1944, the leader of the local Maqui gathered 7000 members in a plan to stage a major attack against the Germans. The Germans learned of the plan, and on June 20, they did a counterattack, forcing the Resistance fighters to flee after taking heavy casualties. Wake and her team retreated with the Maquis on a three-day walk to the village of Saint-Santin.

There are several incidents that Nancy claimed in her later memoir that officials have not been able to verify, but they may be true. One of them is that during the retreat, the group's radio operator left his radio and codes behind, and the SOE desperately needed that radio and the codes to be in touch with London. Nancy said she borrowed a bicycle, rode it to Chateauroux, found the radio, and updated London on their situation. She wrote that she bicycled back to Saint-Santin, traveling 310 miles in seventy-two hours. She reported no interference by the Germans during that ride.

She participated in a raid that destroyed the Gestapo headquarters in Montlucon, in which thirty-eight Germans were killed. The group freed three women who had been forced into prostitution by the Germans. Nancy interrogated the three and decided that one was a German spy. The other two were released, but she demanded that the third woman be executed. Nancy later said she had no remorse about the woman's death.

Nancy killed an SS [Schutzstaffel] sentry with her bare hands to prevent him from raising the alarm during a raid on a German gun factory. After the war, during a TV interview, when the interviewer questioned her about the incident, she said, "They'd taught this judo-chop stuff with the flat of the hand at SOE, and I practiced away at it. But this was the only time I used it — whack — and it killed him all right. I was really surprised." That action proved both her physical strength and her willingness to participate in violence. Nancy's experience contradicts the wartime gender dichotomy that insisted women were incapable of such violent acts.

At the war's end, Nancy returned to England and worked for the intelligence department at the British Air Ministry. In that capacity, she worked in both Paris and Prague before her wanderlust led her to return to Australia. She ran unsuccessfully for several different political offices during the late 1940s. Finding no success in Australian politics, she returned to England in 1951, where she again worked as an intelligence officer in the Department of the Assistant Chief of the Air Staff in Whitehall. After a few years, she married an RAF [Royal Air Force] officer, John Forward, in December 1957.

She and her new husband moved to Australia in the early 1960s. Nancy again tried her hand at politics by running as a Liberal candidate in the 1966 legislative election. Although she nearly won the seat, her attempt led to failure. Finally giving up on politics, she and her husband retired to Port Macquarie, a small town on the east coast.

In 1985, Nancy published her autobiography, *The White Mouse,* the name the Nazis called her because she was so elusive. A TV mini-series, *Nancy Wake*, was released in Australia in 1987 and later released as *True Colors* in the US. To her delight, Nancy made a cameo appearance in the movie. After the series, she was interviewed by many domestic and foreign news agencies, and she loved the attention. Some of her comments during those interviews included: *"I have only one thing to say: I killed a lot of Germans, and I am only sorry that I didn't kill more,"* on life after the war, *"It's dreadful because you've been so busy and then it all just fizzles out,"* and speaking of her time during the war *"I was never afraid. I was too busy to be afraid."*

Her second husband died in 1997, leaving her with few financial resources. Nancy had no children and no other family to help her, so she sold her medals to support herself. She said, *"There was no point in keeping them, I'll probably go to hell, and they'd melt anyway."*

Nancy left Australia for the final time in 2001, moving to the Stafford Hotel in St. James' Place in London. It had been a British and American Forces club during World War II, and the wartime general manager had introduced her to her first "bloody good drink" there. Nancy always enjoyed a good drink, and she spent most mornings having a gin and tonic while she entertained anyone at the bar with her war stories. The hotel manager had a special chair made for her to sit at the bar, and it was designated as "Nancy's Corner." After hearing about Nancy from a hotel patron, Prince of Wales, Charles invited her to Buckingham Palace for afternoon tea. He later paid for her outstanding bills at the hotel in remembrance of her service during the war.

Nancy died on August 7, 2011, just a few days shy of her ninety-ninth birthday. She had requested that her ashes be scattered in central France, and that was done near Montlucon, where she served during much of the war. Some of her medals are now on display in the Second World War gallery at the Australian War Memorial in Canberra.

Several books have been written about Nancy's war contributions, and portions of her story are included in many more that deal with the war years. In 2014, TVNZ (New Zealand) released a docudrama, *Nancy Wake: The White Mouse.*

When remembering Nancy, nothing encapsulates her spirit quite as much as the words of her fellow Resistance officer, Henri Tardivat,

"She is the most feminine woman I know, until the fighting starts, then she is like five men."

Over the years, Nancy received the following awards for her service to the Resistance movement in France:

* The George Medal from the United Kingdom on July 17, 1945

* The Medal of Freedom from the United States with Bronze Palm, 1947

* A Chevalier (Knight) of the Legion of Honor from France in 1970, and an Officer of the Legion of Honor in1988, and the Croix de Guerre with two Palms and a Star

* A Companion of the Order of Australia, 2004

* Returned Services Association (RSA) The Badge in Gold from New Zealand, 2006

*****

Author: Donna Pedace

Donna Pedace's first husband was a US Navy Submarine Service nuclear officer. Her current husband retired from the Army National Guard in Connecticut. Donna researches some of the little-known women who volunteered to work as spies behind Nazi lines during World War II.

W. Howard Plunkett

The Operational History of the F-105 Thunderchief

I began my Air Force career in early 1964 as an aircraft maintenance officer supporting F-105 Thunderchiefs at McConnell Air Force Base (AFB), Kansas. At the time, the F-105 was the Air Force's premier fighter-bomber. The supersonic aircraft looked like the fighter plane it was. Its 20-mm Gatling gun with its six rotating barrels poked out of the left side of its streamlined nose. It had short, swept-back wings that held racks to mount bombs, missiles, and fuel tanks. It had a single cockpit (a feature that pleased its pilots) and an engine afterburner that started with a loud bang as the plane raced down the runway for takeoff. I've been interested in machines since childhood, and I quickly became fascinated with the F-105, especially when I began supporting its combat missions in the Vietnam War.

On 2 August 1964, North Vietnamese gunships attacked the destroyer USS Madox (DD-731), a US Navy spy ship in the Gulf of Tonkin. This attack triggered Navy responses as well as a series of F-105 squadron deployments for a possible war in Southeast Asia. Until then, the mission of F-105s based in the Pacific (as well as in Germany) was nuclear alert as part of the US's Single Integrated Operational Plan (SIOP) that specified retaliatory nuclear weapon attacks by aircraft, ships, and strategic missiles on the Soviet Union, its Eastern European satellite countries and on Communist China. Fortunately, it was a plan that was never done.

Two days after the Gulf of Tonkin attack, eighteen F-105s from the 36 Tactical Fighter Squadron (TFS) were ordered on temporary duty from their home at Yokota Air Base (AB), Japan, to Korat Royal Thai AFB in Thailand. To replace the 36 TFS at Yokota, the 357 TFS deployed from McConnell under "Operation One Buck Two." I was one of the maintenance officers with the 357th during its four months at Yokota. The 357th periodically sent a few F-105s to Osan AB Korea to sit nuclear alert, but this Tactical Air Command squadron was not allowed to deploy to Thailand to fly combat missions over North Vietnam.

In December 1964, pilots and support personnel in the 357th returned home from Yokota to McConnell, leaving their eighteen F-105s for their replacements from the 469 TFS.

Over the next year, F-105 pilots began dropping bombs on North Vietnam and Laos from two Royal Thai Air Force bases in Thailand: Korat and Takhli. On 6 August 1965, I traveled to Takhli as an F-105 maintenance officer with the 562 TFS from McConnell. During my four months at Takhli, the squadron lost six aircraft to North Vietnam's anti-aircraft defenses. Two pilots were killed by malfunctions of their own bombs while flying combat missions. For a while, their deaths depressed the morale of the squadron, but the pace of operations soon put the tragedies behind us. The consequences of war, though, stayed with me.

At Takhli, I sat in on maintenance and intelligence debriefings of many pilots after returning from combat missions. I was astonished at the bravery of these fighter pilots and how many relished the adrenaline high from the dangers in their profession.

I returned home to McConnell in December 1965 and, five months later, received an assignment to a squadron in Germany that flew F-4D Phantom IIs. It was the first of several assignments supporting F-4s, and I never returned to working with the Thunderchief. I came to recognize, however, the differences between the close-knit culture of the pilots and support people of F-105 units and those who flew and supported the far more numerous "Double Ugly" F-4. This awareness stayed with me during my twenty years in the Air Force.

After I retired in 1983, I linked up with two authors working on a book of F-105 photos (*Roll Call: Thud*) and volunteered to develop a history of the Thunderchief for them since neither had worked with the aircraft. Over the next several years, I tapped into primary sources at

215

the Air Force Historical Research Agency at Maxwell AFB, AL. My F-105 history work became recognized by retired F-105 pilots who invited me to their reunions. My history research expanded as I wrote stories they told me. My interest in F-105s has stayed with me for nearly forty years. It has produced five published books on the Thunderchief as well as seven articles in history journals, all based on the F-105's operational history.

***

Books

- *F-105 Thunderchiefs: A 29-Year Illustrated Operational History,* McFarland & Company, Jefferson, North Carolina, 325 pages, 2001.
- *Fighting Cavaliers: The F-105 History of the 421st Tactical Fighter Squadron 1963 – 1967,* with co-author Jeff Kolln, self-published using Amazon's CreateSpace, 415 pages, 2018.
- *Pack Six Blues: The Diary of an F-105 Thunderchief Pilot,* self-published using Amazon's Kindle Direct Publication (KDP), 214 pages, 2020.
- *All F-105 Thunderchief Losses, Vol. 1: 1955 – 1966,* self-published using Amazon's KDP, 311 pages, 2023.
- *All F-105 Thunderchief Losses, Vol. 2: 1967 – 1981,* self-published using Amazon's KDP, 378 pages, 2023.

Articles

- *"Takhli August to December 1964,"* Air Force Museum Friends Journal, Winter 1994.
- "Ozark Lead is out of the Aircraft," *Air Power History,* Spring 2005.
- "The Rest of the Story: Wild Weasel Exhibit," *Air Force Museum Friends Journal,* Winter 2005/2006.

- "Radar Bombing During Rolling Thunder – Part 1: Ryan's Raiders," *Air Power History*, Spring 2006.
- "Radar Bombing During Rolling Thunder – Part 2: Combat Lancer and Commando Club," *Air Power History*, Summer 2006.
- "When the Thunderbirds Flew the Thunderchief," *Air Power History*, Fall 2009.
- "Thud Out: Saying Farewell to the F-105 Thunderchief," *Air Power History*, Summer 2020.

*****

Author: W. Howard Plunkett

W. Howard Plunkett is a retired Air Force Lieutenant Colonel. His twenty-year career as an aircraft maintenance officer began with F-105s in 1964. For the past twenty-seven years, he has researched the history of the F-105 and provided details of F-105 operations to many aviation authors. He lives in Albuquerque.

LÉONIE ROSENSTIEL

Military Patterns

Mama (Annette Rosenstiel), a petite Greer Garson look-alike, was the one who served from 1943-46. She supervised a censorship unit of 1,000 WACs [Women's Army Corps] in Port Moresby, New Guinea, during the waning days of World War II. The whole unit earned a commendation for cracking codes that a few soldiers had attempted to conceal in their letters home. Considering that only 5,000 WACs served in the Pacific Theater, Mama, then a lieutenant, had been the officer directly supervising twenty percent of them. Her military career ended with a supervisory stint at the Port of New York, after which she retired as a captain.

Her stories about tropical New Guinea — its giant, venomous spiders and snakes, its fruits then uncommon in the US, twice-per-day downpours, and extraordinary people — entranced us all. She never told us much about her most painful experiences. Based on Mama's papers that I eventually inherited, she seems to have suffered from PTSD [post-traumatic stress disorder] for the rest of her life. That diagnosis did not exist back then, but the symptoms did. On-going anxiety. Headaches. Bouts of insomnia. Competitiveness at inappropriate moments. Jumping when hearing loud noises. I am equally convinced PTSD played a part in Mama ending up in a commercial guardianship for almost nine years at the end of her life. It was a time when both of us suffered greatly.

Not until I sat down to think about how the military, in general, affected my family did I realize that military actions (and even contemplated actions) affected us all, regardless of where we lived or whether we served down through the centuries. Even those family members for whom I do not have any direct proof that it affected them,

218

I remain convinced that it did. I know these experiences affected me, even though I never served.

I was born in the United States, not in Russia or France, because of the military. One of Mama's great-grandfathers came from Austria-Hungary. All other members of my mother's immediate family had all been born within the boundaries of Imperial Russia. Her father's family consisted of her grandparents and their five sons. Her maternal grandparents had three sons and three daughters.

After 1825, all Russian-born males between the ages of twelve and twenty-five were subject to twenty-five years of military service. If they happened to pick you up before age eighteen, they only started counting twenty years after you reached eighteen. Theoretically, eldest sons were exempt from conscription, but even so, parents always had reason to worry. Bureaucratic "mistakes" often resulted in eldest sons being conscripted for the same twenty-year hitch all others served. Sometimes, the authorities accepted payment to redeem one or more male children from military service. However, buying freedom for too many sons might cost more than a family could afford. Most conscripts died before they completed their obligation to the czar.

My mother's forbears tried to get their sons to the United States before they reached draft age. Except for Mama's father, who seemed to travel back and forth to Europe under several different names, and claiming a new profession and age each time. He told us that, at least once, he had to escape from exile in Siberia to get to the States.

For my father's paternal great-grandparents, the War of 1870 determined their future. Both branches of Dad's French family ended up in the United States.

Salamon Rosenstiel, Dad's great-grandfather, and his family, sympathizers with the social reforms of the Paris Commune, escaped the Siege of Paris after it fell that June. They took refuge in Belgium. While in exile, they all renewed their commitment to remain citizens of France, even signing papers to that effect. The documents also confirmed that they were then in Belgium.

They had no warning that Salamon, the slender, brown-haired family patriarch, then forty-four years old, was about to be sentenced, in absentia, by the Paris Tribunal. French law assumed guilt. Salamon got five years in a penal colony at hard labor. That would likely have been a death sentence for someone his age. And sometimes, they sent the families away with the convicts.

Word of the sentence reached them. The whole family had escaped the Massacre of the Communards in Paris. Now that Salamon had been convicted, they would be subject to deportation to the French penal colony in New Caledonia if Salamon returned to France.

They hid in Belgium, keeping the names of all family members from appearing in any street directories. They must have realized that if they stayed in Europe, they would eventually be found.

In 1874, Benjamin, their eldest child, would turn eighteen. He needed a profession. If he were going to make a living, he would need to list himself as a tradesman in a street directory somewhere. At twenty, as a French citizen, he would be required to register for the French draft anyway. That meant that he would have to declare his next of kin and their location, thus alerting the authorities to the location of the rest of the family. All of them chose to flee once again.

The whole family traveled the more than 500 miles to the port of Stettin, then in Germany, where the authorities were not likely to search for a family that was supposed to be in Belgium. Then too, any pursuers would not expect them to make their escape, as a family, on a cargo ship, so that was exactly how they emigrated.

They declared that their last place of residence had been Belgium. Salamon seems to have traveled under an assumed name and lied about his age.

Salamon himself never returned to Europe. He sent his wife back there on an errand once, using the German name of his original home province (Elsass) and changing both of their first names slightly to give the passport office the impression that they had both been German speakers, born in Germany, not France.

Benjamin started a business making ornaments for women's hats. He had already become a US citizen, but he wanted to return to France for a visit and to buy the raw materials. Before obtaining a passport, he had to obtain a special pardon for his draft evasion from the French consulate in New York.

Benjamin's wife, whom he met in the States, also came from an Alsatian family. She never ceased to tell people that the German Army had turned her family out of their home during the War of 1870. "She was so upset that Gaston [her younger son] married a German girl as his first wife," Dad used to tell me.

The published prison sentence had named Salamon Rosenstiel from Alsace as the convict, but Benjamin had been born in Paris. To deflect attention from his family's Alsatian origins (and hence a possible connection to his father, the convict), Benjamin kept insisting that his family had originated in Paris, not Alsace. That was the story that Dad had inherited and the one that he passed on to me.

My paternal grandmother's birth father was Dutch, and her mother English. If they had any direct military reason for emigrating, I never discovered it. Her stepfather had been born in Alsace. Although a naturalized US Citizen, he was also patriotically French. He did not arrive in New York until 1884.

My Alsatian-American forbears all joined French fraternal and paramilitary organizations, continuing to contribute to French causes all their lives. By 1888, Salamon, the convict, had become the Commander of the Grenadiers Rochambeau, leading them for the New York Bastille Day festivities. My father shared their love of the military and of their adopted country. Dad told us that he sold $1,000,000 in war bonds during World War I. (That would equal more than $22.3 million in 2023.)

Dad looked a lot like Salamon in his youth. He was raised bilingual. Culturally, he was half-French, half-American. He met my mother in a French-speaking social group during World War II. She was multilingual and an award-winning French teacher at the time.

I do not think Dad knew exactly why his family had to leave Europe, except that it had something to do with the War of 1870. At least, that was what he told me. Dad inherited his family's papers in 1936 after his father died, but I later realized he did not have all of them.

Not until 2023 did I find, among centuries of family documents that I had by then inherited, the one pardoning Benjamin for his draft evasion. Dad must have known about that because he kept the proof, but he had kept it secret. He had never spoken to Mama or me about his grandfather's draft evasion. I found out about Salmon's prison sentence through research, so I doubt that Dad ever knew about it.

I wish he had told us about Benjamin! It would have explained a lot. Dad registered for the draft on September 16, 1940. Before that, he had joined the ROTC [Reserve Officers' Training Corps]. He had even started taking a formal course enabling him to join the artillery as an officer.

My parents married in August 1943, when the WAAC (Women's Auxiliary Army Corps) was merging into the regular Army to become the WAC. All previous enlistees were asked to sign up again if they wanted to continue to serve.

Dad had just been reclassified as "available for military service," category 1A. He had a brother, so there was no reason why he ought to expect to get a deferment. He told Mama that he might be drafted at any moment. Mama decided to reenlist, placing herself on a service path that eventually led to the Pacific. Her experiences there induced her to change careers and become an anthropologist.

Meanwhile, Dad suffered through many sleepless nights, waiting for the call-up, trying to get his affairs in order before he would need to leave for basic training. He was devastated, some months later, to be rejected for service. He took to his room, and my grandmother said he would not come out, eat, or talk to anyone for days. Dad said, "I simply couldn't face anyone. They didn't classify me 4F [registrant not qualified for military service], either. They just refused to draft me.

Your mother was serving. My friends were serving. Why wasn't I serving? I felt so guilty!"

Why indeed? It turned out that Dad had grown up in Harlem. Although the draft board never mentioned this to him, all the draftees from Harlem were automatically assigned to Black units. Dad was White.

Dad had friends with flat feet, and other problems, then referred to as "physical defects." They had been given 1A-limited draft status and then assigned to desk jobs. But no, the draft board simply rejected him. He was inconsolable. It was years before he realized that America's across-the-board policy of racial segregation in the military had dictated his rejection.

Dad's inability to serve during World War II was the ultimate family irony. His grandfather had evaded service and then needed permission to rejoin polite society. Dad had badly wanted to serve but was not allowed to do so. He, too, felt that he needed a pardon, but he had no idea where — or how — to get one. Perhaps Truman's integration of the military in 1948 was Dad's equivalent of his grandfather's pardon.

It was easy to understand why Mama's family came to the States. I am still healing from the pain of knowing why Dad's family really came here and what it must have cost them all to keep those painful secrets for more than a century.

*****

Author: Léonie Rosenstiel

Léonie Rosenstiel cared for her mother, Annette, for nine years. Annette had supervised a 1000-Woman's Army Corps censorship unit during World War II. Léonie's book *Protecting Mama*, describing Annette's years under commercial guardianship, won First Place in the 2022 New Mexico-Arizona Book Awards.

EARL W. RUGEN

Cathy's Clown

saw a friend the other day
didn't have that much to say
    Army, Navy what's the use
    patriotism our excuse
drank a beer and reminisced
about the girls we never kissed
    he stayed here and I went there
    did our tours without a care
he rode the waves the Navy way
worked in a galley every day
    I crewed a chopper, fixed it too
    French Indochina without a clue
I had some trouble coming home
isolated, all alone
    drinking, smoking, drugs abound
    went to hell, then came around
now we sit, the sun goes down
he a man and I a clown.

Sally II

we came in fast

    on the double

L.Z. Sally

    there was always trouble

sometimes Viet Cong in the wire

    most times Sally was under fire

our cover fire was always good

    101st Airborne, knock on wood

load the wounded then off again

    if we lost a man it was our sin

we tried to do our very best

    but every day was one more test

lay down at night and start to pray

    then wake up to another day

*****

Author: Earl W. Rugen

Earl Rugen was a proud member of the US Army's 571st dust-off helicopter ambulance unit in Vietnam from 1968-1970. He is a member of the VA Creative Writing Group at the Raymond G. Murphy Medical Center in Albuquerque.

LYNNE SEBASTIAN

The Silver Dollar

They left White Oak at daylight, two men on horseback riding down the narrow track that crossed and re-crossed the creek bed a dozen times between the head and the mouth of the holler. Barely visible in the heavy fog that filled the narrow mountain valley, one was a man in his mid-forties, lean and work-hardened after years of wresting a living from a worn-out hill farm; the other was a boy just turned nineteen. Their black curly hair and strong, regular features marked them as father and son.

At the mouth of the holler, where the creek flowed into the south fork of the Kentucky River, stood a rundown general store. It wasn't open yet, but the old man who ran it was just turning two cows into the farmyard so his wife could do the milking. "Mornin', Ned," he called out.

"Howdy, Hargis," the older horseman replied, "how air you farin' this mornin'?"

"Oh, a touch of the rheumatiz," the old man said, "but hit'll git better onct the fog lifts. So, you're goin' to the Army, are ya, Ernest?"

"Yes, sir," the boy replied.

"Well, you-uns better git down and come in. I'll have my old woman fix ye a bite of breakfast."

"Thankee, Hargis, but we've done eat, and we'd best be gittin' on."

"Well. You be careful out there among them flatlanders, now Ernest."

"I will, sir."

The two rode on, following the river north toward its confluence with the north and middle forks of the Kentucky. As the light grew stronger, the fog began to lift, revealing the small farms and pastures dotting the rich bottomland. Finally, the sun broke through, lighting up the extraordinary living tapestry of reds and russets, yellows and golds and browns that marks the Appalachian autumn. The boy had hoped for a different future — college and a career as a forest ranger, roaming these hills as a caretaker for the magnificent old-growth trees and the creatures who lived among them. But the year was 1939, and the grinding poverty of the Great Depression had extinguished the dreams of both young and old here in the mountains.

They stopped around midday to water and rest the horses. Sitting on the trunk of a fallen chestnut tree, they shared the lunch of cornbread, country ham, and dried apple hand pies that the boy's mother had packed. After a while, they remounted and, leaving the river valley, took a steep and winding track that crossed over the mountains into Estill County. It was midafternoon when they rode into Ravenna, the nearest town on the L&N [Louisville and Nashville] Railroad line. The boy exchanged the chit that the Army recruiter had given him for a train ticket to Covington and a bus transfer to Fort Thomas. The Cincinnati-bound train was due in about half an hour. They sat on a bench under a tree across from the depot while the horses dozed in the shade.

After a long silence, the man looked at the boy and said, "Ernest, you're goin' out into a world that I've never seen and don't know much about. I've studied on what I could do to help ye along the way, but I just don't have anything much to give ye. This is the best I could do." He reached into the pocket of his bib overalls and pulled out a bright, shiny, nearly new silver dollar. "I want you to take this, son, and put it in yer pocket. And you keep it in yer pocket and don't spend it, just carry it with ye. That way, if you was to ever git into a bad place, I'm hoping this might be enough to help ye out. Now promise me you'll hold on to this dollar."

227

Knowing too well what it must have taken for his father to scrape together a whole dollar to give him, the boy felt his eyes grow moist, and he said, "I will, Dad; I promise I'll hold on to it."

The train arrived with the screech of steel wheels on steel track and a great gush of acrid coal smoke. The boy shook hands with his father, hugged the neck of his brown mare, and handed the reins to the older man. "Don't let Virgil ride her," he said. "He's too rough with horses."

His father managed a crooked smile and patted his shoulder. The boy picked up his worn knapsack and climbed the wooden steps to the platform. The conductor pointed out his coach. The boy lifted his hand in farewell, and then he was gone. The older man watched until the train was out of sight. Slowly he mounted his horse and, leading the mare, started on the long ride home.

The boy was as good as his word. Despite many temptations, he kept that silver dollar in his pocket through basic training and two years of active duty. After Pearl Harbor, he carried it in his pocket on the troopship across first to Iceland, then to Scotland, then, by train to southern England, where his Coast Artillery regiment trained for the invasion of France. He carried it in his pocket across the Channel and onto Omaha Beach a few days after D-Day. He carried it through the hedgerows of Normandy and the breakout at St. Lô.

He carried the dollar in his pocket through the liberation of Paris, the air defense of Antwerp, and the Battle of the Bulge. He had it in his pocket when he and his crew hauled their 90 mm antiaircraft gun across the badly damaged Ludendorff railroad bridge at Remagen and helped to fight off the desperate Luftwaffe efforts to destroy this last intact bridge over the Rhine. And he had it in his pocket when he and his comrades reached the Elbe River, deep inside Germany, where they were ordered to wait for the arrival of the Red Army.

Ernest and the silver dollar both survived World War II, mustering out of the Army in June of 1945. He briefly returned to the mountains of eastern Kentucky to try to comfort his mother over the death of her

Viv came around the corner out of the locker room, checking her smart-watch, and almost walked right into the guy.

Oh. Dear. God. Stunning, crystalline blue eyes. At least six foot three inches and all definition, bulk muscle striating all that caramel skin. Not over-done, though. She just bet there had to be an impressive eight-pack under that black tank. Viv had to swallow, hard.

He put out his hand to her for a shake. "Mike Ramos," he said simply.

She didn't take his hand right away. She watched him while she made him wait. He didn't flinch or retract his hand one bit. His intense blue gaze remained tightly fixed on hers.

When she joined her hand with his, the tiny strawberry-blond hairs on her forearm rose. An exhilarating warmth zipped up her arm. She looked on, and apparently, the same thing was happening to him.

"Vivian March," she whispered, in awe of what had just transpired. She eased her hand away from their clasp.

He crossed his amazing arms over his amazing chest. "Vivian, let's get coffee."

Viv was stuck to the spot. She didn't know what to say. She had to admit to herself that there was a definite physical pull, but he was all wrong, totally wrong — angry Vet. Hands off.

"I. Ah ...."

He didn't move. Didn't withdraw.

"You're not right for me." This was so awkward.

"What?" His left brow rose. "Because I'm brown?"

"No," she said with vehemence.

"The missing leg?" he asked, raising the knee of his prosthetic.

"Hell, no!"

"Too many tattoos?"

"Oh, no," she said, in a voice much smokier than she'd intended, trying to stifle a grin.

He reached up and moved a stray tress off of her forehead. "It's coffee, Viv, not a marriage proposal."

"Okay, okay. Where are we going?"

He held the gym door open, and she stepped through. "To my place, of course; I've got my own Espresso machine."

She pivoted and nabbed him with her disapproving gaze, only to find him grinning.

"Kidding! To that coffee shop." He pointed at the cafe across the street.

Smart ass, she thought. But he'd made her smile. He totally got points for that.

As they crossed the street, they stopped a couple of times to avoid a few cars. Then stepped up on to the curb to the side entrance of the coffee shop. He seemed to struggle a bit with his prosthetic. She wondered how recently he'd been injured.

When they were between the two sets of dark brown glass doors, Mike stopped and pulled her to him. The hand holding hers disengaged, and with sure fingertips, he caressed up her arm, leaving tiny chills in their wake. All movement came to a stop when he palmed her cheek. Then looking into her eyes, he lowered his mouth to hers, slowly. Giving her the chance to stop him. God help her, she didn't. This was *so* not her.

The touch of his lips, hot and soft, soothed and excited at the same time. And just when she was totally with it, totally aware of what was really happening, he pulled back.

"There, now we don't have to think about how or when that first kiss is going to happen — it's done," he said with a mischievous grin.

"What? Oh, okay." *That sounded so lame.* Things were moving too fast. At the same time, she couldn't help imagining how far down did those amazing tats go?

She followed him up to the barista. He ordered a black coffee. When he moved aside to give her the chance to order, she stepped up to the counter and ordered an almond milk latte with hazelnut.

As they walked over to the far side of the counter to wait for their drinks, Mike kept his hand at her lower back. She had mixed feelings about that. His proprietary gesture kind of bugged me, but at the same time, the warmth of his hand was ... nice.

An older man who just claimed his coffee stopped and raised his hand to shake her companion's. "Thank you for your service."

She felt Mike's hand drop from her lower back and his body tense beside her. He took the guy's hand for a shake and nodded, but didn't say anything.

She led them to a booth, and she sat before he did, giving her an opportunity to see his face. His expression was tight, and he looked miserable. She reached for his hand and took it in hers. "What's wrong," she asked.

"Nothing," he said. "Drink your coffee." He looked down into his, dismissing her.

Oh, no. Not going to happen. She sat up, leaning toward him, gripping his hand more firmly. "I don't really know what's going on here." She made a movement with her free hand, pointing at him and then back at herself. "But I won't be shut out or dismissed. So, if you want whatever *this* is to continue, *don't* do that again."

His expression went through several rapid-fire changes. First, scary irritated, then morphed into contemplative, ending with his eyebrows pulled down to pure curiosity.

"Okay. But I'm not talking about my deployments."

"Fine. Don't want to hear about them," she responded, taking a sip of her coffee. The creamy and sweet hazelnut flavor flowed across her tongue. "What *do* you want to talk about?"

That wicked grin covered his full mouth again. "I want to talk about how I'm going to get you in the sack."

She laughed at that. "Slow down, Ramos. You can start with being straight with me and not being an asshole."

"Sounds easy."

"Not as easy as you may think." She looked at her watch. "And all that will have to wait for another time. I've got commitments."

He sat back and studied her, question in his gaze.

"What?" she asked, putting the stir-stick in her mouth.

"You're not looking for a wedding dress and kids any time soon, are you?"

"Not in my plans at the moment." But they were definitely in her plans.

"Good."

"Let's go then."

"Kay." She finished her coffee and slid out of the booth seat, securing her gym bag over her shoulder.

He felt awkward disengaging from the booth with his damn fake leg, but it seemed to work without too much fumbling.

Walking back to the gym parking lot, he stopped at his car to pull a flyer from under the wiper.

"You're the one with the black Charger?" she asked with excitement. "What year is it, sixty-eight or sixty-nine?"

"Sixty-nine. You know cars?"

"A little. My dad used to restore classics." She smiled real big at him. Made his heart thump.

"Can I get in?"

"Sure." He tossed her the keys. Her eyes lit up like a kid in a toy store. He loved that.

As Viv scrambled into the driver's seat, he went around and got in next to her. Her enthusiasm was contagious.

"Start her up."

She looked over at him with her eyes alight with excitement. "Really?

"Sure."

She carefully put the key in the ignition and turned her over. The car's finely tuned engine roared to life, then settled into a seductive rumble. She leaned her head back, and the look of delight on her face was amazing.

This was more than wonderful. Viv was smoking hot; she knew her way around the gym; she knew cars and didn't take his shit. He turned to look at her face, and she was staring at him. Staring with that captivating look in her eyes.

He swallowed, and gently grasping her elbow, he tugged, pulling her toward him. She slid across the bench seat, until their thighs touched.

Bringing his palm up to her cheek, he held her there as he sought her mouth. He sipped at the side of her lips and then covered her mouth with his.

His mouth watered as he explored the soft, warm recesses of hers. Her arms twined around his neck as her tongue sparred with his.

She gave as good as she got.

Holy Christ!

***

This is the first chapter of a novel of hope and redemption, available on Amazon in digital and paperback formats

https://www.amazon.com/War-Within-Wounded-Warrior-Romance-ebook/dp/B08VH9S4RH/

*****

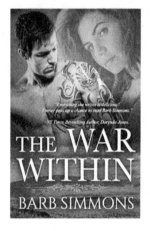

Author: Barb Simmons

Barb Simmons is an award-winning author of romantic fiction and the proud daughter of Lieutenant Colonel John L. Simmons, (Retired) Judge Advocate General's Corps, United States Army. Growing up a Military Brat back and forth between Germany and the DC area was the best.

TED SPITZMILLER

Joining The Army: A Critical Decision

With the Cuban Missile Crisis of October 1962, I looked more seriously at the possibility of being drafted into the Army *soon*. In those days, most young men were obligated to serve in the military in some form. My first thought was the Air Force, and I went down to Montclair, New Jersey, to interview the recruiter. Because I wore glasses, there was no thought of being a pilot, which had been my primary objective as a young boy. I was not impressed with the opportunities, and as the Air Force required an enlistment of four years, I decided to see what the other services offered. Four years was an eternity at the age of nineteen.

The Navy was also four years, and they pushed the nuclear submarine program hard. I was attracted to the obvious civilian job that might follow, such as a reactor operator. However, the first year for those who enlist in the Navy was performing undesirable menial jobs aboard ship before they sent you to a technical school, and there was no guarantee what type of training that might be. So, I ended up visiting the Army recruiter. The Army only required a three-year tour, and they were the only service that would guarantee the specific school for which you enlisted.

I ended my discussion with the recruiting sergeant by agreeing to take the Armed Forces Qualification Test (AFQT), which would determine what career paths might be open to me. I was a bit leery of the testing process as I had not paid much attention to my studies in high school and had graduated at the bottom of my class. However, I was more than pleased when I returned to the recruiter for my test scores a

239

week later and discovered that I was eligible to choose any program in their several hundred-page catalog.

The recruiter was much more animated now that he had a *live one* on the hook and was pushing the Army Security Agency (ASA). These are the guys who, among other tasks, listen in on the communications of the bad guys. But he noted that I would probably have to attend a language school. Having had a difficult time getting through high school English, I looked to electronics.

I was working as a draftsman for the year and a half since graduating high school and thoroughly enjoyed it. Having drawn mechanical and electrical layouts, I had been exposed to these funny squiggly electrical symbols that made up schematic diagrams. Also, I had often been told by many *in the know* that the future was in electronics. However, I didn't have much confidence in my intellectual abilities — the AFQT scores notwithstanding.

One Military Occupational Specialty (MOS) — as the various jobs were called — was a fourteen-week school that led to an MOS of '250', which was a Guided Missile Electronics Technician. What sold me was the location of the school — Redstone Arsenal in Huntsville, Alabama. This was the location where the Army had developed the Redstone missile that became the basis for both the Jupiter-C (that launched our first earth satellite) and the Mercury-Redstone (that flew our first American astronauts to the edge of space). I tentatively applied for that school and took the next step, which was to go down to Newark and undergo the military physical exam. This was completed by Christmas of 1962. I gave little thought that this would be my last Christmas at "home," or in New Jersey, for that matter.

With the beginning of the New Year, I wrestled with the decision, and by mid-February, I signed the enlistment agreement. This was followed quickly by a letter from the US Army with a legal-looking paper that was my guarantee of the school. But it also ended with the phrase "... and will then be assigned in accordance with the needs of the

Army." Essentially, they would provide the schooling but then do with you what they wanted. Fair enough.

I told my boss at the company I was employed (G-V Controls Inc.) of my decision, and they were supportive. They also had a guarantee that they would provide me with a job on my return to civilian life three years hence. I selected mid-March for my induction because I thought the cold weather would be over and I would be done with the two months of basic training before the hot weather began. G-V gave me a nice send-off party and two gifts — a ditty bag and a very nice Parker ballpoint pen (which I still have). Not having done much travel (essentially none) during my life, I really didn't know what a ditty bag was for. Of course, it was one of the most practical gifts I would receive over the years.

I put my car up for sale, as I was only halfway through the "easy" thirty-six months of payments. As I was to earn only $69 a month initially, there was no thought of keeping the car, and there was no equity in it — so I would be without wheels for quite some time.

The morning of March 14, 1963, found me going about the mundane details of breakfast and performing perfunctory goodbyes to my mother, brother, and sister. I had planned on taking the No. 29 bus to the induction center in Newark, but my friend John Sidvers offered to take me down and provided an old gym bag for my meager belongings (the ditty bag and some underwear). He dropped me off at the Induction Center, and we said our farewells. He noted that I could throw the gym bag in the trash when I no longer needed it — that saved the postage.

I knew I was starting a new life at this fork in the road. It was an exciting prospect that held many unknowns. However, it was probably one of the best decisions of my life. I successfully completed the electronics course. Because the top half of the class was sent to advanced schooling, I went to Sandia Base in New Mexico for six months of added training as a Nuclear Weapons Electronics Specialist (MOS 304). (They must have been holding the class list upside down.) They apparently made the same mistake again with the class list when I completed the

MOS 304 training, as I was retained as an instructor in the course I had just completed for the remainder of my enlistment. With that experience on my resume, at the end of my enlistment in 1966, I was able to secure employment with IBM [International Business Machines Corporation], where I learned the ins and outs of computers. March 14, 2023, marks the sixtieth anniversary of my enlistment in the Army.

Ted Spitzmiller receiving a Commendation Award for outstanding performance as an instructor in the Field Command, Defense Atomic Support Agency, at the conclusion of his enlistment in the US Army on March 11, 1966, from General Brown. Note the Naval Captain to the left, reflects the fact that all military services received their nuclear weapons maintenance training at Sandia base during the first thirty years of the nuclear age.

***

A few comments on the military service. A new study from the Pentagon shows that seventy-seven percent of today's young Americans would not qualify for military service without a waiver. It states that the most prevalent reasons for youth between the ages of seventeen and twenty-four were for being overweight (eleven percent), drug and alcohol abuse (eight percent), and medical/physical health (seven percent). A total of forty-four percent were disqualified for multiple reasons. I am more than a bit shocked and concerned that so few of today's young men and women can qualify to serve in the military. What does this say about our culture and our educational system?

*****

Author: Ted Spitzmiller

Ted Spitzmiller's military training in the Army served as the basis for a career in computing while earning a BS and MS degree. He has been a Flight Instructor for over fifty years, earned the Federal Aviation Administration Wright Brothers Master Pilot Award, and published seven books and 100 magazine articles on aerospace topics.

DALE SWETNAM

Gabriel

Dexter (mall security) switched from one monitor to another. On one monitor, he could clearly see Brenda, a security floor walker, strolling through the mall. There was nothing exciting about that, so Dexter switched monitors again. Something caught his eye. He called out to Mel, "There is a suspicious character wandering about in the parking lot."

Mel was at his desk, shuffling paperwork. Without looking up, he answered, "What's he doing?"

"He's looking at cars. Wait! Now one has caught his attention." Dexter became more focused. "He's gonna mess with someone's car!"

Mel looked up from his work, leaned over so he could see the monitor, and watched the "suspicious" character get in the car and drive away. "It's his own car. He was wandering around because he forgot where he parked." Mel turned back to his work.

Dexter frowned in disappointment. "Looked suspicious to me."

"Everything looks suspicious to you."

Dexter switched to a different camera. "That bum is coming inside."

Mel was annoyed with the distractions. He had work to get done. "He's harmless."

Dexter grumbled, "He makes the mall look bad."

"Is he harassing people for spare change? Is he doing anything wrong?"

Dexter watched diligently for something to accuse. "He's walking up the mall."

Mel glanced up from his work. "Shut up, Dexter."

Dexter switched to another camera. "Uh oh! Here comes Nancy."

Mel didn't look up. "Nancy?"

"Ron's wife ... the smoke shop." Dexter smiled with excitement. "They're gonna have another big fight."

***

In the smoke shop, Ron had Herb (an employee) rearranging displays. Ron was lecturing Herb on the importance of "image" when he looked up to see Nancy coming in. "Crap," he muttered, and his mood got noticeably worse.

Nancy was apprehensive. "I called the realtor about that house."

Ron's answer was short and dismissive. "Nancy, I'm working."

"We have to talk about this," she insisted.

Ron turned to Herb. "Watch the front. I'll be right back." He took Nancy by the arm and led her out of the store to a mall bench, where they sat down. "Okay, why the hell can't this wait till I get home?"

Nancy raised her voice, sharp and stern, "You won't talk at home! You won't talk at work! We need a permanent home to raise our son."

Ron squirmed on the bench and looked around to ensure they weren't drawing attention. He didn't want to make a scene. "We've talked! You're just a broken record repeating the same thing over and over! You know I need that money to open another store."

"One store is enough," she said. "Our family is more important than another store."

Ron snapped in an attempt to terminate the conversation, "Nancy, don't bother me at work anymore!"

"If you don't care about family, I won't be bothering you anymore at all!"

"What the hell does that mean?" Ron asked as he watched Nancy leave in a huff, then he got up to return to work. He didn't notice that sliding forward on the bench had pushed the wallet out of his pocket, and it remained on the bench.

Meanwhile, Gabe (the bum) — long beard, britches worn thin, a sprinkling of gray in his dark hair — strolled casually up the mall. He sat on the bench, crossed his legs, and leaned back … quite content with his lot in life. He noticed the wallet and picked it up rather curiously but did not look inside. Gabe looked about, stood up, and walked straight to mall security as if he now had a mission in life.

Shortly after that, while Brenda made her rounds, a voice came on her walkie, "Brenda."

"Yeah, what is it?" She answered.

"Could you come to the office?"

***

Dexter was still fascinated with the monitors when Brenda walked in. Mel was at his desk with the wallet. "Gabe found a wallet," he said. "Looks like it belongs to Ron at the smoke shop."

Brenda anticipated, "And you want me to …."

"Yeah," said Mel. "Could you take it to him?"

"It still has money in it," Dexter added. "It might be a trick."

***

Herb was helping a customer when Brenda entered the smoke shop. Ron greeted her, "Hi, Brenda," he said. "Have you decided to take up smoking?"

"Not today," she said with a smile, and she handed him the wallet. "Is this yours?"

Ron took the wallet while feeling his back pocket to find it empty. "Thank God," he exclaimed. Examining the wallet, he found everything intact, including his money. "Where was it?"

"I don't know," she shrugged. "Gabe found it."

"Gabe?"

"The bum that hangs out in the alley." She smiled as if proud of herself for having participated in a good deed. "I'm sure he could use a nice reward."

"Yeah, sure," said Ron. "I'll give him something."

***

Gabe was digging in a garbage bin in the alley behind the mall. He picked up something, looked it over carefully, then tossed it back. That's where Ron found him. "Are you the one who found my wallet?" he asked.

"Huh? Oh yeah, it was on a bench."

"I'd like to give you a reward for turning it in," said Ron. He tried to hand him a twenty-dollar bill.

"I don't want it," said Gabe. "Thanks."

Ron was confused. "You don't need money?"

"No. I had money once, didn't do much for me." Gabe glanced back into the garbage bin.

Ron was surprised that Gabe was more interested in garbage than money. "You had money?"

"Yeah, I was a stockbroker ... very successful." Gabe paused with a distant gaze. The turn of the conversation brought back a flood of memories. "And I had a wife and a handsome young son."

"Where are they now?" Ron asked.

Gabe turned back to the garbage bin. "I don't need anything."

Ron started to walk away, but Gabe suddenly called him back. "Wait," he said, "there is something I want."

Ron turned back. "What is it?"

"I want you to buy me lunch."

Ron pulled the twenty back out of his pocket. "This should cover it," he said.

"No," Gabe pulled back to refuse it. "I want you to *buy* me lunch, not the money."

"You want to have lunch with me?" Ron frowned. To him, the request was absurd.

"Yes, that's what I want."

Ron was speechless, obviously distressed. He searched his thoughts for an excuse.

"You don't want to be seen with a bum?" Gabe asked.

"It's not that," Ron stammered. He paused, still searching for something non-offensive to say. "It's just … business, you know, it's all about image."

"I understand," said Gabe, and he returned to digging in the garbage.

Again, Ron turned to walk away, but a guilty conscience pulled him back. "I'll be having lunch in Rodrigo's at twelve o'clock. See you then?"

"I'll be there."

Ron gave it a second thought. "Make that one thirty."

***

In Rodrigo's restaurant, a snooty waiter handed out two menus. He kept to Ron's side of the table while staring across at the bum.

Gabe had washed his hands … the only clean part on him. "I don't have any glasses," he said, laying the menu down. "What's the most expensive thing on the menu?"

The waiter smirked disrespectfully. "That would be steak and lobster, $37.50."

Ron raised an eyebrow, then was quite relieved when Gabe answered, "Okay, I'll have a bowl of soup and some hot bread with plenty of butter."

The waiter turned to Ron. "And for you?"

"I'll just have coffee," he said. "I already ate."

Ron kept watch, fearful that an acquaintance might enter and see him lunching with a bum. There was an awkward silence. After the waiter served the soup, Ron made an attempt at conversation. "So, you were a stockbroker?" Ron asked.

"Yeah," said Gabe, "and I was a Marine when I was young."

"Where was home for you?" Ron asked.

"Home?" Gabe looked at Ron blankly. "Spent one tour in the Marines when I was a teenager. Went to some awesome places … places I otherwise would never have been able to go. Had a great time, but all the time, I was busy seeing the world; the only thing I really wanted was to go home."

"You gonna want dessert?" Ron asked.

"So, I served my time and returned home. Or I thought I was going home. My brothers had married and moved out. My friends I'd hanged out with before … I don't know, guess they were off somewhere living their lives."

Ron called out to the waiter, "More coffee, please."

"Everything had changed," Gabe continued. "I had changed. I was a stranger in my parent's house. So, I finally got it."

"Got it?" asked Ron. A fellow businessman entered the restaurant. Ron turned away, hoping he wouldn't be noticed. "Got what?"

"Home is not a place. It's a time of life," Gabe explained. "Grownups might live in houses, but only children have homes."

Ron thought on that for a moment, then, "Is that why you don't have a home?"

Gabe was silent while he spread butter on a piece of bread, then laid the knife back down. The butter melted quickly on the warm bread. "They were killed in a car crash."

Ron was confused for a long moment, then finally asked, "Your wife and son?"

"I busted my ass in the stock market." Gabe tipped up his bowl and drained the last few drops of soup into his mouth. "If you have someone you care about, you want to provide. Without them, money don't mean so much."

"So, you dropped out and walked away?" Ron asked while sipping his coffee. "If you had a family, you'd still be busting your ass?"

"I wanted a good home for my son," Gabe answered. "A home don't mean much of nothin' to me, but, to a child, home is everything."

Ron gave Gabe a suspicious look. "Have you been talking to my wife?"

Gabe asked, "Is your wife a sixty-year-old lady who saves leftovers for me on weekends?"

"No," said Ron.

"Well then, no, I haven't been talking to your wife." Gabe wiped his mouth and gave his full belly a pat. "Okay, I'm done," he said. "Thanks." Gabe got up and left without further comment.

Ron returned to his shop. A customer was leaving as he entered. Herb had the displays laid out just right. "That looks great," Ron noted. "Not too busy this afternoon. You can take off early if you want." He didn't have to say that twice. Herb was out the door by the time Ron finished speaking.

Ron picked up the phone and called his wife. "Nancy, why don't you go ahead and call that realtor? Make an appointment for us to look at that house … okay, sure … yes … I love you too."

As Ron hung up the phone, Brenda walked past the door. She noticed Ron, turned back, and stepped inside. "Did Gabe like his reward?" she asked.

"He wouldn't take it."

"He didn't want the reward?" She was quite surprised.

"He didn't want money, so I bought him lunch," said Ron. "Did you know he was a successful stockbroker?"

"Really?" she asked. "How do you know that?"

"He told me."

"Yeah," said Brenda. "He told me he was a dentist." Through the doorway, Brenda caught a glimpse of a boy dropping a skateboard on the floor. He was just placing a foot on it when she ran out the door. "Hey! Hey!" she screamed. "No skateboarding in the mall!"

*****

Author: Dale Swetnam

Dale Swetnam is a veteran of the US Air Force, trained in the maintenance and repair of navigational computers. He has made use of that experience in the personal computer industry and is now retired and using his free time to enrich the world with a few stories of fact and fiction.

JASMINE TRITTEN

When Life Turns

Sometimes life turns in a completely different direction than expected for unexplainable reasons. It happened in 1987 after I had left Carmel, California, for a glamourous job as an art consultant in an upscale art gallery in La Jolla, hoping to make more money.

For one whole year, I bathed in luxury, expensive clothes and an apartment close by, within walking distance of the beach. I practiced five languages I knew well from growing up in Europe. Some clients lived in exquisite mansions in Beverly Hills. Part of my job was helping them decorate the walls of their gorgeous homes with high-priced paintings ranging from $5,000 - $150,000.

However, during lunch hour one fateful day, my charmed life stopped — as if the universe had other plans for me.

As I walked in the bright sunlight on Girard Street, between palm trees, swinging a paper bag with my sandwich, the face of a young man appeared in front of my eyes for one second. Then everything went pitch black. Next, I lay semiconsciously on the asphalt in a puddle of blood that stained my green silk blouse. An ambulance was right there to drive me to a nearby hospital. In moments of clarity, I remember wailing, "I want to go home!" But the paramedics convinced me to continue toward the emergency room. I had a deep cut on the back of my head, a severe concussion, and a broken tailbone. Not a wishful situation for anybody.

When I opened my eyes, I found myself in a hospital bed with my head wrapped in gauze like a mummy. *Is this a dream or a nightmare?* My whole head throbbed, and I thought it would burst like a balloon. The moment I attempted to raise it from the pillow, the room started to spin around, and the disinfectant smell sickened me. Slowly I lowered my head back down with a trembling chin. An agonizing pain shot through the lower part of my spine and sacrum the second I moved my legs. I hurt all over. *Help! I feel trapped inside my body! I am suffocating! What am I to do?* I let out a whimper. Then I remembered from yoga class how to breathe in air through the nose and breathe out through the mouth to take away attention from my aching body.

"What happened to me?" I asked the doctor, who suddenly stood next to my bed.

"A bicycle hit you," he said while bending over the railing.

"How and where?" I gasped.

"A young man raced his bicycle, with the speed of cars, down a perpendicular street to Girard Avenue, where you walked. Out of control, unable to make the turn with the traffic, he jumped the curb onto the pavement and knocked you down from the front," the doctor continued. "You fell backward and hit your head and tailbone on the pavement with great impact."

"Oh, my God!" Tears rolled down my cheeks in streams. I sobbed when I realized the seriousness of my situation and felt sorry for myself. I could have screamed. *Every cell in my body hurts, and I am all alone.* I thought I was going to die.

My whole life was in jeopardy. I had left Carmel for a better job in La Jolla to make more money, and here I lay one year later, unable to move without a loved one next to me. *Is this karma? What is the lesson here?* I certainly had no clue. *Could it be that I do not need to focus on making money? Why is this happening?* But the universe had a plan for me.

The extra-long recovery time ahead made it impossible for me to work the glamorous job at the Gallery. After five days in the hospital, a lovely couple I had met through my neighbors offered to take care of me in their home for two weeks, feeding me and helping me to the bathroom. Barely was I able to stand on my feet. Returning to my apartment became a considerable challenge. I felt isolated but had a telephone. Hardly any people owned computers then, and iPhones did not exist. Friends from the art gallery brought me food.

This was a tough time, even for a Danish Viking woman. I used to be like a rubber duck, and you can duck me under, but I will pop back up again. However, this time the popping up took longer. Turning to my faith and asking for daily help to get through was the only thing left. So, I prayed and cried — and prayed and cried until I had no more tears.

Luckily, the art gallery owner waited for me to return to work and paid me a small monthly salary. But three months passed, and I still got terrible anxiety at night and when crossing any street. I had no choice but to leave La Jolla and return to Carmel, where I received support from my family and friends.

A fellow I knew offered to pick me up in La Jolla and drive me back to the Monterey Peninsula with my stuff in the back of his covered truck. Bless him. Grateful and sad simultaneously, I waved goodbye to the challenging and stimulating life in the jewel of Southern California. Seven and a half hours later, I arrived in Carmel Valley in a daze.

Friends helped me get settled into a beautiful room with a bathroom of a house next to the rippling Carmel Valley River. The house belonged to an elderly carpenter who lived alone and needed immediate assistance because of a knee operation. In exchange for the room, I took care of an enormous vegetable garden and vacuumed his house once a week. *What a perfect way to heal my body and brain.*

Sitting on large stones next to the stream, listening to the water bubbling over rocks, and watching trout climbing up the rushing creek, soothed my soul and spirit. Under enormous eucalyptus trees, I sat praying and meditating. Family and friends provided the love and emotional support I needed.

However, I went into a severe depression. For the first time in my life, I succumbed to seeing a counselor who told me the accident counted as a loss and that I had not yet grieved my father's death. Until I processed that loss, I would be unable to resolve my current situation.

Stunned, I told my younger son Brendon of the sad discovery. He immediately suggested,

"Mom, how about going to one of the twelve-step programs? It's free and might help you!"

Reluctantly, I dragged myself to a meeting for adult children of alcoholics. Not because I wanted to but only because of not want to disappoint my son. Throughout the session, I sat with my arms crossed in a protective huddle without saying a word. At the end of the meeting, one of the attendees asked if anybody had a burning desire to share something before closing. *In my heart, I know if I don't tell them my story, I will never return.*

So, I raised my trembling hand and spoke of my father's alcoholism and subsequent suicide. Words tumbled in my mouth. Tears flowed out of my eyes. The people in the group handed me tissues. After I finished and sat down, everybody in the room thanked me. *I cannot believe this! They all thank me for sharing something I have been ashamed of all my life. I always thought they would not like me if I told anybody what happened to my dad. Instead, they express gratitude. Wow!*

Later, I told Brendon about the meeting, and he cheered,

"Great, Mom! Try to go to three meetings in a row." He frequently functioned as my private counselor.

Following Brendon's advice, I continued the meetings and learned to speak openly, sharing my feelings and thoughts with people I trusted. The tears continued to flow for months. Since my dad's passing, I had only cried on the inside. Now, liquid seeped out of my body. At least I made progress. The sessions helped me to process my past traumas. *If only these self-help programs existed in Denmark while I grew up. They could have helped my dad cope with his alcoholism, and he might have survived.*

Every day I sat by the rushing river in the afternoons. Peace and harmony filled my soul and gave me strength, hope, and inspiration to start again. Fate brought me back to Carmel Valley, into my inner self, where God resided.

The vegetable garden boomed with greens. I enjoyed planting seeds, tending to the plants, and reaping the benefits later, sharing them with my landlord. Recovery became a slow process, but I improved day by day. There was hope, and my depression subsided. Light shined at the end of the tunnel.

After receiving a lump sum of money from the insurance company of the young man who hit me, I bought with cash a blue Hyundai car and a blue massage table. I signed up for classes in Carmel to become a massage therapist. While soothing and healing my injured head, I could finally make money again. Not as much as in La Jolla, but I was alive. Somebody from above looked after me and guided me.

I attended three twelve-step meetings a week for one year and a half. Finally, one day I said to a friend, "I have now resolved my father's death, my first marriage, and my accident." Two weeks later, I met my prince, my soulmate, a Navy officer who was just about to retire from active duty, and we have been happily married for thirty-two years.

Therefore, when it seems like life has turned for the worse or even disastrous, there might be an underlying good reason for it to happen. If I had not experienced the accident, the pain, and the suffering and returned to Carmel Valley, I might not have found my inner self and resolved my past. As I reflect on this turn of experience, I also recognize I would never have been prepared and ready to enter the most dynamic relationship of my life. For this, I am forever grateful.

*****

Author: Jasmine Tritten

Jasmine Tritten is an award-winning author. She has authored numerous short stories and has published three books. *The Journey of an Adventuresome Dane,* a children's story *Kato's Grand Adventure* with husband Jim, and a memoir *On the Nile with a Dancing Dane.* Jasmine is the wife of a veteran.

JIM TRITTEN

Adjusting to New Realities

I crashed a military airplane in 1979. It only took a few seconds, but the near-death experience would unequivocally and permanently alter the rest of my life. Relationships with my family, work, and my view of myself would never be the same.

Post-Traumatic Stress Disorder (PTSD) was hardly even a fragment in my imagination at the time, so I did not seek counseling, nor was any sincerely offered by anyone. Military medicine was embarrassingly negligent in 1979. A series of unexplained symptoms increased in severity until a highly stressful incident in 2008 brought all my past unresolved issues to a head. I fell into a tailspin, was unceremoniously retired from all work, and was given a psychological disability. I was in total crisis — unable to function in society.

I became a professional patient and sought explanations for what was going on with my body and my mind. After considerable one-on-one counseling, I received a diagnosis. The good news: we know the problem. The bad news: PTSD is a mental illness.

Until you've experienced being diagnosed with mental illness, you have no idea how society treats us. If you only read about the symptoms and the effects in the *Diagnostic and Statistical Manual of Mental Disorders* (DSM), it really doesn't do justice to the impact of the changes we are forced to deal with.

So, imagine yourself running errands alone one fine afternoon, and you see someone you know well — a leader in your community known for their political activism. You watch the individual make eye contact, only to look away and avert their eyes quickly. He ducks into his car, starts the engine, and drives off. Then picture this person as a man of color wearing a clerical collar.

But *I* don't need to imagine. Such an event happened to me, and the only thing I imagined later when I was processing what happened was that maybe I should wear a sign, "Don't worry, PTSD isn't contagious."

Successfully dealing with mental illness on your own is simply *not* possible. It's no more manageable than walking on a broken foot without a crutch.

Following a total meltdown in 2008, I sought help from the Department of Veterans Affairs (VA). But being able to crack the nut of making a case with all the necessary documentation, being correctly classified, approved, and then be scheduled for treatment wasn't an easy task. Getting seen by the VA would take more than a year. In the meantime, I discovered the National Alliance on Mental Illness (NAMI) and took advantage of their support groups and classes.

I transitioned from the initial diagnosis to being part of a new club. I learned what to do next with the aid of excellent clinicians, a well-developed VA program, and peers who volunteer with NAMI. I left my first prescription on the shelf for a month before mustering the courage to take that first pill. I knew that my life would never be the same again once I did that.

With help, I learned the path leading to a predictable and better end state. I mastered coping skills, gained knowledge, grew to tolerate medicines, and changed my environment. Group therapy allowed me to see fragile souls blossom as they meet like-type individuals who suffer the same judgment by society, friends, and family. These folks still deal with unjustified inner shame and share hope for a better life.

I discovered there are "underground" support groups where veterans go who don't want PTSD on their work records. I empathized with them and told my story of being first diagnosed in 1993 and hiding the branding so I could continue to work. That is, until the meltdown. I showed them the results of not seeking treatment. The choice is theirs. At the time, I did not understand the choice.

I write for therapy. I don't want to write about my trauma, and I don't want to write about the negative aspects of my diagnosis and treatment. Instead, I focus on humor and enjoy it when I write a piece that can make others and me laugh. I learned a lot from the VA about emotions. First, to recognize there are emotions other than anger. Second, to describe what happens inside me when I feel different emotions. The last bit is tricky — I have learned to write words that will cause the reader or listener to feel the emotion I felt. I have mastered how to do that using only ink on paper. I started off writing things that made me and others laugh. I now write about things that lead the reader to feel every emotion I have felt while dealing with my diagnosis.

I share my story with vets and non-vets alike. I know it's customary for vets to say no one other than another vet can understand the challenges of military service, but I differ with that opinion. I've obtained excellent care from mental health professionals who've never been in the military or crashed an airplane. I've also learned from individuals diagnosed with various mental illnesses that have nothing to do with PTSD. But they all face the same issues I've encountered, like being shunned by people I know. We debate whether keeping old friends or making new ones is easier.

I have volunteered my time to lead support groups for individuals with all types of mental illnesses. I learn from them, and we help each other. My volunteer activities included entering the high-security mental health units at a county jail and maximum-security prisons. Incarcerated patients in my support groups include my fellow vets — both men and women. Not everyone has what it takes to do volunteer work inside a jail or prison. It is an excellent opportunity for most vets who have what it takes in that environment.

We discuss issues common to anyone with any mental illness. How to get family support, and what to do when help does not come? How do we define recovery? Who else has stopped taking their medicine and not told anyone? Will this PTSD ever go away? How best to process the trauma?

We live in a country where there are finally excellent tools to deal with PTSD and sound programs to reach all veterans who are branded with this diagnosis. The VA and NAMI are both organizations that offer hope to people like me who need to be shown the road to recovery. With help, recovery is possible — and I define recovery as being able to function as well as possible, given the cards I've been dealt. No, my world is not the same as when I could work, let alone when I was a Navy carrier pilot. My new environment is smaller and less complex. And it involves working on my diagnosis every day for the rest of my life. My new reality.

***

Thank you for your service

When US military service members returned home from Vietnam, they were often shunned, spit on, or discriminated against when trying to obtain work. At best, they were ignored for many years and even mistreated by some veterans from World War II — our Greatest Generation. In short, most were not welcomed home or thanked for their service.

The safest course of action was to take off the uniform, stash it in a sea bag or put it in a dumpster, hunker down, and pretend like you never even saw a war movie, let alone thought about serving.

Decades passed, and the social fabric of the nation changed. Many of those who screamed in protest, "Ho, Ho, Ho Chi Min, Ho Chi Min is gonna win," and applauded Hanoi Jane, at some point began to focus their feelings about the Vietnam War into profound disagreements with political decisions and decision-makers. Feelings about the war or politicians were one thing. Feelings about the soldiers, sailors, airmen, and Marines were another.

Many finally realized these men and women were either drafted or volunteered to do what they thought their country wanted them to do in Southeast Asia. As time progressed, there was an apparent national guilt about making the ordinary service member the scapegoat for a war they did not cause, did not understand, but were willing to commit to support as a member of the US Armed Forces.

What was society's new response to American service members? To try to make amends for past insults, veterans today are routinely thanked for their service. All military veterans sign a blank check to give, if needed, their lives, their bodies, and their healthy minds as part of their service in the armed forces. It doesn't matter if they serve in combat, stateside support missions, or in a multitude of small wars. Today's veterans receive a different and justified response from society.

As one who had eggs thrown at him while doing recruiting duty during the Vietnam War, the change in society's view of service members was, and sometimes still is, hard for me to comprehend. As one whose mother was told at work that her son was a baby killer and they hoped he died, I could not grasp why her fellow newspaper reporters would take it out on one of their own for my standing up for my country and doing what I thought was the right thing. Right up until she passed at ninety-nine years old, she still had mental scars from those verbal assaults. What did she ever do to deserve being scorned?

"Thank you for your service." How should I respond to that? I understand it is an attempt to say the right thing, to atone for past behavior, but is it appropriate? Some older veterans do not know how to respond.

I, for one, appreciate the gesture, the offers of special discounts for veterans, for recognition, as a way to make up for facing the crowds on college campuses as draft-deferred students ruined my uniforms with their more than vocal assaults at a different time when military service was not appreciated.

"Thank you for your service" — I always smile and say, "Thank you."

At one point in my life, I wrote the nation a blank check. There was, and is, no expiration date on that check. Millions of young men and women have written that check.

Our nation needs to have the ability to cash those checks when necessary.

"Thank you" for appreciating my service.

*****

Author: Jim Tritten with wife, Jasmine

Jim Tritten is a Navy veteran who flew airplanes off aircraft carriers. He lives in Corrales, New Mexico, with his Danish author/artist wife and two cats. Jim writes for therapy.

LAWRENCE TRUJILLO

In The Night

The night is still
I am restless once again,
A fire burns deep inside me
And has for so long.

I think of my life and its worth
And wonder why it even matters,
Contributions come to mind
No longer mine, who cares.

My journey has been intense
A road with many curves,
Which led me to my wife
My soul mate for life.

Alas! There is beauty in my life
And my life is priceless,
My contributions have been many
They will last forever,
Until the end of time.

Time is for the living
Because of the love of a good woman,
I am alive and life is good
And the night remains still.

War Child

Today, life has new meaning
I am a Soul Survivor
History repeats itself
I'm on a warrior's sojourn

First a child to war
Then a man of war
Now a man of years
Back to the child, with tears

War child, where have you been?

I've been over the water
To the Land of the Dragon People
I was tested in the jungles
I was tested on the ridges

I went prepared to die
I left dead
A joyous return to family and friends
I was still dead

War child, where have you been?

I laid you to rest, buried forever
Alas, you existed in the nether
Exalting in the freshness of new life
Content in the *aether*

It became him
You became me
Taker of life
Giver of life

War child, where have you been?

He creeps out at night, volatile
He's unpredictable, short-tempered
He's no stranger to me
He is blind, he is me
He is PTSD

You think you can kill him
But he doesn't die ... ever
You are the PTSD
You are at journey's end

War child, you're home.

*****

Author: Lawrence Trujillo

Lawrence Trujillo is a US Marine Corps Vietnam combat veteran.

VICKI A. TURPEN

Military Moments in a Marriage

Knowledge and wisdom bring joy and livelihood. Sometimes others seem to make wrong decisions for us. In 1955 America was in the Korean "Conflict." Later the TV comedy M*A*S*H depicted the real brutality and chaos from our memories and friends who served. I was grateful for the humor and reality depicted in the series. We had learned so much from that fight.

A freshman at the University of Kentucky, I was loving school, not "looking for a husband." Then I met Michael Kelly Turpen. From him, I learned to love music and treasure our challenging democratic republic. We were soul companions for sixty-five years.

I was a theater major, the female lead in an Irish play, *The Unanimous Lover*, when Mike suddenly appeared at rehearsal. Struggling with my Irish brogue, I resented his ease in portraying an elderly Irish gentleman. Our director told me Mike's best friend had dropped out, and Mike was delighted to step in. Our friend said with a twinkle in his eye, "Mike wanted to meet you."

I wasn't dating. Mike called every day. On Saturday, we explored the white-fenced plantations in his Chevy convertible, where Man o'War of Kentucky Derby fame resided. That spring day, there were hundreds of birds everywhere. He sang to them, and they answered him. His Grandfather Kelly taught him how. Then he held my hand, singing "A Kiss." I was smitten.

All summer, I lived with my mother in Louisville. Mike worked construction and lived with that same friend. My parents divorced. My father told me, "I will no longer pay to keep you in college; get a job." That was not my plan. As a freshman, I had volunteered to sew costumes. As a sophomore, I was awarded a work fellowship to design and execute costumes for all university performances.

Mike and I shared life. We took up a *Lexington Herald* newspaper route. We ate my meals at the student union or with his family. We created a dozen sandals for *Amphitryon 38*, 30 robes, and four knight costumes for *Murder in the Cathedral*. We "made out" in the green room. Evenings at his house, we did homework. We discussed Plato and Aristotle and worked around a young English teacher who worshiped Moby Dick. Mike knew, "Four pages were wasted describing a whale."

One snowy day he bought me a ring saying, "This is our 'ammunition.'" Mother didn't like Mike. Throughout the summer, we had danced to big bands. On Saturday nights, Mike sang at a piano bar by the Ohio. Mother hated the beer drinking and partying. Having gone through a horrible divorce, fear clouded her mind. The engagement ring made Christmas a harmonious occasion.

I had a delightful time creating costumes for *Tea House of the August Moon* that spring. A lovely native Japanese woman told me that when Dolittle dropped the bombs on Tokyo, they thought it was their planes. She fled to the mountains with a sack of potatoes and a sack of money, dropping one on the way. Fortunately, it was the money. Together we made costumes for the natives and a geisha girl.

I gained inspiration from the scene designer's beautiful floating tea house and his comments that his three years on Broadway were not as rewarding. In *Tea House,* Mike was cast as Old Man Omira. His father came to the performance and afterward asked, "I thought Mikey was in this play. Where was he?" Mike, the born actor.

Mike, however, was not mentally into college. As a radio major, he sluffed off. In high school, he won awards, certificates, and first-place music, speech, and debate honors. He sang opera at colleges. He organized a barbershop quartet singing Christmas carols at the department store. Mike was committed to a summer wedding but not to class work.

I knew beer and cigarettes were mental and physical health problems. Cartons of free cigarettes were everywhere, and too many parties. That was one reason I had stopped dating. Except, we didn't party. We worked hard and talked a lot. His mother had graduated Phi Beta Kappa from a small college in Virginia. His dad, as superintendent of schools, had a doctorate from Columbia. Much was expected from Mike. I asked him, "What have you been doing?"

He answered, "Looking out the window, worrying about my grades." He had just gotten up in speech class and made comments, never prepared an actual speech. In fear before the final, he stayed up all night preparing. After his speech, Dr. Ernie, our friend, said. "Mr. Turpen, please meet me in my office after class."

There he said, "Mr. Turpen, if you could have blessed us with a wonderful speech all semester, why did you waste our time? You didn't respect the class or me and use the intelligence you are capable of. You failed yourself and us. Expect a large fat 'F' for Public Speaking."

Mike flunked out that semester and would be drafted into the Army. Our forces in Korea were facing floods of Chinese communists coming over the border to join the opposition. Many young men were being thrown into harm's way. Others left the United States and went to hide in Canada. Some stayed there, giving up their American citizenship. We had friends whose husbands, sons, and fathers had been wounded or lost their lives fighting with the South Koreans.

Protestors and students around the United States demonstrated against our involvement. The "conflict" was being promoted as the worldwide spread of Communism. Mike and I talked, thought, and reasoned. Mike, a history buff, read a lot. He admired patriots fighting for freedom, the *Bill of Rights*, and the *Declaration of Independence*. He didn't want to be drafted and go to Korea, nor would he ever have crept into Canada. He wasn't sure our present "conflict" had been a wise decision for America. My commitment was to him; Mother had made a lace wedding dress. Would there be a wedding or not? I held my breath.

Sad, amidst his self-inflicted failures, he stumbled to the recruiting office. Wonder of wonders, instead of being drafted, he could experience a different gift from our military, commit to six months of active duty and then seven years of two-week summer camp. We talked. We could schedule our marriage for the short leave after basic. He could experience army life and see if it challenged him. That six months would bless both of us. He would share his money with me. I would go back for my junior year.

That next Saturday, I helped pack his duffle bag, adding a *Bible* and inspiring literature I was studying. We hugged and kissed. Then I sat crying on a park bench. On Monday, I interviewed and got a part-time job at the university career office.

At Fort Knox, Mike was immediately assigned troop leader. He became a confidant of his black sergeant. They were the only men there who had been to college. After four weeks of running twenty miles daily with a backpack, Mike lost thirty pounds; he was all muscle. He found a married Lexington friend. They agreed to share gas when they had passes.

The army changed Mike. His life view and personal experiences were from a small box. Yes, he had all the opportunities promised by the constitution, education, and encouragement, along with love and commitment from his parents. He had the ability to use ideas to reason his way through problems. In the army, he discovered those were gifts not given or used by all young men and women.

He began chewing on words like patience, selfishness, compassion, empathy, and integrity. He had acted out those words on stage. Admitting his own shortcomings now, he was having to deal with a different existence. The elitist protection he had enjoyed in Lexington, Kentucky, was not at all indicative of the world. He experienced a new birth in admitting his own sins and recognizing those of our society.

One night he listened as one kind trooper read a letter another man received from his wife. She and their two children were not getting the army checks, their only income. There was no money for rent or food.

Mike took the husband aside and gently explained that all they had to do was share the mistake with the sergeant and perhaps the chaplain. The army would send the back pay and begin sending her checks. Mike told me the young man looked frightened and did not seem to believe or understand anything he heard.

Before Mike could catch the sergeant or the chaplain, the young man went AWOL [Absence Without Leave] and was arrested and put in prison. It was hard for Mike to admit that some of the men under his command could not read or reason with logic and intelligence to protect themselves.

Mike spent a lot of evenings talking to his sergeant, a kind and thoughtful man. Their personal experiences growing up were quite different. However, they both had loving parents and valued education. Mike just did not understand why the sergeant treated the black members of the troop differently than the white ones.

Mike asked him, "Why are you harder on those of your own race than the other men?" The sergeant explained, "Because life for them will be more challenging. They must be resilient, more determined to achieve, and be respected. Even with all their freedoms, they must prove themselves repeatedly." Today social norms and even religious circumstances can insert unjust barriers to the life of any man or woman. Humans still have a hard time loving each other; often, it has nothing to do with race.

Mike excelled at the shooting range. He loved guns as creations of mankind through the centuries. He knew their history. It made him mad if the movie prop used was the wrong gun for a scene depicting history. He loved hunting and collecting arrowheads with his relatives in Virginia.

Wedding invitations went out. The event was at Duncan Memorial Chapel, Oldham County, Kentucky. Our wedding cost $173. A week before the wedding, Mike called crying, in a panic. He had the symptoms of strep throat. The summer before, he had spent over a week in the hospital with the disease. The doctors would put him in the infirmary; he'd miss his own wedding. I called him back and told him to go pray with the chaplain.

The chaplain at Fort Knox was a Christian Science Practitioner and teacher. Mike and the chaplain prayed together for several hours. The next morning the symptoms were gone. No one else knew. As planned, we were married on Saturday, the third day of September, nineteen fifty- seven. Mike's sister, a coloratura soprano, sang the Lord's Prayer and the youth minister from his Methodist church declared us man and wife. There was such joy.

The next week Mother and I drove him back to Fort Knox. Mike sang "A Kiss" for her, and I knew he was embraced in his mother's heart. He formed a barbershop quartet, and his assignment was managing the fort gymnasium, handing out equipment, and scheduling games. His paycheck and mine just barely covered our rent, utilities, and minimal food.

In 1959 we both enrolled at another university, and Mike was in the honors program every year. We graduated in 1969. Our invitations declared, "The Turpen Children invite you to the graduation of their parents." All five children watched with our parents, and then we all went out for Mike's favorite, Chinese food.

*****

Author: Vicki Turpen

Vicki Turpen was the wife of an Army veteran. She lives with four of her five children on an intentional family farm in the south valley of Albuquerque, New Mexico. She has a Master's in Education from The University of New Mexico. She taught Junior High and High School theater, English, and speech for twenty-two years.

KL WAGONER

Dressing the Dead

My sister and I clutched plastic bags stuffed with the remains of an old soldier's pride as we rushed across the windy parking lot to keep our appointment with the mortician.

In the past week, we had arranged for the casket, music for the service, photos for display, motorcycle escorts, military medals, and ribbons, but I couldn't shake the feeling we had missed something.

My sister stopped me short of the entrance.

We had forgotten the socks. Yes, we both agreed, they were important. Any pair would do as long as they were dark. Thankfully, we had dropped off our father's skivvies the day before.

She left me on her detour to the store, and I pushed through the double doors of the mortuary into a place hushed by heaviness.

Soft lights, serene paintings, and a room full of patterns gentle to the eye were instantly alienating. Here was an elegance I was unaccustomed to, stiff in the classic cut of impeccable furnishings and unnatural neatness. The surroundings were meant to comfort but instead brought a reminder of the dividing line between life and death, the difference between wishes and reality.

Hours seemed to pass as I waited alone on the edge of an overstuffed couch, and time waited with me.

Then my sister burst through the entry doors and paused to gaze around the room. She handed me a bag filled with a dozen pairs of socks. My sister — the ingenious one who could build a boat out of a spool of thread — hadn't been able to decide on such a simple thing as a single pair of socks. She had bought dark blue and black, stretchy and stiff, smooth, fuzzy, and cozy warm. But I understood her dilemma. What would look best with a dress blue uniform? Did it matter if the socks weren't military issue? Since we hadn't found the dress shoes, we decided the uniform wouldn't be the deciding factor. Warm socks would do; the cozier, the better. We didn't want our father's feet to be cold.

An undertaker appeared and, with gentle sympathy, ushered us down a long hall to a solemn grey room void of decoration. He left us alone with our father, who waited on a polished stainless-steel table, naked except for a pair of baggy, white skivvies.

This was not the first time we had stood in an icy room with a loved one between us, determined to do what most considered bizarre. Years before, we found comfort in doing the same for the one who gave us everything, including life. Again, it would be our honor to smooth hair from a face insistent on sleep and dress the outer shell — an expression of final tenderness in this less-than-gracious world.

The long-sleeved shirt slipped smoothly over fingers touched with an edge of shadow, skin that was cool but not cold, firm but not stiff. He fought us as we rolled him from side to side while we pulled his pants over knobby knees and bony hips until, at last, he crossed his legs. That hollow place might never have heard such laughter. With him lying there relaxed and enjoying our plight, we knew he approved of our efforts.

The jacket was more difficult. The problem wasn't the uniform. It still fit more than thirty years after the last time he wore it. And we couldn't really fault our father. We were young children again trying to force clothes onto an unwieldy Ken doll and worrying that the stress on the shoulders would be enough to pop them out of joint. We finally gave up and asked for help.

The undertaker returned and nodded his understanding. There was an art to it, he said, as he stepped up to wrestle with the dead. After he won the battle, he wiped the sweat from his forehead, worked a proper military knot in the tie, and left us alone again.

It was done, and we still had time to touch our father's hands and face and stroke his hair into place. This wasn't a last goodbye — how can you say farewell completely to someone who won't let go? Instead, it was our gift to him and to ourselves. The physical had passed away, but we held on to that superficial silhouette for as long as possible, perhaps because there wasn't much else to cling to.

Our mom had taken the heart of the family with her when she left us for a world without pain. Loving her had been easy. And we knew without a doubt she loved us in return, evidenced by her absolute acceptance of us no matter how huge our mistakes were or how often we made them. She had faults — she had to have — but we never really noticed.

On the other hand, our father was the no-laughing-at-the-dinner-table kind of Father. He handed out the same harsh punishment for spilling milk as for talking back. The kind of drunk who forgot where he dropped his car keys but always remembered where he hung his belt and how to use it. He was the opposite of our mom; his love conditional and impossible to earn. Still, his death left another unfillable hole.

As a child, I wanted to believe he loved me. Aren't Fathers supposed to love their children? But now, time had run out to hear him express what he never had before. Now I was completely incomplete.

The next day, I endured bagpipes playing "Danny Boy" and the melancholy bugle call of "Taps." I flinched each of the three times a sharp military salute cracked the sky. And, as expected, the ground swallowed my father whole.

But it wasn't until later that night, when his friends paid tribute to the old soldier they had dearly loved, that I faced the truth and the lie. The women called him "The Kissing Angel." The men dressed him in humor, in the gold braid of a kind and gracious heart, in the pressed uniform of honor and loyalty. His buddies said, their voices breaking; he was the kind of friend you could always count on.

I listened to every word of praise, unable to say a word myself. It was difficult enough to realize I never really knew my father, but knowing he bestowed precious gifts of himself on others was the most devastating of all.

Even so, I knew what life would hold from that moment on.

My father would stand beside me every time I saw our nation's flag or heard the first notes of "Taps." I would recognize him daily, reflected in my need for perfection, in my own stubborn tendencies. Though he would never let me go, I resolved to be to my loved ones what he had never been to me. When the end comes, I don't want my children to see me — unrecognizable — dressed in a stranger's clothes.

*****

Author: KL Wagoner

KL Wagoner is a veteran of the US Army, as well as the Navy Reserves. She writes short stories and novel-length works of fantasy and sci-fi. Kat will publish *The Last Bonekeeper*, book one in her dark fantasy trilogy, in late 2023 or early 2024. Visit her website at klwagoner.com.

REGINA WASHINGTON

VETERAN

(Very Energetic Touching Every Rank And Nation)

We are strong!

We do no wrong.

Advancing in rank!

Driving the tanks.

Keeping all safe;

In so many ways.

We won't back down!

Taking them to the ground.

You won't hear a sound.

We won't be bound!

Courage, we got.

Bragging we're not.

Only keep marching on!

That's our song.

*****

Author: Regina Washington

Regina Washington, a caregiver, has earned a master's degree and is presently working towards a Ph.D. She loves; education, music, sports, and meeting people. She has trained many others in the mediation process. She's a former member of the International Critical Incident Stress Foundation. She enjoys reading, writing, and cooking. Socializing is an important part of her life.

DAN WETMORE

Images of ICBMs

[26 Jan 1994 - letter to my fiancée, a month into pulling nuclear alerts]

Dear Lynne,

Four-oh-nine of an Ante Meridian, uncomposed and uncomposing on the vertical screen of a SACDIN [Strategic Air Command Digital Information Network] terminal, blue flashes of shrimp lightning swimming straited paths 'cross an electric bay; with me in a grotto that hisses, the sibilance of air angry at being buried alive, mazed through machinery to be breathed by it, desired or no. Hour to shave approaching, Rip Van Winkle up from nap in a curtained closet within another, procrastinating the mundane.

The stretching of this silent time, its excruciatingly syrup flow, brings me wonder that — for every hour you and I have been, done our every thing — that *beyond, below*, there has been somebody pacing these grim spaces, where the chairs are on rails and the coffee pots are shackled fast; paper insurance against the earthquake of incoming ICBMs [Intercontinental Ballistic Missiles]. Every heartbeat, breath, glimpse, texture — the unknowing, the quiet, the timorous, the radiant — each and every has been matched in stride and fall by a bleeping light or a burning indicator; cyclopses of status and standing.

That overwhelms me, daunts all the hopes I never realized I had to be free of measure and shadow. I like to think, I have to *believe*, that we don't owe all our meandering moments to these tethered ones. Otherwise, all those remaining would seem spent in an eggshell much like this one – strong yet unresilient, to which all the king's horses and all the king's men could not put shoulder.

I won't — because I can't — see it so. So I'll look it another way. And strive to see past the day when all our movements are matched by this lurking stillness in barren seeds of stone that refuse growth in the womb most fertile of the world. Only of poorly aping males could this all be.

And I'll strive to live past the time when the tether is taut; when the leash is released and spade of sane nature turns out these tumors to shrink and bleach in a withering warm sun, and God laughs the boom of his sixth sense; the release of breath held so long in wait for denouement in this play on this stage.

I'll live for seeing times unknown, turns of the card, not just the clock. Because while the waiting is the hardest part, a wake would be a parting harder. And maybe that's undue passion, and maybe that's corny, but I'll cry it out before drying all other tears.

Thanks for hearing me, my sweetie.

***

[Summer 94 –
Chris Jarko and I heading to nuclear alert at
Launch Control Center D-01]

The road to Delta has much dirt; slow miles that allow appreciation of the sunflowers that grow in much of it. They stand in rows, a congregation of yellow heads facing east, bowed and stirring in the light of the burgeoning day. All through its passage, those copycat orbs will pay homage, moving en masse to follow their namesake in its trajectory across the wide Nebraska sky.

We, the mobile, turn our attentions in that direction as well, moving across prairie to sequester ourselves in the house of the sun, dug deep within the earth.

Plants and planters do service to the same force, differing merely in the names assigned their deities. Flowers toil in the light of the sun, we in service to sundered atoms. Each seeks the security of that warmth, whether it be as rejuvenation or fortification. And both join in the strange, shifting dance.

Perennials at play in the open breezes crane ever upward, petalled moths to a flame that rides the rim of heaven, but themselves rooted fast, grounded by other gravities. Boys at work, embracing the thermonuclear, wrap themselves in its brilliant shield, yet are wrapped 'round in the chains of a reaction that holds them hard to one course.

One seeks union and can know only distance, while the other knows familiarity and cannot reclaim estrangement. Yet both need the uncomfortable orientation. Without a separation of the searing from the stalk, or the overwhelming from the mundane, vitality would seep away. And without the orange brilliance that hangs from the clouds, or the potency swaddled in its skin of steel, demise would seem assured.

If intimacy is ultimacy, then we are at destination. But an ultimacy of no intimacy colors ground zero as — instead — merely point of departure, leading to conclusion that we are on a map of Möbius as we wend our divagating way through the seemingly flat-ribboned wilds of Wyoming, the nether lands of Nebraska, from which the flowers around us rise, waving our passage in the low animating currents. Whether in kindred greeted, or urged adieu to the foreign and frightening of the affrighted, we cannot tell.

***

Acquittal in Accusation

A cow stared at me as I was going to field today.
Not the passing glance or errant glimpse
of a bovine at its business,
he gave me the full attent of his wooly face,
beady peepers following me long
down the gravel at the mandated 35 miles per hour.

I, en route to provide
the guarantees of WW III,
was shaken from the mundane reveries
which attend that business.

Cow's look was simple and staid,
saying, in the well-grounded insight of them,
"You are but farmer to me;
straw-brimmed, cover-all'ed plodder.
You are all but farmer to me,
plant what seed you may.
In all your boxes, you are still simple men."

There are no blinks in a cow's repertoire,
just eyes closing to dismiss your sight
and terminate the instruction.
And I think the edge in those steely holes
was meant derision,
but I felt it acquittal,
and passed quieter.

- Aug 1996

***

[late summer 96 –

returning to base following 24 hours attending the base]

Outside Albin, westering into burgeoning day, the blue box of an ironic and apt Chevy Suburban crawls past the Friendship Baptist Church where "Everyone is Welcome." Presumably even two blue-suited boys, fresh from the stale confines of a perdition's depth. But stopping's not an option of haste, so on, past the wrought iron script naming the Cemetery Epworth, then its anteroom of a church; stone, one room, sitting every bit the cathedral of its quarter acre.

Out where there's not much, not much is something, and it draws your eye to avid searching. Even to reading the faded tattoo on a windmill's vane: AERMOTOR COMPANY — CHICAGO.

It gives a jolt, contemplating — from the remove of this place's seeming torpor — that one's bustle. In search of an association, superposition shimmers like heat mirage. A sea of rippling grasses abutting bluffs of pine bleeds into semblance of an oceanic lake lapping at precipices of steel and glass, and you've shorted the distance, with wonder that humanity's first self-sustaining atomic reaction, in a converted squash court there under the bleachers of Stagg Field, would ripple so far afield.

So I have to wonder, watching Albin's bunker-from-the-beyond's-worst recede in rearview: If its inhabitants' invitation were put to test … who would pass? If even we slinking Shivas — flouting the holy spirit of creation — would be allowed safe passage through that portal. By the Pater; His patrons; or two dusty prodigals daring without hope, but too tired not to try.

***

The Unbearable of Lightness Being:

A Catenary Tale

I sit keeper of a thread-tethered sun,
star still in waiting,
overdue luminary impatient to its work
to shine o'er all, revealing.

Bright charge, withheld heavens it would home,
pleads needs of nature to rise and survey.
The buoyance of tonnage belied by repose
seeks birthing in the void.

But I hold its flame, deny ascent –
thought higher purpose of lower beings,
frustrating the flight earth-born and -bound
would call its catenary.

Yes, a dim soul here in depths' remove,
I am but clod of this earth,
who – blind to brilliance's station –
do backward count it better

to dark the light of a cursing candle
than illume a single countenance
by the glow of passion's creation's
creation of our passing.

- Fall 1996

***

[27 Jan 1997 - journal entry, pre-empted by notice of a pending
power interrupt]

Last print, boys. She's gonna crash in five. All you aspiring Hemingways better finish your Pamplona runs fast. The bulls of Nebraska Power & Light are about to stop charging ….

What is it about this business of going to ground once a day, seven days a week, four weeks a month, twelve months a year, going on thirty-nine years now? More than most a man's life, little creatures in coveralls about the serious silliness of crisp salutes, stiff upper lips, steely unblinkingness, terse thought.

But what's a fool to do, when fools in deadly serious competition are his company? A one will have at another for no other reason than the other's being other — the other's mere being, for that matter. Though all want to "be," the degrees to which they're willing to "let be" and wish to be "let" lie at opposite ends of the spectrum.

What is it about this business of burying the executioners before the executed? Does it say all that needs to be said about this backward matter? *So* many incommensurables forced into dubious union: scanning the farthest horizon from lowest achievable vantage; delving into deep holes as prelude to arcing bits of rabid metal high through the heavens; framing of polar pursuits of attack and cessation in the same single black vein — the double-speak of the synonyms "execution" and "termination" serving surrogate for the antonyms of beginning and cessation (insider-speak for the beginning *of* cessation); investment in a fleeting peace financed only by the coin of interminable threat of war; a job which, if done right, is done never — finished only *until* the substantive work is begun, failed once it *has* begun ….

How is one to reconcile — to rank and file — incongruous elements which have nary a prayer of achieving a lock step? I don't know. Maybe it's only in an arm's length appraisal that it gains any discernible form. Fish gotta swim, birds gotta fly, nervous energies gotta go to ground or arcing higglety, to someone or other's injury. So perhaps just best, whatever shape those energies would take, to seek firm footing here in the depths sixty feet beneath everyone else's, and add further advantage of gravity's increased company, in hope of lending weight to and forfending flightiness in the machinations we forge.

***

LGM-30G
(silo-launched, ground-targeted missile, 30th type, 7th series)
a.k.a. Minuteman III

Cerberus in deep kennel lay
hard champing at his chain
lolling there in disarray –
three heads all insane.
A mythic beasty, sulfur-sired,
bedraggled, singed and charred,
and tasked – his count'nance never tired –
perdition's gate to guard.

Ingenious ploy, I give it nod,
that lashing of three wills,
odd-numbered for best odds "at odds"
thus dispositioned ill.
It keeps him pacing, snapping taught,
full at his serious play,
all know that none will venture aught
without his bite to pay.

And yet it seems a strange defense,
its logic on me lost;
the keeping of malevolence
and boarding at such cost,
when known the while our charge steadfast,
hard bred to stand us lee,

at first ken of long shadows cast
would from our company flee.

It births a master's harried straits:
Hold fury ill in hand?
Or loose the beast which evil baits,
run rampant 'cross the land?
When man's best fiend's his closest friend
then's seen the coin he pays –
reluctant dawning in the end...
a fence will catch both ways.

Prometheus, you've found new fire,
a fate revised in kind:
embrace the beast with wilding eye,
hope yours it does not find.
The things of gods, best left for them,
not fare for hands so small,
lest strength, less sense – most fearsome mix –
make devils of us all.

- Dec 1997

*****

Author: Dan Wetmore

Dan Wetmore retired with twenty years in the US
Air Force, having served as an ICBM
[Intercontinental Ballistic Missile] launch officer;
Air Force Academy instructor of military ethics and
logic; satellite launch officer, and having worked in
the intelligence community, assessed operational
testing of weapon systems in development and
headed a Wing command post.

BENJAMIN WHITE

Chaplain

The Executive Officer
Was tracking down
A personnel issue
That required insights
       From the base
chaplain
So when he saw him
In the hallway,
The XO called out to him.
       "Hey! Padre!
       Holy Ghost!"

The chaplain stopped
And turned around
For the conversation,
       But I fully expected
       The building
       To be hit by lightning.

***

Chúc mừng Ngày Cựu chiến binh

It was a great reminder
of how diplomacy and unity
have a lowest common denominator
in the interpersonal interactions
    of individuals -
    not governments...

I grew up in America
watching the nightly dire reports
of KIA combat
with a background
of protests in the streets
and on college campuses,
    while she -
    much younger than me -
had grown up
in the reunified peace
of victorious communism,
    yet, our paths crossed,
    and, as one of my students,
she sincerely wished me
a happy Veterans Day -
in her native
    Vietnamese.

***

God Bless Afghanistan

The Taliban
Is poised to take control
Of the soul of Afghanistan
        And those old factions
    Of US allies
Will get back
To where they were
When they chased
The Soviets
Out of there
        And when America
Was simply unaware
Of what military support
Leads to
When every version
        Of God
        Is requested
To bless
A nation
Of choice.

***

LVQ

In one of my many
Trivia traps,
I drive south
On Broadway
   And always get caught
   By the light
At Central
Where – although
There are lofts there now –
   It used to be
   An old high school –
Albuquerque High –
Where Leroy V. Quintana
Graduated sometime before
Going to Vietnam –
   And if he hadn't survived,
America would have had
One less warrior poet
Worth reading
   Letting us know
About the Marine recruiter –
"the biggest of liars" –
Telling the truth
To the assembly of boys
From a stage
   Somewhere in
   Those apartments.

No Need to Thank Me

I

The farms had run out of money
And they was selling eggs
And honey to make ends meet
As farmers felt the heat
To pay the loan
While bankers were on the phone
With auctioneers
To sell off everything
But the tears and anxiety
When impropriety takes the keys
And families move away –
Who could stay in a hometown
Full of debt where regret
Kept hoping for rain
And a good season without
The tractor or the truck breaking
When there was no mistaking
The president's plan to outspend
And withstand the Soviets
While making the Army
The best and only choice –
        And I still recognize
        Your patriotic voice
        Saying what I'm hearing
As you thank me
For volunteering …

***

II

I'd missed the chance in the fall
To go back to school and play ball,
But I didn't have that inclination –
Much less the tuition –
So I was in the position
Of having to make a decision
And went knocking
On the recruiter's door
Where the military wanted
More and more kids like me
Looking for a place to start
To be all we could be
As they offered up
The infantry –
Queen of Battle, follow me –
And I took it
Without looking back
As the contract was sweetened
With a tour in West Germany
After leaving Fort Benning
Where the beginning was a go –
        Though you'll never know
        Taking the oath
        Comes with a lifetime price
Even as you thank me
For my sacrifice …

***

III

I served with Vietnam veterans –
Soldiers among the purest –
Who knew I was no more
Than a camouflaged tourist
Who had to avoid
Admitting that truth or facing
Any military confessional –
I was just riding the trains
And pretending my best
To be a professional
While hovering for two years
Trying to figure myself out
And outlive the doubt
That had sent me to be
An exile overseas
Sitting in the barracks alone
Reading my letters
From back home
While growing into someone new,
Then getting out to the countryside
To decide who that was –
   You will never understand that cause
   Or the specifics of my path
   That provided a viable selection
Even though your different choices
Still thank me for my direction …

***

IV

No drama; no trauma –
Just an enlistment completed
And a discharge with honor
Sending me back to Kentucky
Lucky to have served in peace
Overseas guarding Europe's borders
In front of the Russians
And following orders
To stand tall; stand ready –
Not for a victory parade
Or ticker-tape confetti –
It was all for the duty
I had signed up to do
Counting the days down to wake up,
Fly home, and pursue
The rest of my life
Though it became clear,
Even though I made it home,
I'd never make it back
Having grown too much
And facing the consequence
        Of a uniformed experience
        When I discovered myself
        And the meaning of a purpose
Made no more meaningful
When you thank me for me service …

***

294

V

I'd taken the masculine route
With mortars and grenades
And shouting out until I was hoarse
Running along the bayonet course jumping
Into foxholes and trenches
Thrusting through the rubber guts
Of Soviet representatives,
And I was an expert
With the M-16, keeping mine
Clean and respected
For its locked and loaded
Knock-down capacity,
And I drove an M106
Mortar carrier onto the line,
Refined with precision to aim in,
And I'd have done it again
Except I had a choice
When it wasn't that hard
To change services and go
Into the U. S. Coast Guard
Where I saved lives and gathered
       An appreciation for humanity
       That by comparison
       The Army had made clear,
But I never served the country
So you'd thank me for my career ...

       ***

Ocean Diplomacy

The national news will report
On US-China relations
And both nations are tainted
Painted by politics and policies,
    But on the high seas
Ships sail to places distant,
And freedom
Is consistent with the waves,
The sea gulls, and the hulls
    Of boats making way,
And even when the Coast Guard flag
Is on display and crews
Are enforcing the fisheries regulations
There are still the sensations of liberty
    And independence,
So, when the boarding team got caught
By bad weather and had to stay
Onboard the Chinese fish processor
    Over night
There was no debate, hesitation,
Fight, or impending doom –
The Chinese simply made room
And were gracious hosts,
    And the next day
The American Coast Guard Captain
Sent over a case of M&Ms
Thanking them
For their hospitality –
    Sailors go to sea
And understand
A special brand
Of diplomacy.

***

To the 99%

They have no idea what they're grateful for
Having no experience to compare,
And to share the responsibility
Negates too much individual want
Knowing discipline undermines freedom

Yet, they feel a sense of personal guilt
Obligating them to somehow relate,
Understand, and show appreciation

Falsified in a simplified statement
Offered as five-word patriotism
Reflecting pride in a prideless manner

Yearning for their personal forgiveness
Or trying to present society's
Undying love for what it cannot love,
Respect, or comprehend without knowledge

So, Hollywood images have to fill
Empty concepts of what it means to serve
Reaching out of fantasies and stories
Viewed and relied upon for honesty,
Integrity, and glorious duty
Cheapened manhood can only dream about
Each time it thinks about its liberties.

***

One An Hour: 1716 Hours

The newspaper heading mentions
"Veteran,"
                  And that comes

With its own mystique
Presenting a dichotomy of perspective
Driven by individual understanding,
                  And the story

Is haunted by "suicide"
With its own ambiguity
For those who absently
                  Wonder

And those who absolutely
                  Know why.

***

Warriors Betrayed

Every commercial
For the Wounded Warriors Project
Is a reminder
Of the betrayal
The U. S. Government perpetuates
By shirking the responsibility
To take care of
       The nation's veterans,
And for every
Nineteen-dollars-a-month donation
The lines get longer and slower
At the Veterans Administration
Where the phones ring unanswered
Without enough people or money
       To even answer and say,
"We're sorry"

*****

Author:Ben White

Ben White is the author of *The Recon Trilogy +1, Always Ready: Poems from a Life in the US Coast Guard*, and *Conley Bottom: A Poemoir*. He served as a mortarman in the Army but is retired from the Coast Guard. Ben now teaches at Central New Mexico Community College.

JOSEPHINE WHITE

And Still We Wait

As women who watched the sea of olde, from cliff or edifice on high
We wait today for our loved ones returning from the sky.
The dawn breaks and they're summoned forth to a comradeship they share
While we at home live out our parts to show how much we care.

The days go by and we pretend the thought does not exist –
They won't be back, the loving arms, the lips we briefly kissed.
Be kind once more oh, Temptress Skye and bless the luck of Fate.
Return once more to longing arms of those who chose to wait.

But time moves on and some will fall to Nature's cruel whim
And empty days and empty hours and empty dreams of him.
Surround you now, and so it seems life's plan you can't relate.
For your soul to find true peace of mind, your task is still to wait.

*****

Author: Josephine White

Josephine White's husband flew jet fighters with the New Mexico Air
National Guard for thirty-three years. His unit lost eleven pilots: two in
a mid-air collision in May 1978. After the funeral, she went home and
wrote, "And Still We Wait."

J. ALLEN WHITT

The Door Gunner

When tropic dawn broke in the east,
The sky forewarned of blood.
Montana Kid was standing down,
But Hipshot had to fly.

They met up at the mess tent
For eggs and coffee there.
But amid their silence Hipshot said,
"I won't come back today."

The Kid just gave a hollow laugh.
"Don't joke around like that."
"I dreamed my boots were empty, Kid.
The sign was really clear."

The Kid said, "Aw, don't worry none.
A dream don't mean a thing."
But Hipshot shook his head and said,
"I know my time is up."

*

The crew chief made a final check,
Then yelled, "Let's turn and burn!"
The turbine whined, the rotors flashed,
As they lifted from the pad.

The Huey topped a hazy ridge,
And Hipshot cocked his gun.
While hidden in the jungle below,
A sniper sighted in.

*

Its windshield stitched with bullet holes,
The Huey touched down hard.
There Hipshot lay among syrettes,
Without a tongue or jaw.

When medics brought the body bag,
The Kid asked for time.
His fingers closed his buddy's eyes.
His hands zipped up the bag.

*

The Kid heals slow among the pines,
As forty years go by.
Now his hands tie Copper Johns and nymphs,
Beneath Montana sky.

Yet sometimes eyes that will not shut
Stare through the shroud of night,
And solace lies beyond the stars,
'til dawn restores the light.

*****

Author: J. Allen Whitt

J. Allen Whitt is a Navy veteran of three Vietnam deployments aboard an aircraft carrier as well as a retired Professor Emeritus of Sociology. He has published essays, short stories, and poems. His poem "The Endurance of Letters" won first place at the National Creative Arts Festival in 2013.

CIRCE OLSON WOESSNER

A Quarter Century Later

I miss the sticky fingers around my knees
crumby kisses on my cheek
soft body curled in my lap at naptime
a tousled head topped with a giraffe hat

Longing for ...
Those days of macaroni pasted on construction paper hearts
Those days of wide-eyed innocence and infinite possibilities
Those days when I was his fiercest protector and biggest champion

I wipe up crumbs and coffee cup rings ...
encounter far-off stares
long legs draped over the living room couch-back
— the same head now wears a Veteran's cap

Living for ...
Today where art is lost in bureaucracy, red tape and VA paperwork
Today where innocence and possibilities are long gone with war
Today, where I'm still his fiercest protector and champion

A quarter century later ...

***

PCS no.?

4 AM.

Riding in the backseat of our pickup
My shoulder rests on a flat-screen TV
Headlights slice through the Texas night
Whiff of feedlot — blanketed in a sulfur fog

Another move — like so many before
Instead of maps, we now rely on
navigation from the bored woman on the iPhone

Too warm for nothing; too cold for AC
I shiver in my faded flannel shirt
I've worn these jeans for over a week

My husband's face glows in the dashboard light
 Seconds after I hear a dull splat,
"That rabbit didn't make it"
I say a prayer for the bunny's lost life

The deep plains of Texas
Country and Gospel on the radio
After all, this is God's country

Hypnotized by the dull whoosh of tires on the road
We're jolted awake by a passing freight
Hopscotching between semis in a leap of faith

The tarp's coming loose — has the load shifted?
Are our things flung over Hell's Half Acre?
We won't know till daylight.

How many times have we done this?
Moving from post to base, home to house
Fast food, cluttered motel rooms & interrupted routines
I lost count after 20.

Near-ghost towns, grain elevators, abattoirs
Like the sons and daughters of these dying towns
We move on, heading west

The cooler shifts, hitting my knee
Jarring me out of my thoughts
Breakfast — feed the family
Bottles of grape juice, rolled ham and stale tortilla chips

Behind us, the sky pinks up
Let there be light
Out of the shit, into the day

We're almost home.

$$*****$$

Author: Circe Olson Woessner

Circe Olson Woessner is an Army wife and mother to an Army veteran. She is the founder of the Museum of the American Military Family & Learning Center in Tijeras, NM. Between 2020-2022, she coedited *On Freedom's Frontier: Life on the Fulda Gap, Schooling with Uncle Sam, and Host Nation Hospitality.*

NORBERT WOOD

Memories

It first was heard as whispers
on a breeze so long ago.
From out of the mist of morning
came a breath of magic sweetness,
a calling never seen yet
felt inside one's soul.

Come be with life's beginning;
I will show you where to go.
The voice was with the wind
and promised all that we should be,
yet was only heard by children
or hearts' untroubled souls.

It carried down through canyons
and caressed the fields of grain,
through ancient timberlands
and over rocky plains. It played
with waterfalls and stroked
the placid lakes, and

if you are still and quiet
its whisper might be heard,
for the secret really isn't —
all once knew it well. Listen.
Listen, said the wind
for the sound of life again.

What was lost, was not,
but only hiding from our thought.
It's there to be once more,
for what has always been, remains
not lost, but waiting for our life
again. So much to be enjoyed —

a pool reflecting gossamer clouds,
the butterfly's wisps of concinnate
color, a flower to greet the morning dew,
the lilting voice of a turtle dove,
a leaf dancing with a gentle breeze or
drops of rain singing welcome songs of love.

A world of wonders all about.
Some will ask, *what do you see?*
Answer with a simple smile.
No need to explain such joy.
Behold the beauty of each day;
the gift will welcome our embrace.

But time required a price be paid;
the cost said *new is good* — then
new was soon forgotten and
faded from our thoughts.
We searched for might-have-beens
and so many other ifs ...

These are never found. They
only add to discontent.
What might awaken one's repose?
Is there something to be known?
A candle's light to guide the way?
Think back in time before it's lost.

Is there a truth to be discovered,
found again beneath life's rubble?
Waiting, waiting for a remembered
journey that joins the end to its
beginning — be this so, where
is the warder of such treasure?

As the chalice of each flower
invites the ever-searching hummingbird, so
our memories nourish the multitude of
threads woven into this tapestry of life.
Are not memories the only truth? —
be they real or just imagined.

May dreams be believed, if laced
with fond memories of long ago.
It is with such we learn, and find
our way to cherish the past is to
anticipate our yet-to-be.
Accept with grace life's simple bounty.

Be of two minds, and gently temper
each memory, but do not risk its loss,
for each may be drawn from the
larder of its keep to serve one well.
Nurture such while one is able.
The planted seed will bloom resplendent.

It has been said, *If memories be dreams,*
what wealth we all must have.
They speak of many journeys past,
and future paths that time will offer.
Trust these mystic truths once more.
Know that life is to be lived again.
Memories may tell of grace and beauty;

more of precious loving times.
What's past will not occur again.
Memories linger with us always.
Build upon these footprints in time
and follow each to glorious life again.

***

Lament for Jimminie

There is a cricket here about
Of this I'm sure, there is no doubt

Now it's time I shall assume
Its whereabouts within the room

Hear its chirrup again declare
Look over here by this old chair

Sure enough, I see it squarely
Perched down there quite debonairly

It's coming nearer as if hell-bent
Ever, ever closer with obvious intent

Now upon my foot, how can it be,
Continuing upward to my knee

It goes no further I do see
But surely is looking straight at me

Holes in Our Hearts

My greeting of soft hello
Is answered with a chirrup quite low

I have a thought that does occur
And is somewhat vague provoker

Could it be we have met before
Are you some past contributor?

Like some repeating Oberammergau
Tattooed upon this aging brow

If such a thought be verily true
Who could this be, I have no clue

Surely there is a tale to tell
Like the ever-spiraling caracole

No beginning and never an end
Enough to make one's brain distend

Once again my thoughts reach out
No word is spoken or needed hereabout

In answer comes a chirrup most apropos
Is this a yes, I do not know

Now emerging from the labyrinth of mind
Imagination jostling with a mystery ill-defined

Might this be some mischievous djinn
Or some other answer deep within

It is my friend, of this I'm sure
A soul of someone from my yester year

I give it water and a bit to eat
It seems quite pleased with such a treat

Before we sleep I say goodnight
A low chirrup answer is forthright

A pleasant chirrup greets my new day
My new friend has decided to stay

*****

Author: Norbert Wood

Norbert Wood was born in 1930 and raised in South Carolina and Florida. A University of Florida graduate and an Army combat veteran of the Korean War, Norbert is a lifelong, self-taught artist. He began painting in his seventies and writing poetry in his late eighties.

KAY YOEST

The Mostly Amusing Reflections of a Female Army Officer

How times have changed for women in the military and women in general! I entered the four-year ROTC [Reserve Officers' Training Corps] program at my university in 1973, which was the first year women could do so. I did this unwillingly at the advice of my father, a college professor, who insisted I have a meaningful job to fall back on since I was majoring in music. There were only several females giving it a try; the others dropped out, leaving shy and introverted me for all the glory and publicity until another female joined the following year. My picture was in the newspaper where I was dressed in fatigues with a rifle on my shoulder, holding a powder puff with the caption "Keep the Powder Dry" (referring to gunpowder). Today that seems so ridiculous, but back then, it was funny. Ha! I cringe when I look at that newspaper clipping.

Having been in marching band for many years, I loved "drill and ceremony," where we marched around a local armory near campus responding to commands. Finally, something I could excel in better than the males! And all the physical training we did excused me from all physical education classes; yay! No gymnastics or volleyball. I was a total klutz when it came to taking apart and reassembling various weapons, but I practiced a lot and caught up to the others. The M-60 machine gun was my favorite, and I became very speedy. Too bad it was so heavy; I don't think I could have carried it anywhere as I was very thin at the time with no muscles (which would change later). With an indoor rifle range on campus, I enjoyed trying to shoot accurately in the comfort of an indoor range. Unfortunately, with severe near-sightedness, I was never very good on the rifle range, at yearly pistol practice, or on campus, but I always did my best.

Attending ROTC Summer Camp for six weeks is one of the requirements to be commissioned an officer, and this generally falls between the junior and senior years. College students leading and supervising other college students is a real challenge, much harder than supervising real soldiers. Anyway, with all the physical activity and mess hall food, I gained weight and definitely developed some muscles. I learned to do chin-ups, so I didn't have to do a zillion push-ups before entering the mess hall. We had a Green Beret drill sergeant ensuring this! I'm sure they loved their jobs being detailed to college kids after Vietnam had ended. After six weeks of "fun in the sun" at Ft. Riley, I volunteered for an additional three weeks to shadow a female Army Captain at an Army post in the Personnel branch, which I loved. The work was in an air-conditioned building with reasonable hours!

Women were restricted to only five branches of the Army at the time, so I set my sights on the Personnel or human resources (HR) branch, formally known as the Adjutant General Corps. Now women can enter any branch (Infantry, Field Artillery, etc.) of the Army and any school (Ranger, Air Assault, etc.). We were very limited back in the 1970s. I had no intention of spending more than two or three years in the Army, traveling, and then getting out to pursue a career in the corporate world, but of course, that didn't happen.

My first assignment after graduation and 2nd lieutenant school was Ft. Ord, CA. Little did I know I couldn't afford to live in beautiful Monterey, CA, or Pebble Beach but had to move to Salinas, driving by the lettuce fields daily watching the migrants pick vegetables. I had never eaten artichokes, avocados, or fresh fish because of where I lived, so this opened my eyes to unique and healthier foods. After growing up near the steel valley of Youngstown, Ohio, it was quite an awakening, as were my Army jobs. In my first job, I supervised twelve or more people at Ft. Ord, a mixture of soldiers and civilians, which was very challenging! I developed writing skills I didn't know I had and also coaching and counseling, which have served me well in numerous jobs. But it was not easy.

I eventually took flying lessons at the local Navy Flying Club for some excitement. I obtained a Private Pilot's license and didn't fly again, unfortunately. But I enjoyed the beautiful scenery along the California coast. I won't mention the times I got lost and stuck above the clouds. I did meet my future husband, who was in the aviation branch of the Army, although we didn't marry for a number of years.

With a tough economy in 1980, I opted for an assignment in Germany since traveling had been a goal. Based in Mannheim as a Personnel Officer, I was able to travel, ski, and take prisoner escort flights to Ft. Leavenworth in the US since my friend was the Executive Officer at the Army's stockade in Mannheim. Living in a foreign country definitely opens your eyes to different cultures and languages. I learned some German, which was helpful since I worked for a German company at the end of my civilian career.

Fast forward to more schooling and another assignment in San Antonio, then a jump into the corporate HR field and the Army Reserves after completing a master's degree. Serving in a Reserve Civil Affairs unit in San Antonio was another culture shock as I heard nothing but Spanish during drill meetings. This was in the mid-1980s, and I found out I was a minority, with over 50% of the city Hispanic. Luckily, I had taken four years of Spanish in high school, but I couldn't follow the rapid speech patterns.

A move to Atlanta, GA, brought several more Army Reserve assignments, one of which I was a 3% minority white person in a mostly African-American unit. Command & General Staff followed, which takes three years to complete in the Reserves through night school and summer sessions.

After twenty-three total years, I finally retired as a Lieutenant Colonel. I consider myself fortunate in that I missed all major mobilizations and did not serve in a combat zone. However, my Reserve work supported some of these events, and I made sure any of my soldiers knew we were supporting the combat arms soldiers more than anyone else. Throughout my Reserve career, I worked in corporate human resources in mostly international, well-known companies. Although counseled by job coaches to hide my military service on my resume since I was a female, I insisted on listing it at the end as I was not ashamed of it. Males were encouraged to show their service. That has totally changed today, with corporations seeking out former military, especially junior officers. As I look back, I derived rich experiences from the military that formed my life and career paths. I have no regrets at age sixty-seven!

*****

Author: Kay Yoest

Kay Yoest grew up near Youngstown, Ohio, which was a large steel mill town. She attended Youngstown State University, graduating in 1977. Kay spent the next seven years on Active Duty, then in the Reserves. She retired from the Army in 2005 and has lived in Corrales, New Mexico, since 2015.

This anthology was made possible by a grant from the State of New Mexico Arts Division

NEW MEXICO ARTS

New Mexico Arts (NMA) is the State of New Mexico arts agency and a division of the Department of Cultural Affairs. NMA's primary function is to provide financial support for arts services and programs to non-profit organizations statewide and administer the 1% public art program for New Mexico. NMAs mission is to preserve, enhance, and develop the arts in New Mexico through partnerships, public awareness, and education and to enrich the quality of life for present and future generations.

The NMA Arts & The Military Initiative is deeply rooted in New Mexico Arts' mission to ensure the arts are central to the lives of New Mexicans. New Mexico has 141,558 veterans, with military retirees in all thirty-three counties. 8.8% of the adults in the state are veterans.

The NMA Arts & The Military Program Goals are to create more opportunities for military and veteran audiences — including active-duty service members, reservists, National Guard members, veterans, their families and caregivers, and others — to engage with the arts meaningfully and to build capacity among New Mexico organizations to offer arts programs for military-connected participants.

The New Mexico Arts & The Military program supports arts organizations and collaborates with veteran-focused organizations, creating and expanding opportunities for veterans and active-duty service members to engage with the arts. In 2023, a $2,000 Mini-Grants program was launched to assist organizations in creating and expanding arts programming for military-connected participants. SouthWest Writers Workshop was awarded one of these grants to produce this anthology. We are pleased that the results have reached so many individuals and allowed them to share their stories.

MORE ANTHOLOGIES BY SOUTHWEST WRITERS

A Diversity of Expression

Ramblings & Reflections

Seeing the World in 20/20

SouthWest Writers 2019 Winners Anthology

KiMo Theatre: Fact & Folklore

SouthWest Writers Sage Anthology

The Storyteller's Anthology

Books and e-books available on Amazon.

Writers Helping Writers

SouthWest Writers

SouthWest Writers (SWW) is a nonprofit 501(c)(3) organization devoted to helping both published and unpublished writers improve their craft and further their careers. Located in Albuquerque, New Mexico, SWW serves writers of all skill levels in every fiction and nonfiction genre. We are 95% supported by membership dues and the fees charged for events. Donations are welcome!

At a SouthWest Writers meeting you will hear positive stories about the world of writing and be encouraged by your peers. You'll find helpful people in a crowd of friends—and be inspired.

SWW offers its members a variety of creative challenges every month – opportunities to be published and to learn both the art and business of writing – through the Sage Newsletter and our writing contests.

And take a look at our classes and workshops, as well as the benefits of membership. If you have any questions, please contact the SWW office. Better yet, visit one of our twice-monthly meetings!

www.southwestwriters.com